HOAX

HOAX

A HISTORY OF DECEPTION

5,000 YEARS OF FAKES, FORGERIES, AND FALLACIES

IAN TATTERSALL AND **PETER NÉVRAUMONT**

BLACK DOG
& LEVENTHAL
PUBLISHERS
NEW YORK

Black Dog & Leventhal Publishers
Hachette Book Group
1290 Avenue of the Americas
New York, NY 10104
www.hachettebookgroup.com
www.blackdogandleventhal.com

First Edition: March 2018

Black Dog & Leventhal Publishers is an imprint of Hachette Books, a division of Hachette Book Group. The Black Dog & Leventhal Publishers name and logo are trademarks of Hachette Book Group, Inc.

The publisher is not responsible for websites (or their content) that are not owned by the publisher.

The Hachette Speakers Bureau provides a wide range of authors for speaking events. To find out more, go to www.HachetteSpeakersBureau.com or call (866) 376-6591.

Print book interior design by Red Herring Design.

Photo credits can be found on page 244.

Library of Congress Cataloging-in-Publication Data has been applied for.

ISBNs: 978-0-316-50372-3 (hardcover); 978-0-316-50370-9 (ebook)

Printed in China

APS

10 9 8 7 6 5 4 3 2 1

CONTENTS

To all the con artists and their marks, throughout history, who have kept the human enterprise going

PREFACE

The human condition has always eluded accurate description. At the extremes, people may be monsters or saints. They may be miserly or munificent. Decorous or crude. Brilliant or dumb. But while these wilder manifestations of human behavior tend to be the ones that grab our attention, most of the time we find ourselves somewhere in the middle of any behavioral spectrum you might want to consider.

It is mostly in this gray, ambiguous area of human experience that charlatanism, fraud, and fakery have flourished, doubtless ever since *Homo sapiens* emerged in its modern form around a hundred thousand years ago. In many ways, what has happened over the ages in this vast, equivocal middle ground of human experience tells us a lot more about our predecessors'—and our own—lives than many of the grander events we usually think of as history do; and certainly, no account of our historical soap opera is complete that does not consider this aspect of the human condition.

The tendency that has made this vast swamp of morally dubious incidents possible is pretty familiar and straightforward. No con artist is unaware of how credulous his fellow citizens tend to be, even—or perhaps especially—those who think themselves most highly sophisticated. And every trickster is acutely conscious of the seemingly universal penchant for believing what one wants to hear. Either of these basic human proclivities opens the door for the unscrupulous to exploit their less cynical peers.

In 1165, the Byzantine emperor Manuel Comnenus received a letter from an unknown Christian king, Prester John, whose lands allegedly extended beyond India to the Tower of Babel. Pope Alexander III then sent envoys east, hoping that Prester John would come to the aid of Crusaders in Jerusalem besieged by Muslim armies. Prester John's mythical kingdom, as seen on this 1564 map, became the object of a quest that fired the imaginations of generations of adventurers, but has always remained out of reach.

In contrast, the motivations that have fueled the consequent entrenchment of misrepresentation, fakery, and demagoguery in common human experience are a little more complex; and they are as varied as the species *Homo sapiens* itself. The reason for taking advantage of the innocence, avarice, or preconceptions of others is most commonly simple greed, but malice and personal animosity are also frequent driving forces, as are sheer impishness, the desire for power or influence, a wish to "show the experts," or even the pathetic need to simply be recognized for *something*.

Still, wherever the incentive may come from in any particular case, the dynamic that makes fraud possible is evidently baked hard into that frustratingly elusive human condition. As long as there are people and language there will be frauds and lies, con artists and suckers, the credulous and their gleeful exploiters.

If both human unwariness and the desire to take advantage of it are—and always have been—irredeemably part of the human psyche, then the consequent hoaxes, frauds, and fallacies also provide us with an alternative lens through which to view the vagaries of the past and present. This lens is potentially a powerful one, for while human gullibility is eternal, its expression varies hugely according to the fears, aspirations, and world views of each generation. At the very least, we can confidently claim that what we recount here is not history as written by the victors.

In this book, merely the most recent expression of a splendid historical tradition that dates back at least to Charles MacKay's 1841 *Extraordinary Popular Delusions and the Madness of Crowds*, we have chosen a potpourri of fifty varyingly disreputable episodes that cover around five thousand years of human experience and billions of years of life itself. Since we have tried to keep each entry short, we have provided a few suggestions for further reading at the end of the book; a bit of browsing around on the Web—while remembering that what you find there is mostly without guarantee of factual accuracy—will yield a trove of other information.

Some of the events portrayed in this book are familiar, others obscure. Some involve intentional misrepresentations, while others more closely reflect misguided general preconceptions. Some reveal the depths to which human callousness and meanness of spirit can descend, while—to take a generous view—others actually added to the sum total of human contentment. But, considered together, they hint at two contradictory aspects of the human experience.

One of these is the constancy and durability of basic human nature: our species as a whole has evidently changed not one whit since human beings first began to write down their thoughts and feelings and experiences. The other, in contrast, is how dramatically the sands of history may shift: how our preoccupations and beliefs—and what, as a society, we have been prepared to be deceived about—change with the passage of time.

As authors, we have refrained—wisely, we hope—from attempting to fit any of these fifty episodes into a wider view of history, or of how it unfolds. Human experience is, after all, far too haphazard for that. But we do think that each of them will make its own point. And since it turns out that not all cons are altogether reprehensible—indeed, some fraudsters were actually perfectly genial—we have buried a tiny fraud of our own somewhere in this book. See if you can spot it.

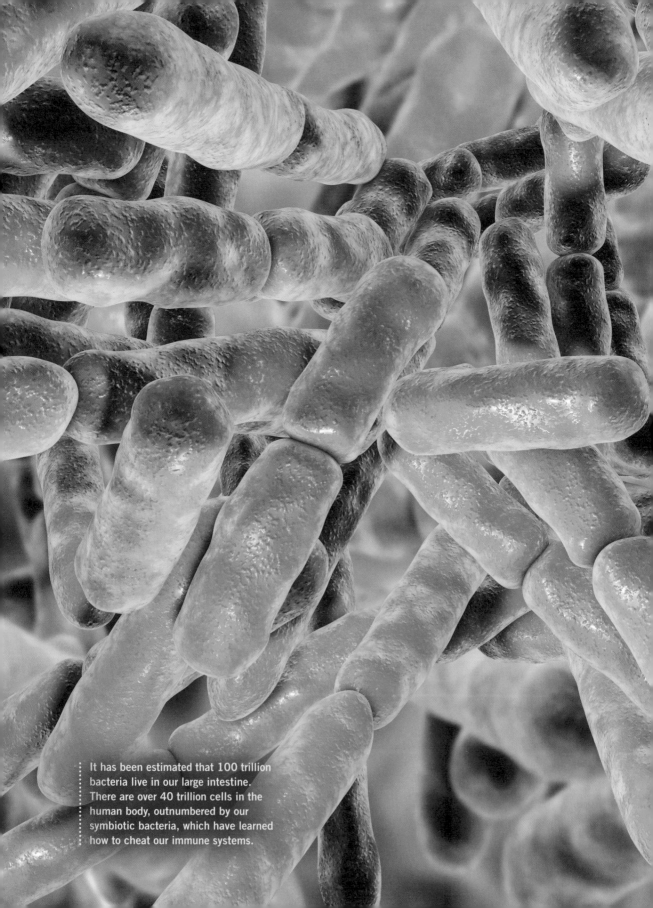

It has been estimated that 100 trillion bacteria live in our large intestine. There are over 40 trillion cells in the human body, outnumbered by our symbiotic bacteria, which have learned how to cheat our immune systems.

EVOLUTION OF THE CON

This book is about the integral place of fraud and fallacy in the human experience. Yet it may help put things in perspective to begin it by pointing out that fakery and deception are hardly unique to our species, *Homo sapiens*. Indeed, it seems that these frequently unappetizing propensities are rampant throughout the entire living world. As we lament the sorry state of the human condition, it is somehow comforting to know we are not alone in our imperfections.

Human beings are intimately nested into the great tree of life that unites all living organisms on our planet, and that stems from a single common ancestor which lived upward of 3.5 billion years ago. That ancestor doubtless shared many of its features with today's microscopic, single-celled bacteria, and it seems that, for all their apparent simplicity, even bacteria engage in deceptive practices.

One of the big biological discoveries of recent years has involved the realization of just how important our "microbiota"—the community of microorganisms that live inside us and on our skins—is to our overall functioning. A major example of this is provided by the plethora of single-celled creatures that have colonized our guts and become crucial to our digestive processes. We have a very active immune system that usually sends out special cells to attack pathogenic invaders, yet our microbiota goes about its business unscathed. How does it pull off this trick? Well, it turns out that the bacteria that have coevolved with us indulge in what is known as "molecular mimicry." In other words, they pretend to be our own cells, the bacterial species known as *Bacteroides fragilis* being especially good at imitating the proteins and sugars that coat the cells in the digestive tracts of humans and other animals.

Females of the firefly genus *Photuris* mimic the courtship flashes of the genus *Photinus*. Male *Photinus* drawn to these flashes are captured and eaten by these "femme fatale" *Photuris* fireflies.

Deception of this kind benefits both the bacteria and ourselves. But false advertising is not always so benign. To us, the intimate flashing of fireflies is one of the more delightful aspects of many a summer evening. But in the world of fireflies, danger always lurks. Usually a firefly flickers in the context of courtship, as males and females of the same species respond to specific patterns of flashes. But females of the firefly genus *Photuris* cheat.

Imitating the flash pattern of another genus, *Photinus*, those female *Photuris* lie in wait for a smaller *Photinus* male. And when he shows up, he gets eaten. In the process, the female *Photuris* gets not only a tasty snack but also a dose of a steroid called lucibufagin, which will discourage jumping spiders from extending a similar courtesy to her. Sometimes crime pays.

Perhaps the most famous example of deception in the animal world is the "brood parasitism" that is remarkably common among birds. It is independently found in five different bird families, though the poster child for this bad habit is the common European cuckoo. A female cuckoo will lay an egg in another bird's nest that very closely resembles the ones laid by the host. Amazingly, seven different variants of European cuckoo, producing different-colored eggs, specialize in parasitizing seven different kinds of host that range from warblers to wagtails.

Sometimes a male cuckoo will attempt to lure a prospective victim out of her nest so that his mate can sneak in to lay her egg. If it is not ejected right away from the host's nest, that egg will incubate faster than the rest and the cuckoo chick will mature more quickly than the host's own. Once hatched, it will do its best to dispatch the competition and to monopolize the food provided by the unsuspecting foster parents. The cuckoo parents can meanwhile relax, relieved of the responsibility of raising their youngsters.

If bacteria and birds are both into deception, then it is hardly surprising that primates do it, too. Actually, cheating hasn't been reported yet among the lemurs and lorises, the so-called lower primates. But among our closer relatives, the "higher" primates, misleading behaviors are rampant. Chimpanzees, for example, are well known for hiding their real intentions from others, especially when such dissimulation involves a lower-status male who is trying to woo an attractive female within view of a dominant male.

Recently a chimpanzee has been reported hiding its intentions from humans, too. A male chimpanzee named Santino, resident at Sweden's Furuvik Zoo, has now apparently gotten in the habit of hiding stones behind logs and hay piles, and then later suddenly snatching one and throwing it at an unsuspecting visitor.

Finally, a study some years ago showed that how often individuals of a primate species typically deceive one another is accurately predicted by how big the brain's neocortex is in the species concerned. This is a measure that places us way ahead of chimpanzees. You have been warned.

About 1 percent (around 100 species) of birds resort to "brood parasitism" by sneaking an egg into a host's nest. If it is not ejected right away, that egg will incubate faster than the rest, and the chick will mature more quickly than the host's own. Some hosts have learned to recognize "foster" chicks by the spots inside their mouths, in what is known as "gape pattern recognition," and will feed them less than their own offspring. In response, parasitic pin-tailed whydah chicks (left) have evolved spots that closely mimic those of the host common waxbill chick (right).

Prop. 1. The 2300 Ọprophetick days did not commence before the rise of the little horn of the H[e] Goat.

2 Those days did not commence aʃter the distruction of Jerusalem & of Temple by the Romans A. 70.

3 The time times & half a time did not commence before the year 800 in wch the Popes supremacy commenced

4 They did not commence after the reigne of Gregory the 7th. 1084 842.

5 The 1290 days did not commence before the year 842.

6 They did not commence after the reigne of Pope Greg. 7th. 1084

7 The difference between the 1290 & 1335 days are a parts of the seven weeks.

Therefore the 2300 years do not end before yͤ year 2132 nor after 2370.

The time times & half time do not end before 2060 nor after

The 1290 days do not begin before 2090 nor after 1374,

The letter written by Isaac Newton in which he predicted the world would end in 2060.

THE END ᴼᶠ WORLD ᵀᴴᴱ AS WE KNOW IT

I f you are like us, you have probably seen more cartoons of men bearing placards that read REPENT FOR THE END OF THE WORLD IS NIGH than you have seen actual people doing so. But such apocalyptic visions are nonetheless ingrained in the human cultural experience—and evidently have been at least since people first began recording their beliefs about their place in the world around them, and about their fears for their own fate and that of humankind in general. An Assyrian clay tablet dating from 2800 BC is gloomily inscribed: "Our Earth is degenerate in these later days. There are signs that the world is speedily coming to an end."

Such perceptions were eagerly adopted by early Christians, who seized upon Jesus's repeated proclamations that the current world was about to end, to be replaced by the coming Kingdom of God. Initially they seem to have expected that catastrophe was just around the corner, although by the end of the first century doubts evidently set in: "But concerning that day and hour no one knows, not even the angels of heaven, nor the Son, but the Father only" (Matthew 24:36, English Standard Version).

Later theologians seem to have taken this wavering as a challenge. For whereas in AD 365 the theologian Hilary of Poitiers returned to the original proposal that the end of the world was imminent, a whole host of his successors soon stepped up to the plate and predicted that the world would end on a specific date in the future: January 1, 1000,

This Assyrian clay tablet bearing the *Epic of Gilgamesh*, dated to 2800 BC, reads in part: "Our Earth is degenerate in these later days; there are signs that the world is speedily coming to an end; bribery and corruption are common; children no longer obey their parents; every man wants to write a book and the end of the world is evidently approaching."

the Christian millennium. Despite the disenchantment that must have followed when the magic date passed uneventfully, specific dates remained in vogue.

Even the iconoclastic Martin Luther—who rejected the Book of Revelation, a favorite source of such apocalyptic embellishments as the Rapture, as "neither apostolic nor prophetic"—expected that the world would end on October 9, 1538. When that failed to occur, he revised the date to 1600, by which time he was comfortably dead and immune from disappointment.

Given the amazing variety of the things that people are manifestly prepared to believe, it is maybe not too surprising that ancient Assyrians and medieval theologians should have bought into apocalyptic predictions. Who knows? They might in the long run even be right, though we shall have to wait and see. More disconcerting is that Sir Isaac Newton, the very embodiment of the Age of Reason that saw the birth of modern science, stood right there alongside them. For it seems that the inventor of celestial mechanics and calculus, the author of the magisterial *Principia Mathematica*, was also a very literal believer, convinced that biblical prophecy was "no matter of indifferency, but a duty of the greatest moment."

For Newton, scriptural prophecies were "histories of things to come," albeit written in arcane symbolic language requiring expert interpretation that he was happy to supply. After years of effort he calculated that the world would end some 1,260 years after the foundation of the Holy Roman Empire, a period that would see us through to AD 2060. "It may," he wrote in 1704, "end later, but I see no reason for its ending sooner." So by the calculations of one of the most outstanding scientists of all time, many of us, at least, can rest easy.

Interestingly, Newton made his conjecture "not to assert when the time of the end shall be, but to put a stop to the rash conjectures of fanciful men who are frequently predicting [it], and by doing so bring the sacred prophesies into discredit as often as their predictions fail."

Not that this sage objective was achieved. For example, closer to our own times, the radio evangelist Harold Camping predicted in 1992 that the Rapture (when, roughly at the time of Christ's Second Coming, believers living and dead would be raised up to join the Lord in the clouds, while the rest of us would be consumed by earthquakes and plagues: blame Revelation again) would probably occur on September 6, 1994. Undeterred by the failure of this happening to take place on schedule, he revised his prediction for the Rapture to May 21, 2011, with the actual end of the world to follow five months later, on October 21.

On his Family Radio network, Harold Camping predicted Jesus would return to Earth on May 21, 2011, followed by five months of fire, brimstone, and plagues that would culminate in the end of the entire universe on October 21, 2011. At age ninety-two, Camping met his own end on December 15, 2013, with Earth still intact.

Events, or the lack thereof, eventually forced Camping to "humbly acknowledge we were wrong about the timing." But meanwhile, he and his associates had pocketed millions of dollars in donations to his Family Radio stations. Camping declined to return these donations after his prognostications failed to turn out as advertised, allegedly remarking, "We're not at the end. Why would we return it?" Sadly, aggressive publicity directed at the 200 million souls he had expected to save incurred significant cost overruns, eventually forcing his network to sell off stations and lay off staff.

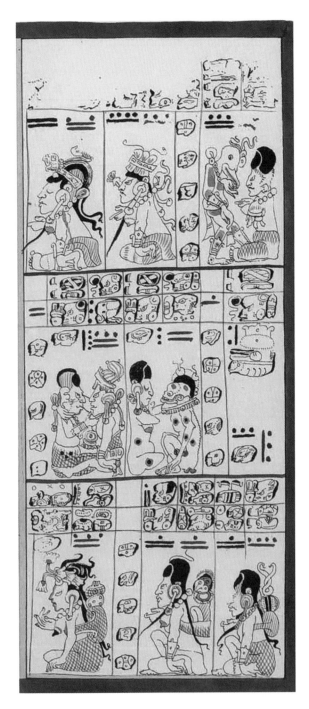

This discouraging experience is unlikely to end such predictions, especially in an age when an all-too-probable meltdown of the Internet could potentially have even more disastrous consequences for human-kind than any number of apocalyptic Horsemen. But why, after so many disappointments, do so many people continue to devour them?

The theologian Lorenzo DiTommaso suggests that such beliefs flourish when problems loom in the material world (as they almost invariably do) and people feel pressured by circumstances. They come, he suggests, from the desire to reconcile two conflicting beliefs: that there is something disquietingly wrong with modern human existence, and that there are nonetheless grounds for hope. The idea that we are hurtling toward some kind of "cosmic correction" is balanced by the promise of salvation, so that "the God of apocalypticism is a God of order, not chaos." And if DiTommaso is correct, the belief in apocalypse is as good an example as you will find of the cognitive dissonance that seems to characterize the human condition so profoundly.

....

Millions logged on to Internet conspiracy sites alarmed that a 5,126-year Mayan cycle concluding on December 23, 2012, would mark the end of the world as we know it. The Dresden Codex, several pages of which are shown here, contains astronomical and astrological tables used to calculate this cycle. This codex is one of only three Mayan codices that survived out of an estimated five thousand; the rest were destroyed by Spanish religious authorities in the sixteenth century.

THE ARK
AT THE **END** OF THE **RAINBOW**

Human experience is finite, which is one reason why the same themes tend to crop up repeatedly as history continues to unfold. One of the most pervasive metaphors in the Western tradition occurs in the biblical account of Noah's Flood, with its none-too-subtle message about how unwise it is for humans to displease higher forces. However, while most of us associate this episode with the Book of Genesis and the Judeo-Christian God, its elements actually go back way before biblical times to ancient Babylon—and quite possibly beyond, although no earlier written records exist.

According to the *Epic of Gilgamesh*, written some 1,500 years before the Old Testament was begun, the gods became so annoyed with the antics of mankind that they resolved to exterminate humans by drowning them all. But one man, Utnapishtim, was warned of this fate in a dream in which he was told to build a roofed boat of specific dimensions that should be filled with "the seed of all living creatures."

This story is uncannily similar to the biblical account of Noah and his flood, although admittedly the hero's name rolls less easily off the tongue. And the two watery legends are, indeed, sufficiently alike to suggest that they had a common origin; or perhaps the later one was directly bootlegged from the earlier. Either way, the story has clearly had enough staying power to repeatedly excite two somewhat contradictory aspects of the human psyche.

The 16,854-foot-high Mount Ararat, located in eastern Turkey close to the borders of Iran, Armenia, and Azerbaijan. It is reported in the Old Testament to be the final resting place of Noah's Ark. As early as 275 BC the Babylonian historian Berossus reported on an ark in Armenia from which "some get pitch from the ship by scraping it off, and use it for amulets."

The first of these is the desire to believe in a truth revealed by a higher power. The second, presumably based in doubt at least as much as in the underlying faith, is a thirst to find some kind of material evidence to back up such convictions. Hence the regular reports in the press that someone has found definitive evidence of Noah's Ark, perched somewhere up on "the mountains of Ararat" as reported in Genesis. Today Mount Ararat is located in far eastern Turkey, though it was more anciently in the territory of Greater Armenia.

"Arkeology," the search for physical traces of the Ark, has a long pedigree. Back in 275 BC the Babylonian historian Berossus recorded that "some parts [of the Ark] still remain in Armenia, and some get pitch from the ship by scraping it off." Since then, numerous intrepid souls have set off in search of those remains, even though a stranded wooden vessel is highly unlikely to have survived thousands of years on the wind-and-rain-swept flanks of a 16,854-foot-high mountain. But the rate of investigation seems to have increased sharply with the advent of TV, and its thirst for sensational material.

In 1949 a Bible college professor called Aaron J. Smith, upset with what he saw as widespread disbelief in the Bible, organized a large-scale expedition to Mount Ararat with the avowed intent of proving the Good Book true. Alas, after following up on various local myths he found no trace of the Ark. Undeterred, in the subsequent sixty years at least one hundred different expeditions have also tried, many spurred by the identification of "boat-shaped" features on aerial photos and satellite images of the mountain's slopes. So unimpressive were the results (many reports turned out to be profitable hoaxes by local Kurds) that some scholars shifted the focus of their exploration to Mount Suleiman in Iran, on the south side of the Caspian Sea. Once more, to no avail.

But finally a story came along that the TV people could really get their teeth into. In 1993 the CBS network aired a purported documentary titled *The Incredible Discovery of Noah's Ark*. This starred George Jammal, an out-of-work actor who told the national TV audience that he had visited Ararat three times in search of the Ark, finally finding it in an ice cave on the mountain's upper slopes. As Jammal described it, the interior of this large icebound wooden vessel was divided into animal pens, and he had hacked off from it a piece of wood as proof of its existence. The other proof was going to be photographic; but alas, Jammal's photographer fell into a crevasse soon after the Ark was discovered, and his body (and camera) were never recovered. This story was razor thin at best, and the show's producers might productively have listened more carefully to the names of Jammal's local Armenian collaborators: "Mr. Asholian" and "Allis Buls Hittian."

Nonetheless, Jammal was the centerpiece of the prime-time program, theatrically showing off his piece of wood as "precious—and a gift from God." His stellar performance

The *Epic of Gilgamesh* recounts how the gods sent a flood to destroy Earth, but instructed one man, Utnapishtim, to build a boat to save himself, his family, and birds and beasts of all kinds. After six days, the waters abated and the ship was grounded. In the Book of Genesis, God decided to flood Earth but instructed Noah to build an ark to save himself, his family, and two of every living thing. After forty days, the waters receded and the Ark was grounded.

An ark built to the dimensions described in the Book of Genesis at the Ark Encounter theme park in Williamstown, Kentucky. What has been the motivation for the endless and fruitless expeditions to find Noah's Ark? Or Bigfoot, or the Fountain of Youth, or the Golden City of El Dorado...what are we looking for?

was backed up by a parade of "experts," each of whom made more extravagant and loopy claims than the last. The reverential host, Darren McGavin, summed up the whole two-hour farrago by declaring that the claims "support the biblical story of the Deluge in every detail." Evangelicals applauded; skeptics harrumphed.

Within a year of the airing, Jammal publicly announced that the entire Ararat episode had been made up. He had never been anywhere near the mountain, and the allegedly ancient wood was a scrap of local pine he had boiled and baked with every condiment he could find in his kitchen. It reportedly smelled of teriyaki sauce, but the TV producers had declined to test its antiquity, as they had failed to fact-check everything else.

Jammal's aim had, in his own words, been to expose the "propaganda" of the "radical religious right"; and after his revelations the CBS brass rushed to recast the "documentary" as "entertainment." But the lesson was already clear: not only can you not believe everything you read; you can't believe everything you see, either.

Noah's Ark remains a phantasm. But the flood recounted in *Gilgamesh* and Genesis may actually have a basis in fact. Around 5600 BC the waters of the Mediterranean burst through into the low-lying and formerly isolated Black Sea basin, not too far from Ararat. Imagine the shock among the basin's resident early farmers when the waters of their formerly freshwater lake rose, drowning the familiar landscape and doubtless many of them as well. It is a shock that still resonates today.

GLADIATORS AND PRO WRESTLERS

Next time you find yourself standing in Rome's mighty Colosseum, trying to imagine the overbearing structure filled with a cheering, jeering, frenzied crowd of citizens consumed with bloodlust as, in the center of the ring, sword- and net- and dagger-wielding gladiators impale one another and Christians are torn to pieces by wild animals, just conjure up the Astrodome on a night when it has been rented by World Wrestling Entertainment. The two forms of diversion have even more in common than might appear at first sight.

As its name implies, for all the threatening, scowling, and posturing that goes on in the ring, the WWE is pure entertainment. Boxers try to hurt one another; WWE wrestlers don't. In fact, even as they slam each other to the floor and stomp on their alleged opponents' heads, they are trying *not* to hurt one another—not always an easy task when the impression they are trying to create is of ultimate violence.

And they go to great lengths to create that violent impression. A video circulated not long ago of the WWE champ Triple H repeatedly banging his opponent Roman Reigns's head on the announcers' table, as the commentator Byron Saxton, himself a former wrestler, seems to be sneaking Reigns a capsule of artificial blood. The episode finishes with Reigns's head an apparently bloody mess, while the crowd predictably goes wild. Real blood, by the way, would have been a violation of WWE policy, which insists on TV-PG programming—though it's hard to see how it was avoided amid all

World Wrestling Entertainment (WWE) shows are not genuine contests, but are purely entertainment based, such as this match featuring star John Cena. They feature plot-driven, scripted, and choreographed matches, and often include moves that can put performers at risk of injury if not performed correctly.

that banging of Reigns's face on the hard tabletop. But for some altogether unfathomable reason, in the absence of real blood the TV-PG rating is maintained.

As wrestling, then, the TV pro version is entirely fake—though its practitioners hate that word, preferring to describe their sport (to the extent that it is accurately described as a sport) as "predetermined." Still, as a form of entertainment that demands high skills in acrobatics, theater, and improvisation, professional wrestling is not at all fake. It is, indeed, highly demanding. Not to injure or to be injured amid all that exertion and activity in the ring takes a great deal of expertise and concentration. But it pays off. As one pro wrestling coach reportedly remarked: "Nobody ever loses a wrestling show."

Naturally, the audience is perfectly well aware that it is being treated to a staged performance. Protected by the anonymity of the crowd, many people apparently like to lose themselves in the illusion of violence. But of course, if anyone were actually to get killed or badly injured down there in the ring, the spectators would instantly subside into a shocked silence. Or would they? After all, tradition tells us that those crowds in the Colosseum responded to all that gore with cries for more.

Recent research, though, suggests that what was going on in Rome was not quite that straightforward. The standard interpretation of gladiatorial combat is that it became formalized as a sort of ritual warfare after the Pax Romana (the Roman Peace) was established around 30 BC. For more than two centuries, the Roman army had been engaged in almost constant war, and with the arrival of peace the gladiatorial tradition allowed for the maintenance of martial skills. To keep those skills sharp, it is argued, such combat was necessarily as savage as the fighting it replaced. But that is to forget the entertainment value of conflict that is staged in front of an audience secure in the knowledge of its own safety.

Although some of those spectacles in the Colosseum and elsewhere were just as hideous as history paints them—especially when they were mass events involving prisoners of war, criminals, Christians, wild animals, and so forth—we should never underestimate the apparently deeply ingrained human need to worship celebrity. And some gladiators indeed became celebrities, famed for their skills in hand-to-hand combat and in making nubile ladies swoon.

Flamma, for example, was one of the biggest names among Roman gladiators. Using a small sword and shield, and armor on only one-half of his body, he terrorized his

In the lower panel of this fourth-century mosaic, a *retiarius* (net-fighter) named Kalendio has thrown his weighted net over a more heavily armored *secutor* (chaser) named Astyanax. In the upper panel Kalendio is on the ground, wounded, and raising his dagger to surrender. The inscription above him bears the sign for "null" (Ø) and his name, implying that he was killed.

The Roman Colosseum was completed in AD 80 and could hold up to eighty thousand spectators. It was the scene of gladiatorial contests as well as massive animal hunts, elaborately staged mock land and sea battles, magic shows, and brutal executions.

opponents in thirty-four combats, drawing huge numbers of spectators. Thanks to Hollywood, though, the most famous to us today is Spartacus, who led a slave revolt that defeated six Roman armies before he was finally brought down. Gladiators were often stars; and the parallels between the present and Imperial Rome are uncannily close: Roman children even played with clay gladiator "action figures."

A-list gladiators were obviously far from expendable. Aside from the fact that these martial artists were expensive to train, the reputations of famous gladiators were hugely valuable to their sponsors, governmental and aristocratic alike. Although most gladiators were nominally slaves, we see their worth in what top practitioners got paid. The emperor Tiberius is said to have found his gladiators so expensive that he had to limit the number of games he staged to stave off bankruptcy, while a century and a half later one of his successors, Marcus Aurelius, was forced to try a salary cap. Maybe this was necessary because by then gladiators even had agents: impresarios called *lanistae*, who supplied them for the games staged by the emperors and the rich. A really famous gladiator with a good agent might fight only a couple of bouts a year, and make enough in that short time to buy a country estate.

Under these circumstances top gladiators could hardly fight to the death, or even risk serious injury. Instead, they often aimed at a broad display of all the fighting skills they had learned over time, thrilling their audiences with virtuoso performances. According to Steven Tuck of Miami University, many gladiatorial contests progressed in three stages. In the first, the fully armed combatants moved in on each other. In the second, when one was wounded (or, as rumor has it, feigned being wounded, even using fake blood), he would regroup and distance himself from his attacker; and in the third, both would discard their shields and weapons and move in to grapple with each other, perhaps even in the formalized style of modern WWE wrestlers.

Although most such contests were won or lost, the ideal outcome of a gladiatorial match involving superstars was for the combatants to fight each other to a standstill, maintain their honor, and live to fight another day. If that wasn't exactly "nobody ever loses," it wasn't too far from it.

Upon his ascension to the imperial throne, Julianus immediately devalued the Roman currency by 6 percent, thus reducing the amount he had to pay the Praetorian Guard. This didn't go over well with the Guard or the people of Rome, who tried to stone him whenever he appeared in public.

THE JULIAN PURCHASE

Before you buy anything, make sure that the seller has title to it. This is the best real estate advice anyone can give you. The second-best advice is for the seller to make sure that the buyer can afford what he's purchasing. Those two golden rules were every bit as apposite back in the days of the Roman Empire, when the largest real estate auction of all time was held.

The Praetorian Guard was founded around 275 BC, and soon came to be the military unit specifically designated for the emperor's protection. At first its members were stationed mainly outside Rome, which meant that although they could rush to the emperor's defense they could not directly control him. But in AD 23 the Praetorian base camp was moved right to the city walls, and the Imperial Palace came under the Guard's constant surveillance. This system provided more efficient protection for the emperor, but also made the Praetorians a more than theoretical menace to the ruler. Thus, in AD 41 the Guard played an active role in the assassination of the emperor Caligula, and subsequently it saw its strength rise and fall as emperors alternately tried to exploit and control it.

But while the Praetorian Guard thus potentially controlled the fate of each emperor, it never became integrated into the larger administrative apparatus of Rome. And as a result, it remained relatively isolated politically. This isolation became particularly

The Roman Empire "stretched from Hadrian's Wall in drizzle-soaked northern England to the sun-baked banks of the Euphrates in Syria; from the great Rhine-Danube river system, which snaked across the fertile, flat lands of Europe from the Low Countries to the Black Sea, to the rich plains of the North African coast and the luxuriant gash of the Nile Valley in Egypt. The empire completely circled the Mediterranean...referred to by its conquerors as *mare nostrum*—'our sea.'"
—Christopher Kelly, *The Roman Empire: A Very Short Introduction* (Oxford University Press, 2007)

apparent in AD 193, which became known as the "Year of the Five Emperors." It began when the increasingly unstable emperor Commodus was assassinated with Praetorian connivance, and the general Pertinax was declared the new emperor. Among the first discoveries Emperor Pertinax made was that Commodus had exhausted the imperial treasury, leaving him short of cash with which to pay his protectors. This was doubly awkward for Pertinax, since while he understandably wished to exert stronger control over the Guard, his inability to cough up their salaries set the stage for confrontation. The upshot was that after Pertinax had ruled for only three months a detachment of Praetorians rushed the gates of the palace in a pay protest, and he was killed.

This is where the story departs from the standard pattern. Instead of installing one of their own—or at least a co-conspirator—as the new emperor, the broke and isolated Praetorians put the Roman Empire itself up for auction. In retrospect, this event marked the beginning of the empire's famous decline, although at that point the territory it controlled was vast, embracing not only the entire rim of the Mediterranean but also much of the Near East and central and northern Europe. One estimate puts the total acreage in AD 193 at around 1.4 billion.

The Praetorians at first feared retribution from the Senate and the Roman population. But when—despite much grumbling—none came, they announced that the empire was for sale to the highest bidder. Most potential purchasers ignored the offer or hurriedly made plans to leave town, but after carousing at a late lunch, and urged on by his wife and a "mob of parasites," the noted soldier and administrator Didius Julianus hustled to the Praetorian camp to make a bid. The other bidder was Pertinax's father-in-law, Titus Sulpicianus, prefect of Rome, who had already been dispatched by the Senate to make peace with the Guard.

The bidding war began, with Sulpicianus inside the Praetorian camp and Julianus bellowing counteroffers from beyond its walls. When told that Sulpicianus had offered every soldier an amazing 20,000 sesterces for the empire, Julianus upped the ante to 25,000. And because the Praetorians knew that they couldn't fully trust any relative of their victim Pertinax, they accepted Julianus's huge bid with alacrity. It worked out to about $1 billion in today's money—or about $1.40 for each acre of the empire.

The problem was, of course, that the Praetorians didn't actually own the empire—or, for all their control of the imperial palace, even its leadership. And although they succeeded in forcing the Senate to declare Julianus emperor, there were people out there with other ideas. One of them was Septimius Severus, a close associate of Pertinax's, who immediately began moving the armies he controlled in central Europe toward Rome.

Meanwhile, lacking sufficient cash to pay off the increasingly unhappy Praetorians, the new emperor Julianus devalued the currency and thereby further upset an already incensed population. A crowd in the Circus Maximus called for the consul to Syria, Pescennius Niger, to take over. Niger declared himself emperor, and also moved his legions toward the imperial city. To complicate things yet further, the Roman armies in Britain and Iberia independently proclaimed as emperor their own leader, Clodius Albinus, who initially allied with Severus. Civil war ensued, and eventually both Niger and a by-then-estranged Albinus were killed in battle with Severus's troops, ending the war.

As all this began to unfold, an increasingly desperate Julianus was trying everything he could think of to neutralize the threat from Severus. He declared him a public enemy; he hired assassins; he ordered the Praetorians against him; he even offered him a co-regency. To no avail. After defeating a Praetorian contingent and offering the rest of the Guard amnesty—though he had the Praetorians who had murdered Pertinax executed—Severus entered Rome, where, even before one of his soldiers killed Julianus, a trembling Senate had recognized him as lawful emperor.

This was the beginning of June, AD 193, a scant nine weeks after Julianus had purchased his imperial title. Reportedly, Julianus's dying words were: "But what evil have I done? Whom have I killed?" And despite his military background, he actually appears to have been of significantly less violent proclivities than the other major actors in this unfortunate story. Indeed, history—written of course by the victor, the austere Severus—has painted him as more interested in debauchery than in the arts of power and governance.

And thus the most spectacular real estate deal of all time ended in tears, not only for the unfortunate Julianus but also for the Praetorian Guard, which Severus disbanded. To both sides, the $1.40-per-acre price tag for the entire Roman Empire might have looked like a good deal at the time—after all, the Praetorians had good reason to distrust the underbidder Sulpicianus, whose son-in-law they had murdered, while in the afterglow of a good lunch Julianus was not to know that he would find the imperial treasury empty, or that Severus would or could move so fast. But then, the true cost of things is often a lot more than is apparent at first sight.

Sulpicianus survived Julianus's death and the arrival of the new emperor Septimius Severus. But due to his having supported the rival imperial claimant Clodius Albinus, Sulpicianus was tried and executed in AD 197.

THE LOCH NESS MONSTER

s the Loch Ness Monster a deliberate hoax? A misconstrual? A tourist attraction? A misbelief? By now it is all of these, and probably more. But it has become so iconic of the human power to believe in bizarre things that it is worth taking a look back at Nessie to get an idea of how one classic myth has grown.

Loch Ness is a narrow, deep freshwater lake that lies along the line of the Great Glen geological fault that bisects Scotland from northeast to southwest. Its waters are notably murky, due to the peaty soils of the basin in which it lies. So who knows what lurks beneath the surface?

The first report of a "monster" in Loch Ness came from Saint Columba, the sixth-century Irish monk who brought Christianity to Scotland. According to Adomnàn of Iona, his seventh-century biographer, Columba was crossing the lake when he saw people burying a man who "was a short time before seized, and bitten most severely by a monster that lived in the water." Shortly afterward a member of his own party entered the lake and was himself attacked by the monster, which the holy man calmly commanded to flee. In Adomnàn's words, "At the voice of the saint, the monster was terrified, and fled." The local Picts were impressed and gave thanks to God for this miracle. Whether Columba actually succeeded in converting them for the long haul is unrecorded, although he did pretty well in Scotland as a whole.

After its skirmish with the redoubtable Columba, the newly skittish Loch Ness Monster was not seen again for well over a millennium. Indeed, the series of sightings that gave rise to the legend as we know it today actually dates only from 1933. According to a report in the *Inverness Courier* published on May 2 that year, Mr. and Mrs. John Mackay of Drumnadrochit had just seen a whale-like creature disporting itself in the loch; and on July 22 a George Spicer reported that he and his wife had seen "a most extraordinary form of animal" crossing the road that skirted the lake. The creature had a lumpy body and a long neck; how it contrived to move is unclear, since the Spicers noticed no limbs. The next month a possibly concussed veterinary student named Arthur Grant, having just fallen off his motorcycle, also claimed to have seen a small-headed, long-necked animal entering the loch.

The first photograph of the mysterious beast was taken on November 12, 1933. After this, sightings took off, until by now around a thousand people have purportedly seen the monster, and blurry photos abound. Many of the latter have been explicitly exposed as hoaxes, most recent among them being a 2011 image of a fuzzy-looking hump (nonetheless hailed as one of the "best ever" Nessie photos) taken by a tourist boat skipper who eventually admitted he was trawling for business.

The first systematic investigation into the Loch Ness Monster was mounted not long after the initial sightings but came up with the peculiarly Scottish verdict of "not proven." World War II intervened, but then during the decade between 1962 and 1972, the "Loch Ness Phenomena Investigation Bureau" conducted sonar and other studies, eventually giving up, too.

The arena was then entered by a team led by the American lawyer Robert H. Rines, and eventually a puzzling sonar image and some associated photographs were secured. After computer enhancement at the Jet Propulsion Laboratory in Pasadena, the hugely indistinct photos were analyzed by Rines and the noted English ornithologist and conservationist Sir Peter Scott, son of the famed Antarctic explorer Robert Falcon Scott. The two men, neither of them with any significant experience of such animals, concluded that they were looking at images of the hind limb, or paddle, of a large aquatic reptile.

In a report in the prestigious scientific journal *Nature* dated December 11, 1975, the pair created the new genus and species *Nessiteras rhombopteryx* for the animal whose paddle they thought they saw (experts at the Natural History Museum in London thought they saw gas bubbles). The name roughly means "wonderful lozenge-fin of Loch Ness," and seldom can either of us remember hearing so much chortling in the rather serious world of taxonomists. In a discussion worthy of an eighteenth-century academy, Rines and Scott solemnly debated to which group of reptiles their new species might be related, though eventually they very responsibly declined to reach a firm conclusion. Just for the record, Nessie aficionados consider the front-runner to be the plesiosaurs, a group of mostly long-necked marine reptiles that went extinct some 66 million years ago.

The rationale for going ahead and naming Nessie on such incredibly slender evidence (the taxonomic convention is to never name anything until you have an actual specimen in hand) was that, whatever it might have been, Nessie was definitely endangered; and you couldn't protect an endangered species unless it had a proper zoological name.

In the 1970 Billy Wilder film *The Private Life of Sherlock Holmes*, the detective encounters the Loch Ness Monster. The thirty-foot model of the monster included a neck and two humps. Wilder did not like the humps and had them removed, despite warnings that this would affect buoyancy. As a result, the model sank.

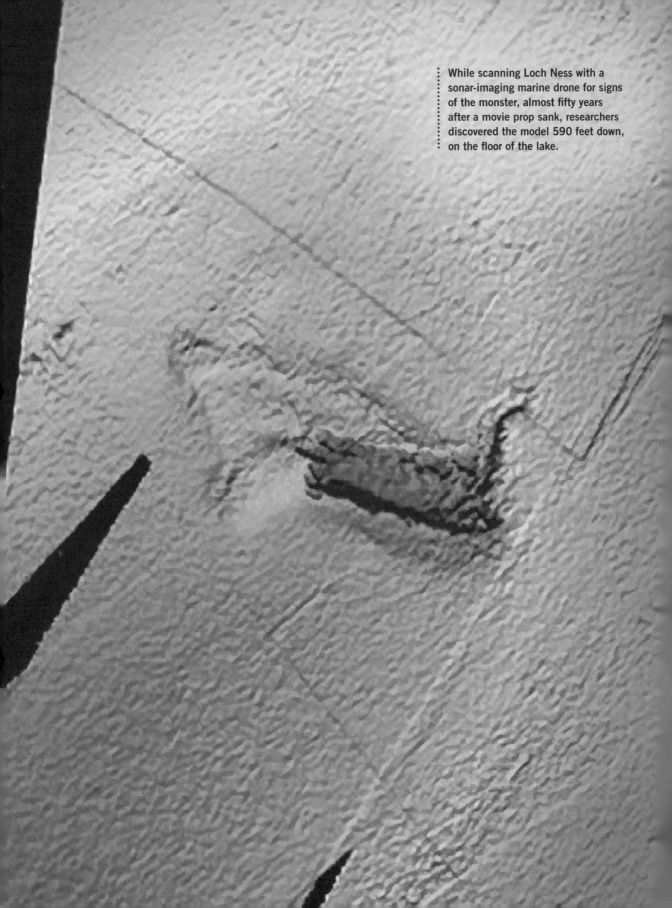

While scanning Loch Ness with a sonar-imaging marine drone for signs of the monster, almost fifty years after a movie prop sank, researchers discovered the model 590 feet down, on the floor of the lake.

Well, okay. For us, the best part of the story is that, as a crossword fan pointed out, *Nessiteras rhombopteryx* is an anagram for "monster hoax by Sir Peter S."

Of course, that was not the end of it. Nessie enthusiasts have recently been using a robotic submarine to image the bed of Loch Ness in search of Nessie's lair—despite a BBC team's conclusion back in 2003, following an exhaustive sonar survey, that there was nothing down there apart from a few shipwrecks. And amazingly, in 2016 the robot did find a monster lurking in the deep. Only it turned out to be a thirty-foot-long model of a long-necked Nessie, with stubby horns and bulging eyes, that had accidentally sunk after being towed out into the lake in 1970 for use in shooting Billy Wilder's movie *The Private Life of Sherlock Holmes*.

If even the great detective couldn't find Nessie (and actually managed to lose it), what hope is there for the rest of us? An excellent question, but we can nonetheless confidently say that the story of the Loch Ness Monster is not over yet. As long as we want a monster to be down there, there will be one—even if it is only a movie prop.

Monsters have been reported in more than sixty-five lakes worldwide. A sampling of these include (with their nicknames): Cold Lake, Alberta, Canada: *Kinosoo*; Lake Nahuel Huapi, Argentina: *Nahuelito*; Lake Ikeda, Japan: *Issie*; Seneca Lake, New York: *the Serpent;* Lake Somyn, Ukraine: *Som*; Lake Kariba, Zimbabwe: *Nyami Nyami*; and Loch Morar, Scotland: *Morag*.

A *Kreuzpartikel* or fragment of the True Cross. "There is no abbey so poor as not to have a specimen. In some places there are large fragments, as at the Holy Chapel in Paris, at Poitiers, and at Rome, where a good-sized crucifix is said to have been made of it. In brief, if all the pieces that could be found were collected together, they would make a big ship-load. Yet the Gospel testifies that a single man was able to carry it."
—*John Calvin, Traité des Reliques.*

THE **PRECIOUS PREPUCE**

P eople have always been morbidly inquisitive, but rarely more overtly so than in early medieval times, when the craze for relics of Christian martyrs was at its height. From its very beginnings, Christian belief had depended on the miraculous, and as the church expanded its area of dominion to cover most of the Western world, grisly physical tokens of miracles and of those who wrought them were in ever greater demand. And wherever there is demand, there is supply, a basic fact that did not fail to escape Christian (and other; see chapter 9, *Sindonology*) entrepreneurs.

Back in the sixteenth century, no less a personage than the Protestant theologian John Calvin complained that if all the alleged fragments of the True Cross scattered in churches and monasteries across Europe were collected together, they would fill a large ship. Irony not being his strong suit, Calvin then felt it necessary to add, "Yet the Gospel testifies that a single man was able to carry it."

Of course, the notably humorless Calvin had political rather than satirical motives for making his observations. And exactly the same thing applied to the Roman Catholics who had diligently filled vast numbers of religious institutions with saintly relics to help cement their grip on a credulously adoring populace. Certainly, political circumstance seems to have been complicit in the appearance of one of the most improbable relics of them all: the infant Jesus's foreskin, allegedly preserved in an oil-filled alabaster box following the traditional circumcision ceremony during which it had been detached from its doubtless unhappy owner.

Having made its literary debut in the apocryphal First Gospel of the Infancy of Jesus Christ of the second century AD, this curious item seems to have reappeared in material form at the turn of the ninth century, when the Carolingian leader Charlemagne was raised by the pope to the hereditary rank of Holy Roman Emperor. Said to have been gifted to Charlemagne by an angel, the sacred prepuce duly found its way to the Basilica of St. John Lateran in Rome.

At this point preputial stories diversify, mostly to account for the eventual presence of the object in at least eight, and by some versions as many as eighteen, widely scattered religious institutions. Many of these mysteriously multiplied preputia disappeared during the upheavals of the French Revolution, but the last of them—believed by many to be the original Roman one that had vanished during the city's sacking by an errant Bourbon army in 1527—survived to be stolen, as recently as 1984, from an Italian parish priest who purportedly kept it in a shoebox stored under his bed.

Much controversy inevitably followed this latter event, although it was widely rumored at the time that the final foreskin's disappearance had not been entirely unwelcome to the Catholic hierarchy. Possibly this sense of relief was due to the insistence of many Catholic theologians that the adult Jesus had ascended intact into Heaven, necessarily taking his prepuce with him. Indeed, the missing tissue was intrinsic to some very elaborate Catholic cosmologies: the late-seventeenth-century theologian Leo Allatius, for example, explained at some length how this disputably dispensable part of the Redeemer's anatomy had become transmuted into the recently discovered rings of the planet Saturn.

To many modern minds, such explanations of celestial phenomena may echo even more strangely than the veneration of saintly body parts itself. Yet sacred physical relics were intrinsic to the spiritual lives of millions of medieval Europeans, filling the void left when pagan gods and idols had been swept away by the triumph of Christianity not too many centuries before. The distinguished nineteenth-century anthropologist James Frazer explained their importance in terms of what he called "contagious magic": relics conveyed the imagined sanctity of the past to the present. They embodied a spiritual quality that could not be experienced directly by mere mortals, and provided a tangible connection between heaven and the noisome earthly realm.

Unlike the holy scriptures, which gave only abstract satisfaction, the veneration of these physical objects involved the physical senses: in medieval times, biting and fondling of relics during the holy days on which they were exhibited was hardly a rare occurrence. Through such intimate contact, as well as by veneration from afar, they lent a corporeal form to the supernatural beliefs that helped give communities their

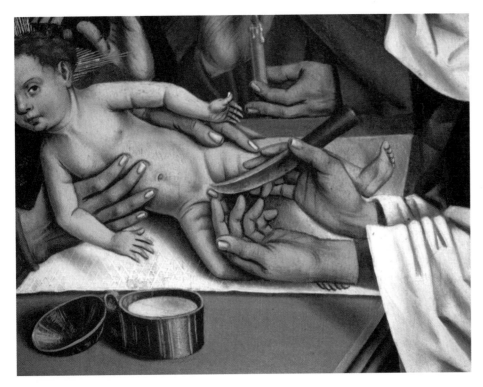

Circumcision of Christ, detail from *Twelve Apostles Altar (Zwölf-Boten-Altar)* by Friedrich Herlin of Nördlingen, 1466.

sense of cohesion. Correspondingly, the control of these often gruesome items also gave the clergy direct leverage over their adoring flocks.

It was as much the political aspect of relics as their theological implications that horrified Calvin, Martin Luther, and other reformers of the sixteenth century, who insisted that a more natural corporeal progression was "from dust to dust." In Protestant northern Europe the reformers' constant exhortations gave rise to an immediate frenzy of statue-smashing and relic-trashing; and while in the Catholic south the veneration of saintly relics continued unabated for another couple of centuries, even there it began to weaken toward the end of the seventeenth century. Not coincidentally, this happened at a time when science was beginning its ascendance, replacing transcendental explanations of physical phenomena with rational ones that could be tested against actual observations of nature.

But we still live in a world of images. We may not overtly worship them or attribute supernatural powers to them, but we are still prepared to pay well over the odds to possess them. When it comes right down to it, the items we value today furnish precious little evidence that essential human yearnings have changed significantly since the Middle Ages. The signed baseball—genuine or forged—is in many ways the new saint's finger.

POPE JOAN

Despite the recent proliferation of celebrity female CEOs and stay-at-home dads, it is still hard to argue that women have achieved parity with men in our society. But in most developed countries things are much better for women today than they were in the Middle Ages, when the lot of female Europeans was a hard one indeed, and women were constrained in ways we currently glimpse in only the most backward of societies.

For any medieval woman to stand out, then, was something altogether remarkable. An ambitious Englishwoman might have looked back to Boudicca, the quasi-legendary Celtic queen who bravely stood up against Roman occupation in around AD 60. Those seeking inspiration from the ancient world might have admired the example of Hatshepsut, who became the fifth pharaoh of Egypt's Eighteenth Dynasty in 1478 BC. The builder of the sublime temple at Deir el-Bahari in western Thebes, Hatshepsut is regarded as one of Egypt's most accomplished ancient rulers; but, probably significantly, the many representations of Hatshepsut as pharaoh show her wearing the stylized pharaonic beard.

In the early Catholic church, women were revered as mothers and as martyrs, but as little more. One outstanding exception was the extraordinary Hildegard of Bingen, born around 1098 in Germany's Rhineland. Through sheer force of character, Hildegard contrived to found her own monastery before becoming an influential visionary theologian and composer of sacred music, though today she is best remembered as a pioneer in natural history and a recorder of the medical practices of her time.

....

OPPOSITE: A granite statue of Hatshepsut, arguably the most important woman ever to occupy the throne of Egypt. She is depicted kneeling and wearing a ceremonial beard.

And then there was Pope Joan. This mysterious figure does not appear in official histories of the patriarchal Catholic Church, but the references to her in medieval and Renaissance Catholic writings are numerous. The first mention of the female pope came from the pen of the chronicler Jean de Mailly in around AD 1250. Jean tells a sad tale:

> A…female Pope…is not set down in the list of Popes…because she was a woman who disguised herself as a man and became, by her character and talents, a curial secretary, then a Cardinal and finally Pope. One day, when mounting a horse, she gave birth to a child. Immediately…she was dragged and stoned for half a league, and, where she died, there she was buried.

Jean's story was picked up by others, most famously soon after by the papal historian Martin of Opava. Martin added various details, including the name of the mysterious pope ("John Anglicus"); that she had been educated in Athens, whither she had followed a lover, dressed as a man; and the place of her death (a lane between the Colosseum and St. Clement's Basilica). He also moved the event back from the early twelfth to the mid-ninth century.

A fifteenth-century hand-colored woodcut depicting Pope Joan giving birth from Giovanni Boccaccio's *De Mulieribus Claris* (Concerning Famous Women).

Sedes marmorea Pontificis in Basilica Lateranensi.

This is a powerful story, and from the beginning it was the stuff of legend, especially dating as it does—if true—from a time when the papacy was a pretty chaotic institution. Over the period in question, popes and antipopes were busily murdering one another, and in 1309 the entire papal court fled from Rome to Avignon and established a new capital there. Still, only rather few independent pieces of evidence hint at a possible historical reality behind Pope Joan.

The first of these is a curious commode-like red marble throne, now in one of the Vatican Museums, on which, between 1199 and 1513 (when the newly minted Protestants began to laugh at them), popes were seated for coronation. This curious article of furniture has a hole in its seat into which, by some accounts, at the investiture, an attending official would put his hand to ensure the presence of testicles. Apparently, on assuring himself of this fact the cleric would cry, "*Testiculos habet et bene pendentes*" ("He has testicles, hanging nicely"). The others in attendance would

A priest checking for the pope-elect's testicles during the investiture ceremony.

joyfully respond, "*Habe ova noster Papa*" ("The pope is virile!"). Popes supposed being celibate, one naturally wonders why all this was considered necessary—unle it was a case of "once bitten, twice shy."

Another odd fact: In the fourteenth century some 170 busts depicting various pope were made for the cathedral in Siena. Three hundred years later it was reported by Vatican librarian that one of them had depicted a female, and had been labele "Johannes VIII, Femina de Anglia"—in other words, Joan. The pope ordered the bu destroyed, but the thrifty folk of Siena simply erased her name and replaced it wi that of Pope Zachary.

Finally, it does seem to be the case that later medieval popes strictly avoided the plac at which Joan reportedly gave birth. Today, a shrine stands on that spot, officially called th Chapel of the Virgin but popularly known as the Chapel of La Papessa. Not long ag the eminent endocrinologist Maria New reported finding a pregnant woman prayir there. When asked why, the expectant mother responded: "I am praying to Pope Joa for me to have a healthy baby." Legend or not, Pope Joan refuses to go away, ar repeatedly resurfaces in modern literature as well as in the daily lives of the faithful.

As intriguing as anything, perhaps, is Dr. New's suggestion that, had Joan in fact existe she could indeed have been technically a woman—and have given birth to a baby- and yet have had the physical appearance of a man. She might even have believed sl was one—hence the surprise at the unexpected birth while preparing for a processio

An event of this kind might have been possible if Joan was what is known as a fema pseudohermaphrodite, having female chromosomes and internal reproductive organ but male external appearance. This is a pretty rare syndrome, but it is well known endocrinologists under the label of congenital adrenal hyperplasia. If this proper describes Pope Joan, she might have had a homosexual liaison with a man, becom pregnant, and delivered a child. Skipping the first part and using artificial inseminatic instead, one of Dr. New's very masculine-looking patients did just that.

THE SHROUD OF TURIN

Not everyone is religious, but religious belief is characteristic of every human society ever documented. Most of us seem to yearn to believe in something existentially larger than ourselves, and for many religion fills that need. Yet religion demands a comprehensive world view, and the world is a complicated place, full of details. In some religions those details are supplied by relics: physical symbols, both of the greater faith itself and of those who most excellently exemplified it and exhibited it in their lives—mythical or otherwise. Relics are, in many ways, the small mosaic tiles that flesh out the bigger religious picture, and to some people they have an even larger significance: they are the glue that holds it all together.

Perhaps the most famous relic of them all is the Shroud of Turin. This is a rough linen cloth, about fourteen feet long and four feet wide, that bears life-size, ghostly yellowish images of the front and back of a tall, naked, bearded, and long-haired man. The man appears to bear bloody puncture wounds on the wrist and chest, as testified by reddish-brown stains on the image as well as smaller lacerations across the forehead. It is believed by many to have been the actual burial cloth in which Jesus was interred— and the image thus is that of Jesus himself.

The Shroud is said to have been brought back from Turkey in 1346 by a French Crusader, Geoffroi de Charny, who later died in the Battle of Poitiers. The first documentary record certainly places the piece in Geoffroi's family church at Lirey before 1390, although that proof of existence comes in the form of a letter from the local bishop to the pope declaring the Shroud to be a forgery.

The Image of Edessa. The sixth-century Syrian scholar Evagrius Scholasticus reported that Abgar, ruler of the kingdom of Osroene (present-day southeastern Turkey), owned a cloth on which Jesus's face had been imprinted. It effected miraculous aid in defense of Osroene's capital city of Edessa against the Persians in 544.

A shadow has thus hovered over the Shroud from the beginning. Nonetheless, in 1453 it was deeded to the Dukes of Savoy, and in 1578 it found its way to the cathedral in the Savoyard capital of Turin, where it has remained ever since. Thousands of pilgrims continue to flock there every year to revere it. Still, despite the Shroud's obvious potential documentary and spiritual importance, the Vatican has never expressed any official opinion on its authenticity.

The Shroud that is now in Turin is actually one of more than forty pieces of cloth of varying sizes that were touted during the Middle Ages as having been used to wrap the body of the crucified Christ. Many of these curiosities were apparently lost during the French Revolution (the French evidently having been particularly diligent collectors of such things); but in addition to Turin, ecclesiastical establishments in Rome; Genoa; Oviedo, Spain; and Cadouin, France, also currently claim to be housing at least parts of the holy winding sheet. All of these textiles are believed to have covered the face of Christ, which of course means that only one of the contenders—at most— can have been part of the true shroud.

In 1988, with Vatican approval, samples from the Shroud of Turin were submitted to three independent laboratories for radiocarbon dating. The dates obtained clustered pretty closely in the period between AD 1260 and 1390, which means that the textile itself was pretty certainly made at some point between the middle of the thirteenth century and the end of the fourteenth. Indeed, in announcing their findings in 1989, the scientists who carried out the dating flatly declared that their results "provide conclusive evidence that the linen of the Shroud of Turin is medieval." The specific date range corresponds very closely to the time at which Geoffroi acquired his souvenir, and the agreement is at the very least extremely suggestive.

The available physical evidence is thus strongly in favor of the conclusion that the biblical crucifixion was already 1,300 years in the past when the cloth was woven, most plausibly in Turkey. The images themselves are rather curious—nothing else

Fourteenth-century French and German legends recount that Veronica was one of the women of Luke 23:27 who followed Jesus along the Via Dolorosa. When she wiped the sweat off his face with her veil, his image was imprinted on the cloth. The last detailed inspection of what purports to be this relic, now housed in St. Peter's Basilica, was in 1907 by Jesuit art historian Joseph Wilpert. He wrote that he saw only "a square piece of light colored material, somewhat faded through age, which bear [sic] two faint rust-brown stains, connected one to the other."

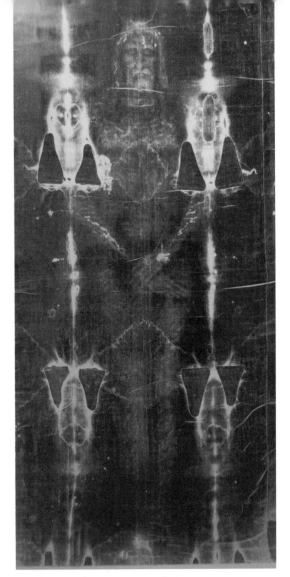

stylistically like them is known—and, strangely, they have some of the characteristics of a photographic negative. Possibly they were made by pressing the linen on a bas-relief model smeared with pigments, although that isn't known for sure. All that is certain is that the images must be younger than the cloth on which they are preserved.

Inevitably, there has been criticism of the dating results: The dating itself was fraudulent, carried out on surreptitiously substituted linen samples. The samples were contaminated by bacteria, or by more recent carbon, maybe from smoke. Or they were taken from a part of the Shroud that had been repaired in medieval times. And so on. But in the event, none of the denunciations has held up under scrutiny.

What is more, there is a much longer list of reasons to suspect the Shroud's inauthenticity. Its characteristics are inconsistent with the accounts of the New Testament; the images lack the expected wraparound distortions and show the medieval stereotype of their subject rather than a realistic Roman-era representation; the images of the front and back of the body do not match up perfectly; the "bloodstains" contain no blood; and so forth.

At this point, then, it is extremely hard to avoid the conclusion that the Shroud of Turin is a fake, albeit an old one, manufactured for the Crusader market at a time when the collecting of holy relics had reached fad-like proportions (see chapter 7, *Sacred Relics*). But maybe the fraudulence of the object itself is beside the point. Sometimes it is more important to preserve what you believe than it is to cleave to fact. Even if it does not date from the time of Christ, the Shroud is a venerable symbol of a system of belief that is of primal importance to its adherents. That system also happens to emphasize the importance of faith. And faith, of course, is necessarily blind.

MICHELANGELO'S
CUPID

During the Renaissance, antiquities were valued far above the art that was being produced at the time. And then, as now, struggling young sculptors found it hard to get their foot on the ladder. One of those aspiring artists was Michelangelo di Lodovico Buonarroti Simoni, now more familiar by just his first name.

Michelangelo's origins were not exactly humble. But the small Florentine bank that his father had inherited failed before he was born, and by the time he was apprenticed to the Florentine artist Domenico Ghirlandaio in 1488, at the age of thirteen, his parents were hardly awash in cash. Yet Michelangelo soon became a wealthy man, and even though his talent had been rapidly recognized, the rate at which his assets grew early in his

This bronze third- or second-century BC Greek statue of Eros may have been the inspiration for Michelangelo's lost *Sleeping Cupid*.

41

career can hardly be accounted for by the early commissions he is known to have received. Unsurprisingly, then, Michelangelo's youthful affluence has occasionally invited suspicions that much of his money might have been made through producing fake antiquities that he sold off the books.

Without doubt, the most audacious (and controversial) suggested forgery of this kind is the famous *Laocoön and His Sons* that resides now in the Vatican, and that is revered as one of the ultimate masterpieces of Classical art. The official (and quite possibly true) story of this extraordinary (and extraordinarily well preserved) statue is that it was found by workers digging near the "Seven Halls" on the Esquiline Hill, one of the famous Seven Hills of Rome.

Using a description supplied by the historian Pliny the Elder, who died in the AD 79 eruption of Vesuvius, experts at the time identified the sculpture as the most celebrated of many Classical representations of Laocoön (a Trojan priest of Apollo) and his two sons being attacked by a pair of serpents. The piece Pliny had originally seen in the palace of Emperor Titus had been sculpted in Rhodes early in the first century BC by three sculptors, Hagesandros, Athenodoros, and Polydoros.

On its discovery in a vineyard in 1506, the Vatican *Laocoön* was missing its main subject's right arm—hardly surprising in a piece thought to be more than a millennium and a half old. After its purchase by Pope Julius II, the statue was restored with the arm extended, although Michelangelo objected that the elbow should be bent—something that was far from self-evident just from looking at the broken shoulder.

When the missing arm was inexplicably discovered in a builder's yard five and a half centuries later, in 1957, Michelangelo was proven right. How could he have known?

Whether or not the evidence is compelling that Michelangelo actually enriched himself by faking the Vatican *Laocoön*—something that was clearly within his uncanny ability—is for those viewing and studying the sculpture to decide. But the artist was well known in his own time for his accomplished copying of old drawings (allegedly he returned some of his copies to the owners, and kept the originals), and in his early impecunious days he was definitely responsible for at least one faked Classical sculpture.

As recounted in Giorgio Vasari's classic 1550 book *Lives of the Most Excellent Painters, Sculptors, and Architects*, in 1496 the twenty-one-year-old Michelangelo sculpted a sleeping Cupid in Classical style that was praised as exquisite by all who saw it. One early viewer, Lorenzo di Pierfrancesco, remarked that "if you were to bury it and treat it to seem old and then send it to Rome, I'm sure that it would pass as an antique and you would get far more for it than you would here."

Is the statue of *Laocoön and His Sons* one of the finest examples of Classical sculpture, or is it one of the most fantastic forgeries of all time, created by none other than Michelangelo?

Michelangelo duly aged the piece, and through a dealer it ultimately found its way into the hands of Cardinal Riario of San Giorgio. When the cardinal was tipped off to the fraud he demanded his money back; but, impressed by the artist's talent, he allowed Michelangelo to keep his cut. Subsequently, in an age during which well-faked antiquities were often publicly admired, the Cupid actually did much to establish Michelangelo's reputation.

Eventually, Vasari says, the sculpture found its way into the possession of Duke Valentino, who presented it in turn to the Marchioness of Mantua. In Mantua, it entered the fabled Gonzaga collection, one of the most astonishing assemblages of artworks of all kinds ever put together—though, sadly, no complete catalog of the twenty-thousand-plus pieces it contained was ever compiled.

Michelangelo's artistic achievements were Promethean.

With a decline in the Gonzaga family's fortunes, much of the collection was sold off between 1626 and 1630 to King Charles I of England, an avid collector of art. Once in London, the Cupid found its way with many other masterpieces to the Palace of Whitehall, which had for a century been the main residence of the kings of England.

The last documentary evidence of the Michelangelo Cupid is to be found in the diary of Samuel Pepys, in his entry for December 6, 1665:

> Up betimes, it being Fast day, and by water to the Duke of Albemarle, who came to town from Oxford last night. He is mighty brisk, and very kind to me, and asks my advice principally in everything. He shews me a curious Sleeping Eros done by Michel-Ange sent from White-hall for his charge of the Admiralty; and so I home by water again, and to church a little.

After this, no more is known of the Michelangelo Cupid. If it remained in the Duke of Albemarle's residence overlooking the Fleet River it was certainly destroyed in the Great Fire of London the following year. And yet, had it remained in Whitehall, it would have suffered a similar fate. In 1698 the Palace of Whitehall itself burned down in a mighty conflagration that, in the words of the diarist John Evelyn, left "nothing but walls and ruins," and that carried away numerous other Gonzaga masterpieces as well as Hans Holbein's mural *Portrait of Henry VIII*.

Perhaps cheeringly, the Cupid's fiery fate may not mean the final demise of Michelangelo fakes. Not very long ago the *New York Daily News* quoted Columbia University art historian Lynn Catterson as saying: "There might be a few more Michelangelos we don't even know about that are hiding in Greek and Roman galleries pretending to be antiquities."

PSALMANAZAR

MEMOIRS of ****.

Commonly known by the Name of

GEORGE PSALMANAZAR;

A

Reputed Native of FORMOSA.

Written by himself

In order to be published after his Death.

CONTAINING

An Account of his Education, Travels, Adventures, Connections, Literary Productions, and pretended Conversion from Heathenism to Christianity; which last proved the Occasion of his being brought over into this Kingdom, and passing for a Proselyte, and a Member of the Church of England.

LONDON:

PRINTED FOR THE EXECUTRIX.

Sold by R. DAVIS, in Piccadilly; J. NEWBERY, in St. Paul's Church-Yard; L. DAVIS, and C. REYMER, in Holborn.

MDCCLXIV.

M.ʳ George Psalmanazar.

I n the early eighteenth century Londoners' notions of the farther-flung reaches of the world that their homeland would soon dominate were still decidedly hazy. Dark-skinned Africans were no longer a complete novelty in the British capital, but the continent from which they came was still largely known only from sparse and often fantastical travelers' reports; and, among other things, it was believed that Africans' complexions were dark in direct response to the tropical sun under which they lived—for after all, Europeans, too, darkened in tropical latitudes.

Since ignorance of the Far East and its inhabitants was almost equally profound, it is maybe not so remarkable that, in 1703, a blue-eyed, fair-complexioned polyglot who had adopted the name of George Psalmanazar found himself welcomed in London society as a native of Formosa (today's Taiwan).

Brought to the city by an Anglican missionary who had encountered him in Amsterdam, the exotic stranger quickly became an indispensable accessory at fashionable social events. At one society dinner after another, his fellow diners looked on in awe as he

In his posthumous *Memoirs*, George Psalmanazar admitted he had fabricated his harrowing tale of an innocent "Formosan," kidnapped by Jesuits and imprisoned by Calvinists, who had finally reached the welcoming shores of Anglican England. The masquerade had worked initially because he had tailored it for an Anglican audience suspicious of Calvinism, and predisposed to hate the Catholic Church.

chewed his way through platefuls of raw meat (Formosans, apparently, never cooked their food) and babbled in a language unlike any they had ever heard before.

Psalmanazar's rapid acceptance into the higher echelons of London society doubtless had a lot to do not only with the story he told of himself but also with the place where he told it. He had, he said, been born in Formosa as a pagan, but then been kidnapped by a Jesuit missionary who took him to Europe and tried to turn him into a Catholic. Anglican hearts warmed as he described how he had resisted conversion and, after sundry adventures, escaped to Holland, where he resolutely rejected the advances of the equally detested Calvinists. In a small society with a limited range of distractions and an intense curiosity about the larger world of which it was just becoming aware, the mysterious and intriguing Psalmanazar quickly achieved rock-star-like fame.

The "Formosan alphabet," which is comprised of twenty letters written from right to left, is a mishmash of Hebrew, Greek, and nonsense.

Emboldened by his social success, in 1704 Psalmanazar published *An Historical and Geographical Description of Formosa, an Island Subject to the Emperor of Japan*, written in a mere two months. Clearly familiar with the ethnographic literature as it existed at the time, he presented in this bestseller an elaborate account of life and customs in Formosa. Apparently, Formosans walked around naked except for a modesty plate made of silver or gold. They dined mainly on snakes, although in case of infidelity a husband might eat his wife. The sun, moon, and ten stars had originally been worshiped; monotheism had intruded later, and at the beginning of every year eighteen thousand young boys were sacrificed to the new god, their hearts roasted on metal grills.

Excessive as this stuff might sound to modern ears, none of it would have seemed unduly outlandish to people thirsty for knowledge of the unknown and exotic, and familiar with existing accounts of Inca and Aztec ceremonies. And Psalmanazar's greatest achievement was to provide a hugely convincing description both of the Formosan language—which he spoke with an accent nobody could pin down—and its orthography. So persuasive was his entirely made-up account that he was invited to Oxford to teach the language to aspiring missionaries, and German linguists were still quoting his "Formosan alphabet" well into the middle of the century.

But this was also an age of skepticism, and many in London worried about the alleged Formosan. Things came to a head at a meeting of the Royal Society, during which

Psalmanazar showed amazing adroitness under interrogation by the astronomer Edmond Halley and his colleagues. (For more on Halley, see chapter 33, *Pseudoplanetology*.)

For example, when Halley inquired how long the sun shone down Formosan chimneys (something that could be checked against astronomical observation), Psalmanazar declared that in Formosa chimneys were built with an angle, so that the sun *couldn't* shine down them. When another interlocutor questioned the fairness of his skin, he explained that the Formosan upper classes to which he belonged lived "in cool shades, or apartments under ground," thus retaining their pale complexions. A visiting French clergyman objected that Formosa was Chinese, not Japanese, to which Psalmanazar replied that he was confusing Formosa with "Tayowan," which was actually a different island.

You might call the Royal Society event a draw, but as time passed and more reliable information about the real Formosa seeped into England, Psalmanazar's claims to Formosan origin became increasingly untenable. His missionary sponsor left to become a military chaplain in Portugal, and the man himself gradually faded from the social scene, ultimately becoming a poorly paid scribbler on Grub Street, the center of London's burgeoning pamphlet industry.

Ultimately Psalmanazar wrote a memoir, published posthumously, in which he withheld his real identity but admitted that his accounts both of Formosa and of his own history were manufactured. His origins remain obscure, but it seems most likely that he was born Catholic in rural southern France, from which a genius for languages had allowed him to escape, and ultimately to be discovered by his Anglican sponsor.

The Idol of the DEVIL

According to Psalmanazar, the Formosans gave up idolatry in favor of devotion to a single powerful god, in whose honor they built a gigantic temple where "the hearts of 18000 young Boys, under the Age of 9 Years" were sacrificed on the first day of each year.

Psalmanazar's smooth ability to impress those he met, to fend off awkward questions, and to maintain his improbable Formosan imposture were remarkable enough. But perhaps the most astonishing thing of all was his later friendship with the literary giant Samuel Johnson. The two met when Johnson was still a struggling writer on Grub Street and Psalmanazar's glory days were well behind him. When Johnson's friend Hester Thrale asked him who the best man was that he had ever known, he unhesitatingly replied, "Psalmanazar." The odd couple would spend hours talking in the ale houses of Holborn and the City of London. One wishes one could have been a fly on the wall.

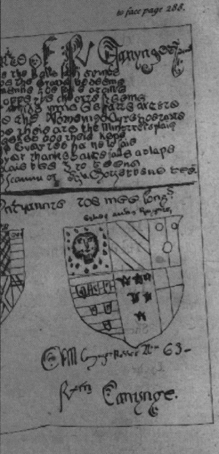

to face page 288.

POEMS,

SUPPOSED TO HAVE BEEN WRITTEN AT BRISTOL,

BY THOMAS ROWLEY, AND OTHERS,

IN THE FIFTEENTH CENTURY;

THE GREATEST PART NOW FIRST PUBLISHED FROM THE MOST
AUTHENTIC COPIES, WITH AN ENGRAVED SPECIMEN
OF ONE OF THE MSS.

TO WHICH ARE ADDED,

A PREFACE,

AN INTRODUCTORY ACCOUNT OF THE
SEVERAL PIECES,

AND

A GLOSSARY.

Published by Mr. Tyrwhit, Clerk of ye H. of Commons.

LONDON:

Printed for T. PAYNE and SON,
at the MEWS-GATE.

MDCCLXXVII.

THOMAS CHATTERTON

n 1752, when Thomas Chatterton was born in a country schoolmaster's house near Bristol, male life expectancy was not much above thirty-five years in an England poised on the brink of the Industrial Revolution. Times were hard for all except a small privileged elite. Thomas's father died before the birth of his son, leaving his young seamstress wife to eke out a precarious living for herself, two children, and her mother-in-law. As a result, the young Chatterton's only formal education was at the equivalent of a trade school.

This was an inauspicious start for a boy who grew up loving beauty and poetry, surrounded by history in the church at which his uncle was the sexton. And things only got worse when the Bristol lawyer to whom he was apprenticed at the age of fourteen tore up the poems he had written in his meager spare time and, as was his legal right, forbade him to write more.

Under these circumstances, the precocious but socially awkward Chatterton was obliged to write clandestinely, an activity he had already begun while in school. His earliest surviving poem was written when he was eleven years old, and his first work to be published appeared in a broadsheet called *Felix Farley's Bristol Journal* when its author was not yet sixteen. This precocious publication consisted of an entirely imagined fifteenth-century account of the inauguration of Bristol's Old Bridge over the river Severn, written on the occasion of the opening of the New Bridge in 1768.

Chatterton's principal ploy, however, was to write poems on parchment scavenged from his uncle's church, and to present them to potential patrons and publishers as the work of Thomas Rowley, a fifteenth-century Bristol monk who celebrated the rich mythical past of his home city in archaic and lyrical verse.

In Chatterton's world, social connections offered the only prospect of advancement for someone with literary pretensions and a conspicuous lack of resources. One early benefactor was William Barrett, a Bristol surgeon and antiquarian, who innocently published a number of Rowley manuscripts—acquired in 1768—in his *History and Antiquities of the City of Bristol* of 1789. Others were less generous, among them the aesthete Horace Walpole, who at first showed interest but later rejected the manuscripts he had been offered as forgeries. Perhaps it takes one to know one, since Walpole had himself tried to pass off his own first novel, *The Castle of Otranto*, as a genuine medieval work.

In 1770 Chatterton extricated himself from his apprenticeship and decamped for London. There he published a wonderful variety of pieces—parodies, satires, poems, political commentaries—under his own name, but found himself little rewarded by miserly editors. So, living frugally in an attic in Holborn, he turned back to Rowley. Alas, to no avail; even the slow-paying *Hamilton's Town and Country Magazine*, which had published Rowley's "Elinor and Juga"—the only one of Chatterton's poems to be published in his lifetime—rejected the subsequently much-admired "An Excelente Balade of Charitie."

By this time, Chatterton was growing desperate. Far from having become a poet whose fame would lift his family from poverty, he was starving in a London garret with not even the barest hint that his prospects might improve. He toyed with the idea of becoming a physician, and even wrote to Barrett asking for help in getting a job as an assistant surgeon on a merchant ship. But in August 1770, when walking in a

To the simultaneously materialistic and sentimental society of his time, Thomas Chatterton's poverty and untimely suicide represented the Romantic martyrdom of the poet, as depicted in Henry Wallis's 1856 painting.

churchyard, the preoccupied poet stumbled into an open grave. Having been helped out by a companion, Chatterton remarked that "I have been at war with the grave for some time now." Three days later he drank arsenic in his attic room and died, three months shy of his eighteenth birthday.

In his short life Chatterton had published only a single poem, and at the time few noticed his passing. Yet before long there was a Rowley revival. In 1777, the Chaucer scholar Thomas Tyrwhitt published a Rowley anthology in the belief that the poems were genuinely medieval, though he was more hesitant in a second edition published the following year. No matter; whether or not commentators believed in the authenticity of Chatterton's poetry—and it was a matter of huge controversy—it was being widely read.

William Wordsworth, born the year Chatterton died, and his near-contemporary Samuel Taylor Coleridge, his cofounder of the English Romantic movement, were both deeply influenced by Chatterton's work; for, whether or not the archaisms of Rowley's verse were true to their supposed times, the poetry itself is exquisitely crafted, embodying a compellingly nostalgic yearning for the mythic past. John Keats identified with Chatterton in his poem "Endymion," and Percy Bysshe Shelley reverently alluded to him in his "Adonais: An Elegy on the Death of John Keats." Wordsworth wrote of "Chatterton, the marvelous Boy."

Thus was born the Romantic myth of the struggling artist ending his own life in a sparsely furnished garret and thereby, through poignancy as much as anything else, lending additional meaning to his life and work, so cruelly cut short. Questions of economic inequity, and of the tragedy of thwarted originality, also intruded into the heated discussion of Chatterton's death. And it has even been suggested, more prosaically, that the poet had accidentally overdosed on arsenic taken to cure himself of a venereal disease.

The gravestone of the poet John Keats who also died young, at age twenty-five—though of tuberculosis rather than suicide. "Endymion," which Keats dedicated to Chatterton, begins with the line "A thing of beauty is a joy for ever."

But over time the most enduring interpretation—and the one everyone wants to believe—has been the Romantic one. Accordingly, the most famous nineteenth-century vision of Chatterton is the one painted by the artist Henry Wallis. It shows a deathly pale poet expiring elegantly by the light of a single attic window. Perhaps appropriately, the model who sat—or more properly, lay—for this elegiac scene was the novelist and poet George Meredith, who later penned the immortal words "Ah, what a dusty answer gets the soul / When hot for certainties in this our life!"

Hardy Rodenstock (left) and James Tien Pei-chun (right), chairman of the Hong Kong Chamber of Commerce, each holding a bottle of the "Thomas Jefferson" wine. Tien was one of sixty people, including many well-connected Chinese and Japanese businessmen and officials, invited by Rodenstock to a weeklong 1998 Château d'Yquem Festival. Most of the guests were wealthy, new to wine, and not particularly knowledgeable about it.

THOMAS JEFFERSON'S LAFITE

ood wine not only contributes wonderfully to the quality of civilized life, but in its more prestigious manifestations it is a symbol of status and savoir-faire. Still, there is a serpent in Eden. As long as one wine has been valued above another, wine fraud has been omnipresent. The eighteenth-century BC Mesopotamian Code of Hammurabi contained several provisions relating to wine sellers, one of them prescribing drowning as a punishment for cheating on the price of a drink, and in the first century BC Pliny the Elder—among many others—complained of the quantity of fake wines sloshing around the hostelries of ancient Rome, particularly of his expensive favorite, the amber Falernian from a celebrated hillside vineyard in Campania.

Closer to our own day, one particular wine fraud stands out among many. While residing in Paris as ambassador of the United States between 1785 and 1789, the oenophile Thomas Jefferson rapidly learned to distrust wine merchants, vigorously advocating direct purchase from the producer. So perhaps it is only appropriate that the most notorious wine scandal of recent times involved allegedly centuries-old bottles with purported Jeffersonian associations.

The property of a flamboyant German wine collector named Hardy Rodenstock, these bottles began appearing at auction and at select wine tastings during the 1980s, and they were remarkable not just for their age—the hand-blown bottles were engraved with the years 1784 or 1787—but also because they bore the initials *Th. J.* The wine was said to have been found in a walled-off cellar of a recently demolished house in Paris, and the strong implication of those engraved initials was that the bottles had been destined for Jefferson, but had not reached him by the time he returned to the fledgling United States.

The first bottle was auctioned in London in 1985. It was a 1787 Château Lafite, a particular Jefferson favorite, and it went for a whopping $156,000: four times as much as anyone had ever paid for a bottle of wine. Sadly, when its purchaser, the publishing magnate Malcolm Forbes, put it on public display under hot lights, the cork shrank and fell into the bottle. Wine—especially old wine—oxidizes quickly when exposed to air, so now nobody will ever know how well that fragile pale amber liquid (unlike white wines, which darken with age, red wines like Lafite grow lighter) might have survived.

At tastings over the years that followed, other bottles from the same cache yielded mysteriously varying results, but this didn't stop Rodenstock from selling several more

....

Thomas Jefferson kept meticulous records of his wine purchases. There is no mention of the 1787 Château Lafite that Rodenstock claimed to have discovered, either in Jefferson's notebooks, recently digitized by the New York Public Library, or in the archives of the Thomas Jefferson Foundation at Monticello.

from his stock privately, at huge if undisclosed prices. One of these—another 1787 Lafite—was eventually sent to a laboratory for chemical testing, and while the sediment that adhered to the bottle's sides was found to be compatible with a two-hundred-year age, the liquid itself was not.

The endgame began only after the wealthy American collector Bill Koch acquired four of the allegedly Jeffersonian bottles from various sources. Plans were made to exhibit these, and Koch's representative Brad Goldstein contacted the experts at Monticello, Jefferson's Virginia home. But while the future president had been a meticulous record keeper, a diligent search turned up no documentation that he had ever ordered the wines concerned—or indeed any others from 1787, something that had actually been known since 1985, before the first bottle had been sold.

Smelling a rat, Koch went straight to a private investigator, who turned to high tech. All wines bottled today contain cesium-137, a radioactive isotope that is present in the atmosphere solely due to nuclear weapons testing and such accidents as the meltdown at Chernobyl in 1986. Since cesium-137 did not exist before the first atomic tests were conducted in 1945, it should not be detectable in a wine from the eighteenth century. Doubtless to Koch's disappointment, when it was placed in a gamma-ray detector, the bottle yielded inconclusive readings, with no significant cesium levels. The wine inside it was indeed compatible with being fairly venerable, if not necessarily two hundred years old.

Undeterred, Koch and his experts continued to investigate, testing many bottles from the Rodenstock cache, including the original Forbes bottle and others from Lafite and the Château d'Yquem. Using powerful microscopy, they determined that the engraving on the "Th. J" bottles had been made using a modern dental drill, rather than an eighteenth-century hand file or cutting wheel. The dates and the initials had apparently been faked. Further searching duly turned up a couple of German technicians who provided affidavits that it was they who had engraved the bottles. However old those bottles and the wine within them might have been, there were no Jeffersonian associations.

Most wine drinkers are of modest means, and may have limited sympathy for high rollers who gamble on expensive bottles of what is, in the end, a perishable commodity that needs to be drunk—something that Bill Koch himself recently acknowledged, when he reportedly consigned about half of his cellar to auction. Sadly, much of it will probably be bought by people for whom wine is more to be displayed and talked about than to be enjoyed.

But the most alarming fact of all is that if you are an average wine drinker you are just as much at risk as the high rollers are, because fraud is even more rampant at the end of the market at which most of us drink. In 2012 the venerable house of Labouré-Roi, one of Burgundy's largest wine producers and shippers, was slapped with charges of

Unlike most other radioactive isotopes, cesium-137 is anthropogenic (human-made), an artifact of atomic bomb explosions. Starting with the first Trinity test on July 16, 1945, trace amounts of this isotope entered the atmosphere. Bill Koch hired French physicist Philippe Hubert to test his purported Jefferson wine for cesium-137, which, if it had been present, would have proved the wine was not from the eighteenth century. The test results were inconclusive.

fraud that involved a staggering 1.5 million bottles of wine, destined for consumers all over the world. The fraud involved everything from mislabeling (the easiest and most widespread form of wine faking) to blending inferior wines with more highly reputed ones that sold at higher prices; and, after Labouré-Roi's owners were arrested, the affair ended in the company's sale to another wine producer.

In the famous Italian "Brunellopoli" scandal of 2008, allegations flew that pricey Brunello di Montalcino wines had been adulterated with inexpensive table wines trucked in from elsewhere; and in 2016 it was reported that counterfeiters in the Italian town of Selvazzano Dentro were labeling cheap Prosecco sparkling wine as the product of a major Champagne house. The list of wine frauds goes on and on; and given that the market is pretty poorly policed, there is no end in sight to this kind of fakery.

As long as some wines sell for more than others do, and as long as consumers have no way of verifying that what they think they are seeing is what they are getting, the temptation to cheat will always be there. And if you were thus to conclude that the only absolute shelter any wine consumer has from fraud is to drink only the cheapest wines, all the time, you would probably be correct. But then again, who wants to do that?

THE BOY WHO WOULD BE BARD

Despite the recent rash of literary reworkings of William Shakespeare's themes, you would think that the legendary playwright would almost instantly have become an icon not to be directly trifled with. For what mortal human could have the hubris to seek to match wits with the Bard of Avon? You might reasonably imagine that to be the case; but, if so, you would be wrong.

One of the most mysterious things about Shakespeare—a man of words, after all—is the paucity of handwritten words he left behind, in an age when people necessarily wrote by hand. His plays were all posthumously published from secondary sources, and there is little physical evidence that he corresponded with anyone. The few examples of his signature appear on legal papers. Rarely since Homer has anyone who bequeathed posterity such a gift of words left so little actual documentary evidence of his own daily existence. And of course, anytime a vacuum of any kind exists, you can be assured that someone will emerge to fill it.

Born in 1775, William Henry Ireland was an unhappy child, frequently beaten at school for a lack of attention to his teachers. At home he was no better appreciated. His unmarried and distant mother posed as a household maid to his father, Samuel, a wealthy author of widely read illustrated travel books; given this unusual domestic arrangement, perhaps it is unsurprising that Samuel was hardly nurturing. One thing

One of William Henry Ireland's most audacious frauds, a letter purportedly written by Shakespeare to his wife, Anne Hathaway.

his father did offer, however, was a house filled with curiosities of all kinds, and above all an enthusiasm for everything Shakespearean. "To possess a single vestige of the poet's handwriting," Samuel told his son, "would be esteemed a gem beyond all price."

Anxious for his father's approval, the young William Henry browsed widely in his extensive library. In one of Samuel's books he found a facsimile of Shakespeare's signature. He also became fascinated not only by the poetic forgeries of Thomas Chatterton (see chapter 12, *Romantic Suicide*), who had died only five years before William was born, but almost certainly also by the purportedly ancient Gaelic "Ossian" poems published by James Macpherson from 1760 onward. Literary forgery had something of a cachet at the time, and evidently William Henry seized on this genre as a potential way to secure his father's approbation.

The young Ireland had been apprenticed to a lawyer in whose office ancient parchment documents abounded, and he had also learned from a chance acquaintance how to make documents look old by using special inks and then heating them. Combining these advantages, William Henry began at some time in 1794, at the age of eighteen, to forge ancient-looking documents. They included a deed that bore Shakespeare's signature. Declaring that he had found them inside a trunk in a friend's attic, he triumphantly presented these curious articles to his father. And, as he had hoped, Samuel was overjoyed to have this "gem beyond all price."

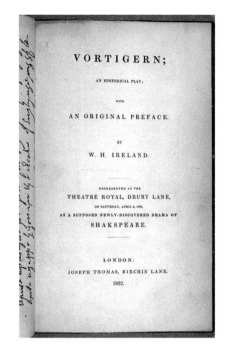

Vortigern was given credence because it showed up after the young Ireland had produced numerous deeds, letters, and other documents attributed to or associated with Shakespeare, all of which had been authenticated by scholars.

....

But William Henry did not stop there. More Shakespearean documents followed, including love letters to wife Anne Hathaway, books annotated in Shakespeare's hand, a declaration of loyalty to the Protestant faith, a partial manuscript of *Hamlet*, and the entire original manuscript of *King Lear*. Barely able to contain his joy, Samuel Ireland invited numerous experts in to authenticate the finds. Upon receiving their approval—to William Henry's surprise, one savant even found evidence of a seal that positively associated the document concerned with the Bard—he published them in a volume called *Miscellaneous Papers and Legal Instruments Under the Hand and Seal of William Shakespeare*.

Emboldened, William Henry then produced the manuscript of an entire unpublished Shakespearean play, *Vortigern, An Historical Play*. The competition for first performance rights that followed was eventually won by the famous playwright Richard Brinsley Sheridan. Meanwhile, though, as the public browsed through *Miscellaneous Papers*, doubts began to descend, nowhere more than in the mind of the Irish Shakespeare specialist Edmond Malone.

Amid a growing flurry of debate as to whether any of the manuscripts were genuine, Malone published a long and damning inquiry into their authenticity on March 31, 1796, just two days before *Vortigern*, a tale of medieval treachery and paternal displeasure followed by disaster, was due to open (on April 2; allegedly, Samuel Ireland had vetoed a proposal to open it on April 1). Although crowds were still flocking to the Ireland residence to admire and fondle the original manuscript (Samuel had found it necessary to limit public hours), even Sheridan had by then come to have his doubts because, though no great fan of the Bard, he had expected more "poetry" than he found in the play. What eventually won him over was the great age of the parchment on which it was written.

The capacity crowd in the newly expanded Theatre Royal in Drury Lane was accordingly tense as the curtain rose on the play's opening performance. The audience was reportedly polite at the beginning, recognizing one (plagiarized) Shakespearean touch after another. But after the skeptical actor John Philip Kemble began to ham it up in the title role, mirth began to prevail, and the crowd grew restive. After the curtain fell,

Shakespeare (left) had no hand in *Vortigern*. Recently, however, an international group of scholars, using computerized textual analysis, have suggested that Christopher Marlowe (right) collaborated with Shakespeare on the three *Henry VI* plays, and may be the primary author of *Henry VI: Part 2*.

fighting erupted between those who believed they had just seen a new Shakespeare play and those who felt cheated. Calm was restored only after Kemble announced that further showings of *Vortigern* had been canceled—to be replaced, appropriately enough, by Sheridan's own *The School for Scandal*.

While most reviews the next day were scathing, William Henry Ireland himself felt a burden beginning to lift from him. A few months later he shed it entirely by publishing a full confession, entirely exculpating his father and pinning his own folly on his youth (while suggesting that his detractors were being particularly malicious because they realized they had been fooled by a mere child).

In contrast, Samuel Ireland couldn't bring himself to face the awful reality. Even as the sales of his books plummeted, he continued to deny the fabrication right up to his death some four years later. William Henry's attempt to impress his father had created a permanent rift between the two.

Still, the story doesn't end there. Although *Vortigern* never took its place in the Shakespearean canon—and could never have pretended to, if today's standards of literary criticism and technological analysis had applied back in the eighteenth century—it has not been forgotten as a literary curiosity. On November 19, 2008, more than two centuries after it was written, it was performed for a second time, at Pembroke College, Cambridge.

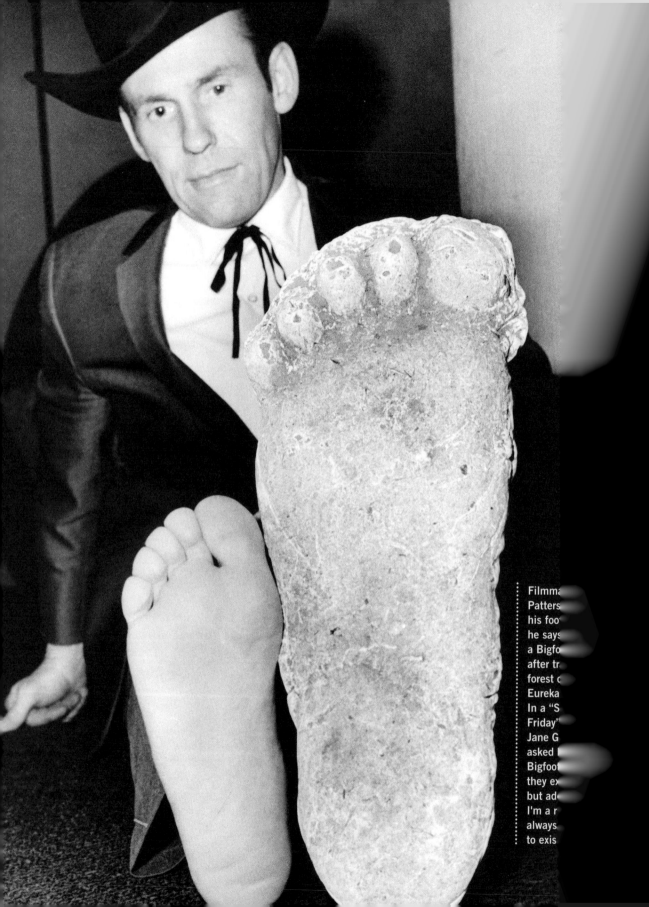

THE SAGA OF **BIGFOOT**

America loves its legends, and holds on to them at all costs. Perhaps no American legend is more tenacious than that of the Bigfoot, aka Sasquatch. This mysterious creature, half ape and half human, was first reported from the Canadian Rockies back in 1811, by a fur trapper. Since then, according to the Bigfoot Field Researchers Organization (BFRO), almost five thousand "credible" sightings of these implausible hominoids have been reported from every state in the Union except Hawaii, along with several hundred more from Canada. That works out to a couple of dozen Bigfoot spottings a year, suggesting that, in the public mind at least, these strange anthropomorphic beasts are a lot more common than one might have thought.

A roadside sign posted in the mountains above Colorado Springs, Colorado.

And yet, for almost two hundred years after that first sighting in Alberta, and in woods increasingly infested by backpackers, hunters, tree huggers, loggers, nature lovers, botanists, fleeing criminals, and mountain men, nobody ever stumbled over the remains of a dead Bigfoot. The typical Bigfoot observation was of a shadowy figure shambling across a forest path or flitting between the trees, vanishing before even a blurry photograph could be taken. Not infrequently, observers reported grunts, howls, or screams reverberating out of tangled vegetation nearby, and occasionally people thought they had seen whole Bigfoot groups. But somehow, tangible physical documentation, the sort that a scientist would accept, never seemed to be available.

Not that there was a lack of scientists who were anxious to find such documentation. Grover Krantz, an anthropologist at Washington State University (and whose own skeleton is now preserved at the Smithsonian Institution as proof of his existence) was one of them, spending an entire career on the lookout for Bigfoot remains. To the end, he believed he hadn't found them simply because bones just don't preserve on the acidic forest floor; after all, he reasoned, he had never found bear remains out in the backwoods, either, although he knew the bears were out there, presumably in far larger numbers than the Bigfoot had ever been.

For long years it remained true that, apart from eyewitnesses' often garbled stories, some blurred and indistinct photographs and the odd footprint or unidentifiable hair were basically the only tangible evidence that this strange creature of the woods actually existed. But in 2008, for a brief moment, all that appeared to change.

In August of that year two residents of the state of Georgia, Matthew Whitton and Rick Dyer, respectively a sheriff's deputy and a used-car dealer (but both also co-owners of a company set up to take tourists on Bigfoot-seeking expeditions) reported finding the body of a dead Bigfoot in the northern forests of their home state. At a press conference in California—a Bigfoot epicenter—Whitton told a room packed with enthralled print and TV reporters how the pair had encountered the deceased Bigfoot on the banks of a stream, deep in the woods. He had then stood guard over the body for several hours while Dyer went to fetch a truck.

Then the real drama started. As the two men dragged the massive corpse through the trees to the vehicle, three live and doubtless angry Sasquatch showed up, dogging their tracks all the way to the truck. This must have been a very alarming experience indeed, for, as Whitton and Dyer described the body, their Bigfoot (a male) was seven feet, seven inches tall and weighed five hundred pounds. Its hands were almost a foot long, and its feet were considerably larger. Walking upright, those enormous pursuing Sasquatch must have towered frighteningly over the two men and their heavy load; yet in the end the pair managed to heave the body into the wagon and whisk it away to be frozen.

The story made headlines and was ubiquitous on national TV, although all that Whitton and Dyer and their associate Tom Biscardi produced at the press conference by way of material evidence were some indistinct photos and some vague talk of DNA. Indeed, one observer at the conference expressed deep disappointment with the finders' presentation, and particularly with the absence of the Bigfoot cadaver itself. Still, Biscardi also noted how the press was lapping it all up: no tough questions, no demands to see the body. Everybody, it seemed, *wanted* this to be true.

But it couldn't last. After the initial heady rush, reason intervened. A DNA sample proved to be a mixture of human and opossum; and when the body finally appeared and was

Frame 352, the oft-reproduced "look-back" image from the Patterson-Gimlin film that allegedly depicts a female Bigfoot. Filmed by Roger Patterson and Robert Gimlin in 1967, it has been the subject of ongoing debate about its authenticity. Years later, Patterson and Gimlin declared they should have shot and preserved the creature to silence naysayers.

thawed out by "Bigfoot experts" at the BFRO, it proved to be a rubber ape suit with artificial hair. In short order, it was revealed that the entire episode had been fabricated.

But why? What did the three men have to gain except the most fleeting of fame, followed by derision outside the Bigfoot community and excoriation within it? Well, it appears that the most immediate aim, especially in Biscardi's case, was to attract more of the Bigfoot tourist business, from which the BFRO had been doing extremely well. The hype surrounding the press conference, he hoped, would establish him as the world's premier Bigfoot hunter, the guide to whom tourists seeking to see the Bigfoot for themselves would inevitably turn.

And that raises the real question. People are often blinded to long-term consequences by the prospect of short-term gain. Nothing surprising there. But what about the tourists? Why should anyone be attracted by the vanishingly remote possibility that an improbable half-man, half-ape chimera might be prowling the backwoods of North America—a continent that had never sheltered any hominoids at all until our own species, *Homo sapiens,* arrived there at some time between thirty thousand and twenty thousand years ago (see chapter 38, *Misguided Archaeology*)?

Perhaps this fascination with Bigfoot has something to do with an obscure and atavistic nostalgia resulting from the fact that *Homo sapiens* has not always been the only representative of its family on the planet. Indeed, there is evidence that at least four different human species coexisted in the Old World as recently as forty thousand years ago. And it is almost certainly our species that is responsible for the disappearance of the other three. Might it be that some abstruse form of guilt at being the fratricidal sole survivor drives us to wish the Sasquatch and its Himalayan cousin the Yeti into existence?

POYAIS

How soon they forget. When humans finally figure out a way to engineer their own destruction, it will probably be through making a mistake they've made many times before.

In the early eighteenth century, at a time when France claimed a larger part of what is now the United States than England did, a Scottish financier named John Law set up the Compagnie d'Occident to exploit a royal monopoly on development of the huge Mississippi Territory. By promoting this enormous terra incognita as a land

An 1827 engraving purporting to depict the Port of Black River in the nonexistent Territory of Poyais.

A 1791 map intended to promote John Law's Mississippi Company in Germany.

of untold mineral wealth and boundless promise, Law pumped up his company's and other prices on the French stock exchange in what became known as the "Mississippi Bubble." French citizens were urged to emigrate, and prisoners were even released from Paris jails on condition that they marry prostitutes and sail to Louisiana (chained together).

All that these unfortunate emigrants found was a vast area of insect-infested swampland already occupied by unfriendly residents, and many died. Back in France, though, Law was concurrently obtaining control over the French currency and eventually over all French foreign trade. In 1720, when the bubble inevitably burst, the already fragile French economy was rocked to its foundations, paving the way for the revolution that was to occur some sixty years later. Law himself fled France, and for the rest of his life appropriately eked out a living as a professional gambler.

Fast-forward a century, and there appeared on the Scottish scene a promoter named Gregor MacGregor. Scion of the clan that had produced the famous hero Rob Roy, MacGregor was already renowned for his military exploits in a South America that was busily throwing off the Spanish colonial yoke.

Not only did MacGregor have impeccable Scottish and military credentials; he was also, he claimed, cazique—prince—of the country of Poyais, a swath of territory along the Black River on Honduras's Mosquito Coast. This part of the world already had a special place in the Scottish heart, lying close to the site of the Darien scheme. Hatched in 1698, the Darien enterprise had involved a plan to implant Scottish colonies on both the Atlantic and Pacific sides of the Isthmus of Panama, in a sort of anticipation of the eventual Panama Canal. The plan had been scotched, if you'll pardon the term, by the hated English, who had then gone on to assemble the largest empire the world had ever known.

The charismatic MacGregor showed up at a time in which returns on conventional savings were low, and moral hazard—the urge to seek higher and riskier gains by any means available, however dubious—was accordingly rife. The Scots thus listened avidly as he spun them tales of a land so bounteous it could yield three crops of maize in a year. Fruit grew everywhere, game abounded on the landscape, and even the riverbeds yielded not gold flecks, but gold nuggets. All that this Nirvana lacked was capital to develop it and the people to settle it (though the few natives already there were, MacGregor promised, friendly).

The indefatigable MacGregor proved to be a superlative salesman, and on the relatively sophisticated Scottish financial market of the day (not for nothing had John Law been a Scot), perhaps it is not altogether surprising that, at a time of economic expansion, he succeeded in raising some £200,000 in bonds (about $4 billion in today's money) for the development of Poyais. What is more difficult to understand is his success in persuading seven shiploads of Scots to emigrate to a country that had no official—or even, as it turned out, unofficial—existence.

A Bank of Poyais "dollar," printed in Scotland. Gregor MacGregor sold these worthless notes to his would-be settlers, taking their real British currency in exchange.

A nineteenth-century cartoon of Gregor MacGregor, "Cazique of Poyais," imprisoned in France awaiting trial for selling bogus land share certificates. After much legal wrangling, he was acquitted of all charges.

The first two ships departed London for Honduras in September 1822, carrying some 250 passengers. On arrival two months later, the prospective settlers found nothing awaiting them. As the *Guardian* put it the following October: "When the emigrants arrived at San Josef, nothing could exceed their anguish at finding, where they expected a fine flourishing town with nearly 2000 inhabitants, only two or three ruined huts." Most of the prospective settlers believed they had arrived in the wrong place, but they went ahead anyway, building houses and planting crops in the poor sandy soil.

Inevitably, disease and privation soon took their toll and hope rapidly faded, especially after the local chief turned up and revoked a small land grant he had made to MacGregor three years earlier. So deep was the settlers' despair that, as reported by the *Guardian*, "Hellie, a shoemaker, who had obtained the appointment of shoemaker to the Princess of Poyais, shot himself as he lay sick in his hammock."

It is absolutely gut-wrenching to try to imagine this poignant scene; worse yet, within a year of arriving most of the other settlers had followed Hellie into oblivion. Eventually a passing timber boat carried the survivors to what is now Belize, and when word of the catastrophe made its way back to Scotland, the British navy was dispatched to retrieve the other five settler ships.

MacGregor's scam has been held up as perhaps the most ambitious of all time, and MacGregor himself as the quintessential master of the principles that have governed the most successful con jobs ever since. He traded on the trust of Scots in one of their own; he exploited his military celebrity for all it was worth; he wore an immaculate uniform festooned with foreign decorations; he projected an aura of unassailable authority; he promised his investors prestige as well as riches in a time when good honest returns were hard to come by; and in addition to all this, he offered them a chance to address a festering historical grievance. By all rights, the illusory Poyais should have been an impossible sell, but the charming and totally unfeeling MacGregor had unerringly pushed all the correct buttons.

The fraud itself had been impeccably executed. But questions remain. Why was it that only after unsuccessfully trying the same trick again in France did the fraudster finally flee to Caracas (where a statue was erected in honor of his contribution to Venezuelan independence), when he could easily just have taken his enormous Scottish bond profits and run? Why, after selling his bonds, did he stay in the game and organize the ill-fated settlement expedition? After all, he must have known it would all end in calamity.

The best guess is that at some point MacGregor had actually come to harbor a genuine fantasy about Poyais, and had begun to believe his own propaganda. Of course, even then his sincerity would have been fake at best; but if you can fake sincerity, you have it made.

FAKED PHOTOGRAPHS

We are just old enough to remember a more innocent time when people would utter the phrase "the camera never lies" in all sincerity. In our jaded contemporary society you are more likely to hear this old cliché used with heavy irony, if you hear it at all, but it is relatively easy to cast one's mind back to a simpler world in which the fidelity of photographic images to nature seemed self-evident. For until photography was first invented in the early nineteenth century, all visual representations of the external world were necessarily processed through the eyes, minds, and hands of artists, and everyone knew that no two artists would ever represent the same face or scene identically. Human perception and dexterity always intervened to influence the final result, and the application of paint to canvas was self-evidently a more subjective process than the simple impingement of light upon a retina.

The new technique of photography, in contrast, appeared to offer our predecessors a level of objectivity that no previous visual medium had ever claimed. After all, the camera itself did nothing to alter the scenes that unfurled before it, and the resulting images resulted purely from chemical reactions that proceeded according to scientific laws rather than to human artifice. Fair enough; but there is still a fly in the ointment: There is always a photographer behind the camera. And, as James Baldwin once

OPPOSITE: In 1920 photography expert Harold Snelling was asked to examine the fairy photographs taken by the young cousins Frances Griffiths and Elsie Wright. He declared that they were "genuine unfaked photographs of single exposure, open-air work, show movement in all the fairy figures, and there is no trace whatever of studio work involving card or paper models, dark backgrounds, painted figures, etc." The cousins later admitted that these were precisely the techniques they had used.

wrote, "It is said that the camera cannot lie, but rarely do we allow it to do anything else, since...the camera sees what you want it to see. The language of the camera is the language of our dreams."

Baldwin was actually being rather generous, because photographs had regularly shown what the camera had not seen since long before the advent of Photoshop. Indeed, the very first faked photo was apparently made as far back as 1840, right at the beginning of photography's technologically experimental early period. When a cruel deception by a friend of his rival Louis Daguerre denied Hippolyte Bayard the French Academy of Sciences' official recognition as one of the founders of photography, Bayard simulated his own suicide, illustrating it with a print of his own apparently drowned body.

Bayard's gruesome little joke opened the floodgates to a plenitude of photographic deception, especially among those who claimed that the camera could in fact see more than the eye did. In a time of intense interest in the spirit world (see chapter 19, *Communing with the Departed*), photographers claiming to capture ghostly presences did a flourishing business. In the United States perhaps the most famous practitioner of the art was William Mumler, whose very first photograph is said to have been a self-portrait in which an ethereal image of his dead cousin appeared, accidentally or otherwise.

In a nation grieving the numerous dead of the Civil War, Mumler sensed a huge business opportunity, and he rapidly gained a reputation for his ability to capture images of the dead alongside those of the living. His most famous client was Mary Todd Lincoln, whom he photographed not long after her husband's assassination. Mrs. Lincoln is seen seated, while the spectral presence of the bearded president looms behind her, his hands on her shoulders.

The technique Mumler used to obtain this complex image was double exposure, something that led to his own exposure as a fraud when astute observers spotted that some of the supposedly supernatural images were those of people still alive. In 1869 he was sued in what one is tempted to call a show trial by the impresario P. T. Barnum, who demonstrated in court how easy it was to forge a spirit photograph; and although in the end he was acquitted, Mumler's photographic career was over.

Not so photography of the unseen world. As late as 1920, the novelist Arthur Conan Doyle, inventor of that ultimate rationalist Sherlock Holmes, enthusiastically wrote in the widely circulated *Strand Magazine* of the self-portraits with tiny winged "fairies" that had recently been taken by a pair of young girls in an English garden. He later cited these photographs at length in his 1922 book *The Coming of the Fairies*. The images then reemerged periodically as items of press interest, and it was not until 1983 that the girls, by then elderly women, admitted having faked them.

William Mumler's most famous photograph of Mary Todd Lincoln with the "spirit" of Abraham Lincoln hovering over her. Mumler grew wealthy producing spirit photographs for grief-stricken clients who had lost relatives in the Civil War. P. T. Barnum purchased some of these photographs as examples of humbug for his American Museum.

TOP: Stalin wanted a photograph of a Soviet flag hoisted atop the German Reichstag, the heart of the "fascist beast," in time for International Workers' Day on May 1, 1945. Photographer Yevgeny Khaldei was able to reach the building only after Russian soldiers had finally cleared it on May 2. With a large flag, sewn from three tablecloths, he and three soldiers who happened to be passing by scaled the ruined building, where he took this historic photograph.

BOTTOM LEFT: In the original photograph, the soldier hoisting the flag is wearing two wristwatches.

BOTTOM RIGHT: Leaving nothing to chance, Khaldei not only added smoke for dramatic effect but also removed one of the wristwatches, as two would imply the soldier had been looting.

Fairies in a rural garden are pretty harmless, but photographs have not infrequently been doctored to rewrite history. A classic Russian revolutionary image is a 1920 photo by G. P. Goldshtein that shows Vladimir Lenin haranguing troops about to leave for the Polish front. In the photograph as originally published, his Central Committee colleagues—and potential rivals—Leon Trotsky and Lev Kamenev are seen next to the podium from which Lenin speaks. Following Trotsky's fall seven years later, both Trotsky and Kamenev were removed, and for the rest of the Soviet period Lenin appeared alone.

It is not always people who are erased from propaganda photos of this kind. One of the most famous images from World War II is Joe Rosenthal's photograph of a group of marines raising the U.S. flag in Iwo Jima on February 23, 1945. Two months later, a Red Army photographer named Yevgeny Khaldei packed an improvised Russian flag and left Moscow to join the Soviet troops who were then sacking Berlin. His intent was to obtain a pro-Soviet image as powerful as Rosenthal's.

Khaldei took three soldiers to the roof of the Reichstag, posed them with his flag, pressed the shutter, and immediately flew back to Moscow. His photo would become a definitive image of the war; but before it was published he made a key change to the negative. He carefully erased one of two wristwatches that one of the soldiers had looted from hapless civilians. For added drama, he later added dark clouds of smoke to the skyline.

Items may be added to photographs, or taken away, or changed in any number of ways. And in the age of Photoshop the products of such "improvement" are probably a lot more common than unadulterated images among the millions we are bombarded with. Indeed, in 2015 the World Press Photo Contest was forced to disqualify a full 22 percent of its finalists after experts had concluded that they had been altered or manipulated "beyond the currently accepted industry standard."

The immediate reasons for doctoring photographic images are as endlessly diverse as human desires, but the underlying motivation seems to be pretty constant: we all know how we want the world to look, and often fixing photos is the only means we have to make it look that way.

Poe's works were not conspicuously acclaimed during his lifetime. Initially his importance in literary history was due to the influence his poetry and short stories had on the late nineteenth-century French Symbolists, especially Charles Baudelaire. Today Poe is recognized as one of the foremost progenitors of modern American literature

EDGAR ALLAN POE AND THE GREAT BALLOON HOAX

O n the morning of Saturday, April 13, 1844, readers of the *New York Sun* awoke to headlines blaring ASTOUNDING NEWS!…THE ATLANTIC CROSSED IN THREE DAYS! This then-almost-unimaginable feat had been achieved in a "flying-machine…employing the principle of the Archimedean screw for the purposes of propulsion through the air."

The story that followed contained a painfully detailed account of how a gas-filled, airship-shaped balloon carrying an astounding eight passengers, among them the celebrated English balloonist Thomas Monck Mason, had been accidentally blown across the Atlantic following a failure of its spring-driven and windmill-like propellers. Conveniently, the vessel was said to have made landfall on a remote island off the coast of South Carolina, far away from easy journalistic verification.

This was big news in the balloon-mad city of New York, which considered itself the gateway to America. The first balloon flight ever launched from Manhattan had taken off more than five decades earlier (on August 7, 1789), and balloon rides had subsequently become a routine form of daredevil amusement for the city's more affluent citizens.

Nonetheless, in 1844 ballooning was still in its infancy as a form of practical transportation. The farthest a balloon had ever traveled was the five hundred miles claimed for a voyage between the English port of Dover and the German city of Weilburg in 1835, by a craft piloted by none other than Monck Mason. The aviator's new achievement of a flight seven times as long now promised great things for America's Gateway.

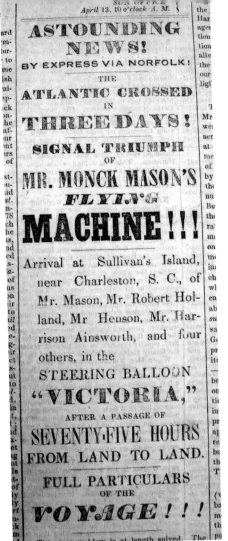

ASTOUNDING
NEWS!

BY EXPRESS VIA NORFOLK!

THE

ATLANTIC CROSSED

IN

THREE DAYS!

SIGNAL TRIUMPH

OF

MR. MONCK MASON'S

FLYING

MACHINE !!!

Arrival at Sullivan's Island, near Charleston, S. C., of Mr. Mason, Mr. Robert Holland, Mr Henson, Mr. Harrison Ainsworth, and four others, in the

STEERING BALLOON

"VICTORIA,"

AFTER A PASSAGE OF

SEVENTY-FIVE HOURS

FROM LAND TO LAND.

FULL PARTICULARS

OF THE

VOYAGE !!!

A front-page announcement in the April 13, 1844, *New York Sun*. According to the story that followed, the famous European balloonist Thomas Monck Mason had succeeded in flying across the Atlantic Ocean in seventy-five hours.

The excitement, alas, didn't last. On April 15, just two days after the story had broken, it was retracted, purportedly on the basis that it couldn't be confirmed. But, more informally, the story goes that on the very day of its publication the story's drunken author had shown up in front of the *Sun*'s building in downtown Manhattan and had begun loudly warning a gathering crowd that he had faked the whole thing. Apparently, nobody much was listening. As he himself later wrote: "The *Sun* building was literally besieged....I never witnessed more intense excitement to get possession of a newspaper....I tried, in vain, during the whole day, to get possession of a copy."

The author in question was no ordinary faker. He was the struggling writer Edgar Allan Poe, who had arrived in New York a scant week earlier, reporting in a letter to his mother that he was down to his last $4.50. The $50 the *Sun* is said to have paid Poe for his article would thus seem to have been a more than adequate reason for writing it in the first place (or, more accurately, for plagiarizing most of it from sources such as Mason's own account of his epic Dover–Weilburg flight). Desperate for cash, Poe could have just grabbed the money and left. So why would he have taken the initiative in denouncing his own fabrication?

Part of the reason is undoubtedly that Poe, a man whose emotions often trumped his moral principles, harbored a strong resentment toward the *Sun* and its editor. This grudge had originated with a highly fantastical series of articles the paper had published nine years earlier. These alleged that, using a revolutionary new telescope from the new vantage point of South Africa, the English astronomer Sir John Herschel had seen winged but otherwise humanlike creatures walking on the surface of the moon, along with a whole bestiary of other creatures. The series was a sensational success, and the circulation of the *Sun* zoomed from some 2,500 to 19,000 copies per issue, at the time a world record.

Poe's problem was not with the fact that the series was entirely fraudulent—although never formally retracted, it became legendary as the "Great Moon Hoax"—but with his belief that the hugely profitable idea for it had been plagiarized from him without compensation. Only two months earlier, he had published a short story, "The Unparalleled Adventure of One Hans Pfaall," which consisted mainly of a supposedly autobiographical manuscript by an individual who had contrived to visit the moon using a hot-air balloon. Poe clearly felt taken advantage of by the editors of the *Sun*, and even somewhat upstaged by them, notwithstanding that he had himself plagiarized some of the circumstantial detail in his story from Herschel's writings.

Still, why did Poe wait nine years to take his revenge? Maybe we can find a clue in his 1850 short story "The Imp of the Perverse," in which he explores the murkiness of human motivations. With astounding circumlocution, Poe's protagonist describes an inexplicable, "radical," and "primitive" impulse that is sometimes "absolutely irresistible," and forces one to "act without a comprehensible object." Gradually it becomes clear that the narrator is describing his own predicament, as he "peer[s] into the abyss [growing] sick and dizzy," and realizes that he is "one of the many uncounted victims" of this impulse, the voice in his brain that is compelling him to confess a murder committed many years before. And although he realizes "I am safe—I am safe—yes—if I be not fool enough to make open confession," eventually, with pounding heart and constricted lungs, "the long imprisoned secret burst forth from my soul."

Poe has surely put his finger here on an aspect of the human psyche that bears heavily on the experience of any fraudster, even if he or she is the only person who knows—or even could know—that fraud has been committed. For only the most pathological of liars could remain entirely oblivious to the inchoate feeling that Poe describes. It may well be the imp of the perverse that explains why he stood on the steps of the *Sun* building that morning in 1844, confessing his fraudulence to an unheeding crowd who only wanted to enjoy the lie. And it also probably explains why he was drunk when he did it.

A print published in the *New York Sun* as part of the "Great Moon Hoax," purporting to show lunar human-bats, unicorns, and other imaginary creatures discovered by Sir John Herschel from his observatory at the Cape of Good Hope.

During séances, Henry Slade claimed that spirits wrote messages in chalk on small slates placed under the table. Actually Slade was writing these "messages from the dead" using tiny pieces of chalk held in his mouth, in the fingers of either hand, or between the toes of either foot.

SPIRITUALISM AND EVOLUTION

LEAH.   KATE   MARGARETTA

T he two sisters Margaretta and Kate Fox evidently became bored living in mid-nineteenth-century upstate New York. To amuse themselves, they fooled their mother and elder sister, Leah, into believing that they were communicating with departed spirits via what they called "rapping." This involved suspending an apple on a string and repeatedly bouncing it

In 1848, upstate New York teenagers Kate and Margaretta Fox convinced their older sister, Leah, and soon many others, that the "rappings" they heard were spirit communications. Under Leah's management, the "Rochester knockers" achieved international success as mediums until 1888, when Margaretta and Kate confessed the rappings were a hoax. Margaretta recanted her confession, but their reputation was ruined and in less than five years all three were dead in abject poverty.

against the floor to make mysterious sounds that they eventually developed into a code. So convincing were the girls that their Spiritualist séances took off like wildfire, first locally, then nationally. All three sisters eventually became professional Spiritualist mediums, and they were joined by swelling numbers of other practitioners using a host of different techniques. Eventually, though, they grew bored again—or maybe just felt guilty—and in 1888 they went public about the fraud, demonstrating how it was done and declaring it "an absolute falsehood from beginning to end."

Not that anyone much listened; by then the horse was long out of the barn, and all over the Victorian world Spiritualist mediums were happily convincing grieving family members that for a fee they could contact their departed spouses or children. One such practitioner was Henry Slade, an American trickster who plied his trade on both sides of the Atlantic. His specialty was slate writing, which involved a small chalkboard on which written messages from the Other Side would miraculously appear while it was hidden under a table.

Having been caught out in New York scrawling messages with chalk held between his toes, as well as surreptitiously substituting boards, Slade went to London in 1876 to try his luck. Unfortunately for him, some well-connected skeptics were lying in wait. Among them were the famous natural historian Charles Darwin (see chapter 23, *Deathbed Conversions*), coinventor of the theory of evolution by natural selection that underpins all biology today, and his able wingman, the anatomist Thomas Henry Huxley. A highly practical man, Huxley actually taught himself many of the Spiritualists' tricks. These included the curious ruse of snapping his toes inside his shoe to make rapping noises at varying volumes (he recommended rapping wearing thin socks and wide shoes).

The story is well known of how the wealthy Darwin, who had been mulling over his theory for many years, was surprised early in 1858 to receive a manuscript from Alfred Russel Wallace, an impoverished biologist who was scraping out a living by collecting museum specimens in what is now Indonesia. When he read it, Darwin was flabbergasted, for in many ways Wallace's theory was identical to his own notion of natural selection.

On the subject of Spiritualism, however, their theories diverged. While the strictly materialist Darwin thought natural selection applied across the board, Wallace couldn't see how it might pertain to humans, who he thought had a much larger brain than the one they actually needed to get by. *Homo sapiens*, he wrote, has "something…not derived from his animal progenitors—a spiritual essence [that] can only find an explanation in the unseen universe of Spirit."

Soon after Slade arrived in London, he found himself entrapped by Huxley's protégé Edwin Ray Lankester, who paid to attend a séance and then snatched a supposedly blank slate that turned out to have a message already written on it. Lankester turned Slade in to the law, and the Spiritualist found himself on trial for fraud. Darwin, who had lost his own daughter at age ten and deplored the "clever rogues" who preyed on victims' grief, ponied up the then-handsome sum of ten pounds to help pay the costs of prosecution.

But on the other side, there was his old comrade-in-arms Alfred Wallace. So lacking in guile himself that he was simply unable to see it in others, Wallace had generously agreed to be the star character witness in Slade's defense.

When the trial began in 1876 all London was abuzz, and the courtroom was packed. The situation demanded drama; and drama there was, aplenty. Darwin's financial contribution helped the prosecution bring in John Nevil Maskelyne, a professional magician who—much like James Randi in our own times (see chapter 43, *Homeopathy*)—elegantly showed the court how the Spiritualist's tricks were done. He challenged Slade to cause writing to appear on a closed-up slate in open court, but Slade sidestepped his invitation by saying that the spirit of his late wife, Allie, whom he was allegedly channeling, had vowed never to do such a thing.

In his testimony for the defense, Wallace, a man universally respected for his integrity, declined to speculate on whether slate writings were caused by spirits. But he nonetheless declared his belief that Slade was honorable, and "incapable of an imposture."

It was not enough. Although in the end the judge conceded that Spiritualism itself was "a sort of new religion," he found Slade guilty of fraudulently representing his tricks as paranormal phenomena and sentenced him to three months' hard labor. The conviction was later overturned on a technicality, and Slade fled to Germany to continue his Spiritualist shenanigans.

Ironically, one of the leading advocates of Spiritualism in Victorian England was the novelist Arthur Conan Doyle, who actually owned a Spiritualist bookshop not far from London's Westminster Abbey. At the apex of his literary fame, Doyle abandoned his Sherlock Holmes stories and devoted himself to the study of the paranormal. He went on to write twenty books on Spiritualism, and claimed to have communicated with the spirits of such deceased luminaries as Cecil Rhodes and Joseph Conrad.

At the height of his literary fame, Sir Arthur Conan Doyle decided to abandon writing fiction and devote himself to the study of paranormal phenomena. "Holmes is dead," he declared. "I have done with him." He went on to write twenty books on communicating with the dead, automatic writing, fairy photographs, ghosts, ectoplasm, telepathy, and a two-volume history of Spiritualism.

Maybe it is symbolic of the conflicted human condition that the man who invented Sherlock Holmes, the most rational detective of all time, fell prey to the cynical heirs of the Fox sisters.

William Thompson, whose deceptions inspired the *New York Herald* to coin the term "confidence man."

THE ORIGINAL CON MAN

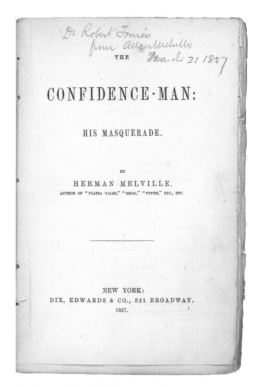

N o book dealing with frauds, fakes, and fallacies could avoid eventually mentioning the original confidence man, baptized with that title by the *New York Herald* back in 1849. The con man's name was actually William Thompson, and by today's standards, his scam was laughably simple. As the *Herald* put it, "He would go up to a perfect stranger in the street, and being a man of genteel appearance…would say after some little conversation, 'have you confidence in me to trust me with your watch until to-morrow'…the stranger…supposing him to be some old acquaintance not at that moment recollected, allows him to take the watch."

One reader who was impressed by the *Herald*'s story of "The Arrest of the Confidence-Man" was Herman Melville, who went on to enshrine the profession's newly acquired name in the title of his otherwise fairly unsuccessful novel *The Confidence-Man: His Masquerade*, published in 1857. Earlier in the nineteenth century, practitioners of the craft had often been known as "diddlers," for the character Jeremy Diddler

Herman Melville's *The Confidence-Man: His Masquerade* borrowed its title from the headline of the *New York Herald*'s 1849 story about William Thompson. Set on a Mississippi steamboat on April Fool's Day, Melville's last novel satirized several nineteenth-century literary celebrities including Henry David Thoreau, Nathaniel Hawthorne, and Edgar Allan Poe.

in James Kenney's 1803 farce *Raising the Wind*; and their skills had already been subjected to literary scrutiny at the hands of no less than Edgar Allan Poe.

Poe clearly considered the practice of deception to be hard-wired into the human condition. Indeed, he not only went so far as to define "man…as an animal that diddles," but also suggested that "had Plato but hit upon" this formulation after he had been reproached for defining humans as featherless bipeds, "he would have been spared the affront of the plucked chicken."

It is hard to imagine anyone falling for William Thompson's rather crude ploy today. Or is it? Maybe it was all in the performance, something that is hardly captured in the brusque newspaper report. After all, it is the job of the con man to conscript his mark into a conspiracy, or at least into an implicit mutual understanding of some kind. Over the years, the stories told by petty con artists have tended to become more elaborate; but in many ways the story itself is just the icing on the cake, or the means to the end; it is the relationship it helps create between fraudster and mark that is the critical thing.

Edgar Allan Poe, not above a good hoax himself (see chapter 18, *Aerial Feats*), understood that very well. In an 1843 essay, inspired by Kenney's character and subtitled "Diddling Considered as One of the Exact Sciences," he nailed the essential qualities of a successful diddler. These included what he called minuteness (keep the scale small—an injunction since widely honored in the breach); a keen sense of self-interest (to keep the conscience at bay); ingenuity and audacity; and perseverance, nonchalance, impertinence, and cheerfulness (all key elements in the performance). Despite his subtitle, Poe clearly considered diddling to be, in essence, one of the dramatic arts.

The most famous list of rules for successful con artistry, "Ten Commandments for Con Men," is attributed to Victor Lustig, a polyglot Austrian who certainly knew what he was talking about. Knowing that the relationship between the scammer and the mark was the key to any successful fraud, Lustig framed his rules to apply to the performance, rather than to the product—though in his view, fast talking was for magicians, not for con men. Indeed, Lustig's first two commandments are to be a patient listener, and to never look bored. He understood that any relationship is a two-way street, and his third and fourth rules involve taking note of the mark's religious and political opinions, and agreeing with them. Most of the other commandments involved commonsense advice about appearance and demeanor.

Lustig is famous for selling fake money-printing machines to clients who were necessarily of questionable probity. But without doubt his greatest coup was selling the Eiffel Tower for scrap. The tower had been built specifically for the 1889 Exposition Universelle in Paris, and had been scheduled for dismantling in 1909; but in 1925 it

FEDERAL BUREAU OF INVESTIGATION
U. S. DEPARTMENT OF JUSTICE
WASHINGTON, D. C.

Fingerprint Classification

19 27 W II 19

26 R I

WANTED

ROBERT V. MILLER, true name VICTOR LUSTIG, **with aliases:** VIKTOR LUSTIG, COUNT LUSTIG, BERT LUSTIG, VILSTER LUSTIG, BERT LAUSTING, ROBERT LAMAR, ROBERT DUVAL, COUNT DUVAL, GEORGE DUVAL, "THE COUNT", VIKTOR FOSTER, VICTOR FOSTER, CHARLES GROMAR, CHARLES GROMER, CHARLES GRUBER, ALBERT GRAUMAN, VICTOR GROSS, FRANK HERBERT, GEORGE BAKER, EDWARD BAKER, C. H. BAXTER, JOHN R. KANE, R. U. MILLER, VICTOR MILLER, ROBERT MILLER, R. B. MILLER, CHARLES NEVERA, NOVERA, CHARLES NOVERA, ALBERT PHILLIPS, G. R. RICHARD, J. R. RICHARDS, GEORGE SCOBEL, EDWARD SCHAEFFER, EDWARD SCHAFFER, EDWARD SHAFFER, GEORGE SHOBO, GEORGE SHOBOL, GEORGE SCHOBEL, CHARLES TAYLOR, ROBERT G. WAGNER, R. G. WAGNER, ROBERT GEORGE WAGNER, G. R. WERNER, "THE SCARRED".

FEDERAL

ESCAPE ACT

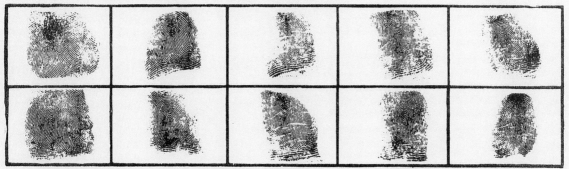

DESCRIPTION

Photograph taken May 10, 1935.

ARREST NUMBERS

Age, 45 years, (Born October 1, 1890, Hostinne, District of Urchlabi, Czechoslovakia); Height, 5 feet 8 inches; Weight, 165 pounds; Build, medium; Hair, brown; Eyes, grey; Complexion, sallow; Scars: 2½ inch scar on left cheek bone. Criminal Specialty, confidence game.

Viktor Lustig

#6667, P.D. Denver, Colorado.
#5552, P.D. Omaha, Nebraska.
#17454, P.D. St. Louis, Missouri
#21429, P.D. Los Angeles, Calif.
#36959, P.D. San Francisco, Calif.
#26664, P.D. Detroit, Michigan.
#15380, P.D. Indianapolis, Indiana.
#6254, Bureau of Identification, Crown Point, Indiana.
#B-52324, P.D. New York, New York.
#8675, P.D. Oklahoma City, Oklahoma.
#5849, P.D. Ft. Worth, Texas.
#12443, S.O. Miami, Florida.
#——, U.S. Secret Service, New York, New York.
#——, U.S. Marshal, Del Rio, Texas.
#——, Erkennungsamt der Bundespolizeidirektion, Rossauerlaende 7, Wien, IX., Oesterreich.

Robert V. Miller is wanted for escaping from the United States Detention Headquarters, New York City, New York, September 1, 1935 in violation of Public Law No. 233 of the 74th Congress of the United States.

Law enforcement agencies kindly furnish any additional information to the nearest office of the Federal Bureau of Investigation, United States Department of Justice.

If apprehended please notify the Director, Federal Bureau of Investigation, United States Department of Justice, Washington, D. C., or the Special Agent in Charge of the office of the Federal Bureau of Investigation listed on the back hereof which is nearest your city.

Issued by: JOHN EDGAR HOOVER, DIRECTOR.

(over)

The wanted poster issued after Victor "the Count" Lustig escaped from Federal Detention Headquarters. He made his exit from a third-floor window in full view of hundreds of New York City passersby, using nine bedsheets knotted together.

Some of Lustig's $51,000 in counterfeit banknotes, discovered in a Forty-Second Street subway locker.

was still there, and in fairly poor condition. Posing as a ministry official, Lustig invited six scrap metal dealers to submit bids, and selected one as the winning bidder.

When the mark's wife became suspicious about the speed and secrecy with which the deal was being conducted, Lustig "confessed" that he was living beyond his functionary's salary and was seeking a bribe. Reassured by this evidence of corrupt business as usual, the mark paid out the scrap money, plus the bribe; Lustig decamped for Vienna with a suitcase filled with cash. His victim was too embarrassed to complain, so the smooth Austrian returned to Paris and tried the same scam again. This time, though, he was turned in to the police. Managing to evade capture, he fled to try his luck in America. There, after successfully scamming the notorious gangster Al Capone, he was nabbed by the feds with a suitcase stuffed with $51,000 in counterfeit banknotes. He was sentenced to twenty-one years in Alcatraz, and died in prison. His death certificate listed his occupation as "apprentice salesman." In retrospect, it is clear that Lustig had already overreached on the second Eiffel Tower deal, and would have done much better to heed Poe's advice and to stick with "minuteness," at least to the extent to which any deal involving the Eiffel Tower could be minute.

And that brings us back to William Thompson, who surely practiced con artistry in its purest and most "minute" form. For Thompson offered his victims nothing. He didn't concoct extravagant stories; he didn't even lie. He only asked for his victim's confidence, after having built it up over a few minutes' conversation.

W. C. Fields is famous for his declaration that "you can't cheat an honest man." And that is perfectly true if your particular scam appeals specifically to your mark's greed, as so many do. But if all you want to do is to steal just what an individual has in his hand, the calculation is different. If—and only if—you are a good enough diddler, you can evidently steal an honest man's watch from right under his nose. For all his simplicity of concept, the original con man was also one of the best.

THE DAVENPORT TABLETS

Myths are both invented and believed for many reasons, not all of them honorable. When settlers began to push westward in the decades after the American Revolution, they were entering a landscape that had already been occupied and altered by Native Americans for many thousands of years. Among the most remarkable reminders of that long history was a huge number of large man-made mounds and earthworks scattered over a vast area of the Midwest, and particularly in the Mississippi and Ohio Valleys. Reluctant to accept that these amazing structures could possibly have been the product of the Indians with whom they now found themselves in often violent competition for territory—for clearly, they could hardly have been engineered by those "savages"—the settlers began to confect the myth that the earthworks were the product of a "lost race" of mound builders.

Not only did this entirely fictitious story of a vanished civilization help the settlers explain what they saw around them, but it also made the Indians they were forcibly displacing appear to be themselves intruders on the territory the newcomers were trying to annex. What is more, the myth allowed the settlers to see themselves in the role of heroes who were reclaiming the landscape on behalf of civilization, using methods no more reprehensible than those the Indians had doubtless earlier used to sweep aside the peaceful mound builders.

Nobody had the slightest idea who the mound builders had actually been, but in most versions of the myth they were (of course) of European or maybe Asian origin, or perhaps even citizens of Atlantis who had been forced to migrate when their continent sank beneath the waves. Anything but Indians. Beliefs like this reinforced the comfortable idea that the newcomers had some sort of ancestral claim to the land they were now taking away from those currently in possession.

In one of the most elaborate popular accounts, in his 1833 best-selling book *American Antiquities and Discoveries in the West,* the writer Josiah Priest proposed that the spectacular mound at Marietta, Ohio, had been built by Roman soldiers who had found their way to the New World along with a motley assortment of Egyptians, Greeks, Scandinavians, Scots, and others. Looking for evidence to substantiate imperialist claims of this kind, amateur antiquarians among the settlers delved into mounds all over the Midwest. At various sites some of them reported uncovering tablets inscribed

in obscure languages, all purporting to prove in one way or another that the mounds were not of Native American origin. There were the Grave Creek Stone (1838), the Kinderhook Plates (1843), the Newark Keystone and Decalogue (1860), the Bat Creek Tablet (1889), all of them long ago exposed as hoaxes; and then, most famous of all, there were the Davenport Tablets.

In 1877 the Reverend Jacob Gass, newly arrived from Switzerland, dug out two tablets bearing inscriptions and drawings from a mound near Davenport, Iowa. These impressed the local intelligentsia enough to get Gass elected to a group calling itself the Davenport Academy of Sciences. The academy set up a committee to study the two plaques, and a third one that turned up later. They all bore "Mound

A Clovis point (left) dated to about 13,000 years ago from Shawnee-Minisink, Pennsylvania, and a Solutrean "laurel-leaf" (right) dated to about 21,000 years ago from Burgundy, France. The perceived similarities between the two led some archaeologists to theorize that European Ice Age people sailed to North America, bringing with them the Solutrean technology that provided the basis for the later Clovis implements. Others have seen this interpretation as part of a long history of minimizing the cultural achievements of indigenous Native Americans.

The ancient Indian burial mound at Marietta, Ohio. It was speculated that Roman soldiers built it.

Builder hieroglyphics" in addition to an astronomical chart and graphics depicting cremation and hunting.

One committee member soon denounced these curious objects as fakes, but the initial consensus was that they were genuine and proved that the mound builders had not been Indians. In the words of the influential advocate Charles Putnam, published in the journal *Science* in 1884: "These relics seem to show a more complex social life, more abundant and varied artistic products, and a higher status altogether, than can be deemed consistent with the views of those who hold that these Mound-builders were merely the ancestors of our present Indians, and in the same state of culture."

This declaration did not go uncontested, and it unleashed a debate that ultimately saw a deep cloud of suspicion settle over the tablets. Indeed, the members of the Davenport Academy themselves soon concluded that the plaques had been planted by unidentified proponents of the mound-builder theory, whose ideas so closely meshed with what society wanted to believe about the origin of the earthworks.

It has been argued that the motivations for the hoax also extended to personal jealousy: as a distinguished outsider who had grabbed a lot of publicity, the rather boastful Reverend Gass was envied and disliked by many of the academy's members. Some of this odium was clearly justified, because subsequent investigation showed that Gass may have by no means been innocent in the fraud: he and his family were no strangers

to archaeological fakery, and over the years are thought to have been embroiled in a whole slew of questionable dealings.

Yet, despite all its many dubious aspects, the issue of the Davenport Tablets has stubbornly refused to go away. As recently as 1976 a Harvard professor named Barry Fell argued in a best-selling book that the inscription on the astronomical tablet had Egyptian, Iberian Carthaginian, and Libyan elements. He suggested the tablet was proof that "Iberian and Punic speakers were living in Iowa in the 9th Century B.C.... the settlers had presumably sailed up the Mississippi River to colonize the Davenport area." Never underestimate the staying power of a good myth. The story itself is often much more important than its accuracy.

So beware especially of origin myths, which are the most tenacious myths of all. Paleoindian cultures are renowned for the elegance with which their members manufactured stone tools (no easy skill to master), and certain early North American implements closely resemble in some respects those made by the Solutrean people who lived in western Europe between about 22,000 and 18,000 years ago. Almost inevitably, a few years ago the suggestion was put forward by otherwise reputable scientists that ancient Europeans had sailed to America in that ancient time frame, bringing with them Solutrean knapping techniques that were later imitated by Paleoindians of the Clovis culture. First the Native Americans couldn't have made their own mounds; now they couldn't even have invented their own stone tools.

BREATHARIANISM

P eople in developed countries are obsessed with dieting. Mostly that is because we are anxious to lose excess weight, of which in modern economies there is a great deal around; and just how difficult this process turns out to be is evident in the soaring sales of largely unread (or unfollowed) diet books, and in the speed with which diet fads come and go.

Another major motive for eating a diet of a particular kind involves worrying about what exactly it is that one consumes. Reasons for such concerns are diverse. Some involve issues of principle and taste (with which there is famously no arguing). Others turn on questions of physiological appropriateness (though when it comes to diet humans are, like their ancient ancestors, the ultimate generalists, and nobody has been able to show that there is

A Difcourfe upon Prodigious

ABSTINENCE:

OCCASIONED

By the Twelve Moneths FASTING

OF

MARTHA TAYLOR,

The Famed *Derbyfhire*

Damofell :

Proving That without any Miracle, the Texture
of Humane Bodies may be fo altered, that Life may
be long Continued without the fupplies of

MEAT & DRINK.

With an Account of the Heart, and how far it is in-
terefſed in the Bufinefs of Fermentation.

By *John Reynolds.*

Humbly offered to the

Royall Society.

London, Printed, by *R. W.* for *Nevill Simmons,* at the Sign of the
three Crowns near *Holborn*-Conduit : and for *Dorman Newman,*
at the Chyrurgeons Arms in *Little Brittain.* 1669.

John Reynolds, *A discourse upon prodigious abstinence...*, 1669, title page.

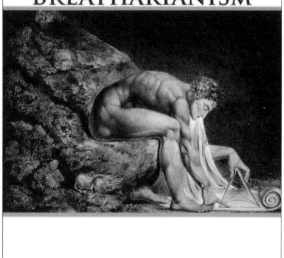

According to the "science" of breatharianism, by using the sun's energy, humans can manufacture chemicals necessary for cellular metabolism in the same way plants absorb energy from light for photosynthesis.

any such thing as an "optimal human diet"). And some people simply seem desperate to rid their bodies of "toxins." In this last case, an uneasy relationship with the ultimate product of the alimentary canal seems to produce a yearning to empty the tract altogether, with the aim of eliminating from the shrine of the body anything that might be construed as impure.

And then, of course, there are the breatharians. These are folks who, sometimes to fatal effect, have concluded that they can get by without eating at all—or who at least like to make other people think that they can. Over the years there have been enough of them to inspire a name for the state they aspire to: "inedia," the ability to live without food. The story of inedia goes back at least to the sixth century BC Sanskrit compendium *Sushruta Samhita*, one of the foundational texts of Hindu medical practice.

The most celebrated nineteenth-century case of this curious condition was that of a Welsh child called Sarah Jacob, born in 1857. The story goes that, after health issues at the age of ten, the young Sarah lost her appetite and eventually gave up eating altogether. Her parents energetically publicized her "miraculous" ability to go without food, and the gaunt child eventually became a minor tourist attraction, and a source of substantial revenue for her family.

After a year or so of this, a committee was appointed to look into suspicions that Sarah might have been snacking on the quiet, and following two weeks of scanty surveillance, it reported that no cheating was involved. Sarah's celebrity skyrocketed as a result, but substantial doubts nonetheless persisted. Accordingly, at the end of 1869 Sarah was checked into Guy's Hospital in London to be watched continuously by a team of nurses. Soon the child grew weak, and her parents were urged to feed her. They refused, and after only eight days of fasting the poor Sarah died. Naturally enough, of starvation.

The public was outraged. Sarah's parents were put on trial and were jailed following a verdict of criminal negligence. Not only science and common sense but also the courts had finally affirmed the amazing truth that people cannot go long without food. It is no coincidence that it was shortly after this episode, in 1873, that the renowned physician Sir William Gull first diagnosed anorexia nervosa as a pathological condition.

But of course, we are dealing here with *Homo sapiens*, and it is a well-known trait of members of that species never to learn from experience, especially that of others. Extreme fasting, recognized since antiquity as a method of attaining religious enlightenment, or at least as a fast track to hallucination, has been co-opted in the service of any number of bizarre belief systems. Among the most radical such expressions is the aforementioned breatharianism, named for the declaration, made in the early 1920s by the German Catholic nun Therese Neumann, that "one can live by the Holy Breath alone." By any standard this was an immoderate formulation, eliminating water as well as food from the diet.

Since Therese survived to die of a heart attack in 1962, one might be forgiven for wondering if she actually practiced to the letter what she preached; nonetheless, according to an article in London's *Daily Mail*, by 2007 the world had an estimated five thousand breatharians and "light nutritionists," the latter imbibing the occasional glass of diluted fruit juice—strictly to eliminate toxins, you understand.

One of the most prominent breatharians of recent times was an Australian financial adviser named Ellen Greve—or, as she preferred to be known, Jasmuheen. She lectured worldwide on the subject and gained a quite extensive following. Rather embarrassingly, in the late 1990s a reporter discovered that her home refrigerator was packed with food (which she said was for her convicted fraudster husband); as a result, she was challenged by the Australian TV program *60 Minutes* to prove that she could live for a mere week with no nutrients other than air.

After two days under medical supervision in a hotel room Jasmuheen began showing signs of physiological stress. Blaming this on polluted air from a nearby highway, she demanded a change

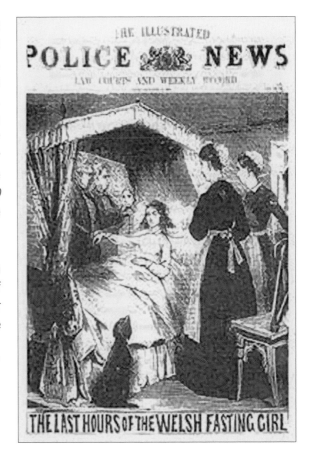

THE ILLUSTRATED POLICE NEWS

LAW COURTS AND WEEKLY RECORD

THE LAST HOURS OF THE WELSH FASTING GIRL

To test the claims made about "Fasting Girl" Sarah Jacob, on December 9, 1869, she was isolated in a room at Guy's Hospital in London. Without food for eight days, she died on December 17. To nobody's surprise, the cause of death was starvation.

Therese Neumann, the German Catholic nun who claimed to have survived for thirty-nine years on nothing more than a daily Communion wafer and a sip of water. Note the stigmata.

of venue, to a remote mountainside. But her condition continued to deteriorate until the TV people discontinued the experiment after a total of four days, fearing for her life—although Jasmuheen claimed it was because they "feared it would be successful." Sadly, not long afterward the starved and emaciated corpse of an Australian environmentalist called Verity Linn was found on a lakeside in Scotland. Her diary revealed her devotion to Jasmuheen's teachings.

Breatharians often call science to their aid, and there is even a *Complete Science of Breatharianism* full of "scientific" mumbo-jumbo purporting to demonstrate exactly how, with the right frame of mind, you can imitate plants and produce adenosine triphosphate, a chemical crucial to cellular metabolism, simply by using the energy in the sun's rays. As far as the rest of us knew, we had to assemble this vital molecule from precursors present in the food we eat. No wonder Wiley Brooks, founder of the Breatharian Institute of America, was once allegedly spotted leaving a 7-Eleven with a hot dog, a Diet Coke, and Twinkies.

Emma and Charles Darwin were first cousins, descended from Josiah Wedgwood, founder of the famous Wedgwood pottery company. Even though both the Darwins and the Wedgwoods were nonconformist Unitarians, Charles worried that his growing doubts about creation would offend Emma. Emma believed deeply in an afterlife, and wanted them to "belong to each other" for eternity.

THE **LADY HOPE**

L et's admit it right away. Charles Darwin (see chapter 19, *Communing with the Departed*), father of the idea of evolution by natural selection, did indeed attend Christ's College, Cambridge, with the vague idea of becoming a clergyman. But this did not necessarily signify a strong religious belief, for in 1828 a life in the church (or the military, which Darwin would have even more greatly abhorred) was pretty much a default option for any male member of the minor gentry who lacked strong career ideas. What is much more important is that Darwin's aimlessness did not last long, and that he left Cambridge with a strong commitment to the study of geology and natural history.

Darwin came from a nonconformist Unitarian family, but he attended a Church of England school and doubtless started off in life with rather conventional Victorian religious views. When he embarked on his epic round-the-world voyage on the sloop *Beagle* in 1831, he even had in mind to look for "centres of creation" in the far-off lands he was to visit.

Instead, though, this thoughtful observer rapidly found himself beginning to doubt the Bible as literal history; and by the time the voyage was over, and he had begun to court his future wife, Emma, his faltering faith seemed poised to threaten the burgeoning relationship. For Emma was a devout Christian, and was reluctant to marry anyone with whom she could not anticipate spending eternity.

As Darwin's religious devotion faded and he elaborated his evolutionary ideas, his abiding respect for his wife's beliefs and feelings made it difficult for him to go public with his developing new view of the living world. Indeed, that reluctance—along with the scientific and social fuss that this very retiring individual knew his evolutionary ideas would cause—is generally reckoned to have been one of the principal factors

The parlor in Charles and Emma's house in Down, England. In a letter written shortly after publication of *On the Origin of Species*, Darwin mused: "With respect to the theological view...I own that I cannot see...evidence of design & beneficence...I am inclined to look at everything as resulting from designed laws, with the details, whether good or bad, left to the working out of what we may call chance.... I feel most deeply that the whole subject is too profound for the human intellect. A dog might as well speculate on the mind of Newton."

that inhibited much earlier publication of Darwin's *On the Origin of Species*. That great work eventually appeared only in 1859 (when Darwin was fifty), after a younger colleague, Alfred Russel Wallace (see chapter 19, *Communing with the Departed*) had come up with a very similar formulation.

Nonetheless, Darwin's diaries and correspondence make it very plain that through the mid-nineteenth century he was consistently losing faith in conventional Christianity—even as he collaborated extensively with clergymen on both sides of the Atlantic and continued to attend the local Anglican church alongside his wife. In his autobiography, published in 1876 when he was sixty-seven years old, Darwin was very specific. He had, he wrote, been "very unwilling to give up my belief." But in the end, while "disbelief crept over me at a very slow rate...[it] was at last complete."

Enter the Lady Hope. Born in Australia to devout English parents, Elizabeth Reid Cotton became well known in England as an Evangelical campaigner in the temperance movement. In 1877, at the age of thirty-five, she married Admiral Sir James Hope, thereby becoming the Lady Hope. Following the admiral's death four years later, she continued her evangelical and social work in London. She wrote novels and several best-selling tracts, and for a while she lived not far away from the Darwins, just across the Sussex border from their residence at Down House, in Kent.

DARWIN AND CHRISTIANITY

BY LADY HOPE.

It was on one of those glorious autumn afternoons, that we sometimes enjoy in England, when I was asked to go in and sit with the well known professor, Charles Darwin. He was almost bedridden for some months before he died. I used to feel when I saw him that his fine presence would make a grand picture for our Royal Academy; but never did I think so more strongly than on this particular occasion.

He was sitting up in bed, wearing a soft embroidered dressing gown, of rather a rich purple shade.

Propped up by pillows, he was gazing out on a far-stretching scene of woods and cornfields, which glowed in the light of one of those marvelous sunsets which are the beauty of Kent and Surrey. His noble forehead and fine features seemed to be lit up with pleasure as I entered the room.

He waved his hand toward the window as he pointed out the scene beyond, while in the other hand he held an open Bible, which he was always studying.

"What are you reading now?" I asked, as I seated myself by his bedside.

"Hebrews!" he answered—"still Hebrews. 'The Royal Book,' I call it. Isn't it grand?"

Then, placing his finger on certain passages, he commented on them.

I made some allusion to the strong opinions expressed by many persons on the history of the Creation, its grandeur, and then their treatment of the earlier chapters of the Book of Genesis.

He seemed greatly distressed, his fingers twitched nervously, and a look of agony came over his face as he said: "I was a young man with unformed ideas. I threw out queries, suggestions, wondering all the time over everything; and to my astonishment the ideas took like wildfire. People made a religion of them."

Then he paused, and after a few more sentences on "the holiness of God" and "the grandeur of this Book," looking at the Bible which he was holding tenderly all the time, he suddenly said:

"I have a summer house in the garden, which holds about thirty people. It is over there," pointing through the open window. "I want you very much to speak there. I know you read the Bible in the villages. To-morrow afternoon I should like the servants on the place, some tenants and a few of the neighbors to gather there. Will you speak to them?"

"What shall I speak about?" I asked.

"CHRIST JESUS!" he replied in a clear, emphatic voice, adding in a lower tone, "and his salvation. Is not that the best theme? And then I want you to sing some hymns with them. You lead on your small instrument, do you not?"

The wonderful look of brightness and animation on his face as he said this I shall never forget, for he added: "If you take the meeting at three o'clock this window will be open, and you will know that I am joining in with the singing."

How I wished that I could have made a picture of the fine old man and his beautiful surroundings on that memorable day!

[At one of the morning prayer services at Northfield Lady Hope, a consecrated English woman, told the remarkable story printed here. It was afterward repeated from the platform by Dr. A. T. Robertson. At our request Lady Hope wrote the story out for THE WATCHMAN-EXAMINER. It will give to the world a new view of Charles Darwin. We should like the story to have the widest publicity. Our exchanges are welcome to the story provided credit is given to THE WATCHMAN-EXAMINER and marked copies are sent to us.—THE EDITOR.]

Elizabeth Reid Cotton, aka the Lady Hope, claimed she visited Charles Darwin while he lay dying at Down. According to a later embellishment of her story, he confessed, "How I wish I had not expressed my theory of evolution as I have done." Lady Hope's initial story, reproduced here, appeared on August 15, 1915, in the *Watchman-Examiner*, an American Baptist newspaper.

Darwin died in 1882 after a protracted illness, while Lady Hope continued her good works, becoming an admirer of the American evangelist Dwight L. Moody. Having been cheated of her inherited wealth by Gerald Fry, a notorious con man of the day, she moved to America in 1913. There, as reported by the Boston *Watchman-Examiner*, she made an extraordinary claim before a 1915 gathering of Evangelicals. She had, she said, visited the aged Charles Darwin at Down House shortly before his death.

Apparently, when Lady Hope arrived at Down, the gracious old man was sitting in bed, reading the Bible. After receiving his visitor warmly, he commented on the passage he had been reading in the "grand" Epistle to the Hebrews, and went on to apologize for his science. "I was a young man with unformed ideas," he said. "To my astonishment, the ideas took like wildfire. People made a religion of them." After speaking of the "holiness of God" and "the grandeur" of the Bible, Darwin went on to invite his guest to speak to an audience of his tenants, servants, and neighbors about Jesus Christ and the salvation he offered.

Darwin's family was appalled. His son Francis is reported as saying, "Lady Hope's account of my father's views on religion is quite untrue.…He could not have become openly and enthusiastically Christian without the knowledge of his family, and no such change occurred." Darwin's daughter Henrietta commented that "the whole story has no foundation whatever." Henrietta's brother Leonard described the encounter as "purely fictitious." And a mutual friend of Darwin and Lady Hope, the social activist J. W. C. Fegan, also went out of his way to observe that "the interview as described by Lady Hope…never took place."

Never mind. To many, Lady Hope's account of Darwin's late-in-life conversion is just too good to resist. She embellished it in a 1920 letter to a colleague that saw publication in 1940. After that her story attained the status of legend among creationists, who saw the great man's return to orthodoxy as a substantiation of their own beliefs. As a result, an extensive literature has accumulated that extolls Darwin's alleged turnaround, and his devotion to the Gospels.

In response, evolutionary biologists have not only pointed to the inherent implausibility of Lady Hope's story but also emphasized that their belief in evolution is based on the overwhelming evidence that has accumulated in support of Darwin's big idea, rather than on what anyone else might claim he thought about religion in his old age. Nonetheless, the idea that Darwin repudiated evolution on his deathbed simply won't go away.

Interestingly, while predictably enough most creationists have glommed eagerly on to the Lady Hope story, some creationist websites have actually rejected Lady Hope's account of Darwin's "deathbed conversion." Apparently their authors prefer to relish the idea that Charles Darwin is roasting in hell for all eternity rather than to feel validated by his alleged change of heart.

THE **PRIORY** OF **SION**

f you visit Paris and a whole lot of other European locales during the summer, you will find it hard to avoid hordes of tourists brandishing dog-eared copies of Dan Brown's 2003 internationally best-selling novel *The Da Vinci Code*, much as you'll see the rest of us clutching guidebooks. In search of the places where key scenes in the novel played out, these good folks are presumably under the illusion that the historical events to which the novel alludes actually took place. The mundane truth, however, is rather more…well, mundane.

The novel's contorted plot revolves around the notion that Jesus Christ did not die celibate, as the Bible claims, but rather had already married his acolyte Mary Magdalene. Following the crucifixion of Jesus, the pregnant Mary fled to France, where she gave birth to their child, Sarah. The descendants of Sarah eventually founded the Merovingian dynasty, which ruled the Frankish territories between the fifth and eighth

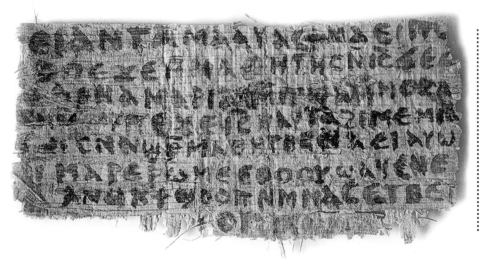

In 2012 the discovery was announced of a papyrus fragment bearing Coptic text that read, in part, "Jesus said to them, My wife." It became the object of heated controversy until Harvard Divinity School declared in 2016 that it was a forgery.

According to Priory of Sion documents, Mary Magdalene was married to Jesus. After his crucifixion, she fled to Marseille, France, pregnant with their daughter, Sarah, whose descendants established the French Merovingian dynasty.

OPVS·DOMINICI

centuries. The Merovingian bloodline continues today, protected by a mysterious sect known as the Priory of Sion.

As the story goes, the Knights Templar are the priory's military wing, and over the years the sect's leaders have included such luminaries as Leonardo da Vinci, Sir Isaac Newton, Victor Hugo, and Jean Cocteau. The Vatican has been at pains to suppress all this for the best part of two thousand years, because the priory's secret jeopardizes its central claim of Saint Peter's apostolic succession.

This makes a great tale, if not one that withstands particularly close scrutiny. But alas, its origins do not go back two thousand years, or even two hundred, for that matter; for it was assembled piecemeal from an unlikely jumble of elements that go back to 1886 at best.

In that year, the priest in the village of Rennes-le-Château in southern France began the reconstruction of his dilapidated church and residence, apparently using funds illicitly gained from "trafficking in masses"—selling masses for the souls of the departed—most of which he probably never performed.

During the reconstruction process the priest reportedly found ancient documents that bore evidence of Jesus's marriage and offspring. Local tradition had it that a huge treasure—the ostensible source of the renovation money—was also involved; and even though at that point nobody had seen the records themselves, the legend was later embroidered and disseminated by one Noël Corbu, who in the early 1950s had turned the priest's mansion into a hotel and was anxious to promote his business.

Beginning in the 1930s, and continuing right through World War II, a French monarchist named Pierre Athanase Marie Plantard founded a series of fringe right-wing activist groups, none of which got any serious traction. These cliques became increasingly esoteric until, in 1956, Plantard set up the Priory of Sion, a fraternal organization named for a famous local hill. It was aimed politically at supporting low-cost housing for the masses; but ideologically it strove for the values of medieval chivalry. Characteristically, it was a disaster, and in an unexpected twist Plantard wound up in jail for child abuse.

During the early 1960s the newly liberated Plantard was eking out a living as a psychic. At that point he met Corbu and learned about Rennes-le-Château, and by 1964 he was ready to recruit the story to his own advantage. Reviving his recently created Priory of Sion, he manufactured an ancient history for it, going back to the Crusades.

As he told it, Plantard was only the most recent grand master of very many, citing a luminous group of predecessors (including Leonardo and Newton) whose names he had actually borrowed from a Rosicrucian list. According to the new account, the Priory had been established specifically to protect the Merovingian connection (as revealed in the Rennes documents) from the Carolingian dynasty that had succeeded the Merovingian monarchs.

To substantiate his claims for the priory's deep roots in time, Plantard and an associate, the artist Philippe de Chérisey, forged on parchment a number of supposedly historical documents (the *Dossiers Secrets*) that they then contrived to have inserted into the collections of the National Library of France, in Paris. Their co-conspirator Gérard de Sède, a former pig farmer turned fantasy writer, then "researched" the embellished Rennes/Priory story using the documents that were now in the library, and published it in his book *L'Or de Rennes*, which appeared in 1967.

In the version of the tale recounted by de Sède, the Merovingian connection was noticeably absent. That detail was later restored by a British actor named Henry Lincoln, who consulted the National Library archive (believing the *Dossiers Secrets* to be genuine) and produced a series of BBC television programs on the subject. Subsequently, with coauthors Michael Baigent and Richard Leigh, Lincoln turned the Rennes legend into a 1982 bestseller titled *The Holy Blood and the Holy Grail*. This book contained the fully embroidered story presented as fact, and concluded rather anticlimactically that the Holy Grail of legend simultaneously symbolizes both the womb of Mary Magdalene and the sacred bloodline of which she was progenitor.

Predictably enough, expert critical acclaim for *The Holy Blood and the Holy Grail* was sparse, and the book was as widely derided by historians as pseudohistory as it was bought by the credulous. Still, it offended enough Catholics to be banned in the Philippines, while others were equally repulsed by its claim that *The Protocols of the Elders of Zion*, a fraudulent 1903 Russian anti-Semitic tract that described an alleged Jewish conspiracy to dominate the world, had actually been based on a similar Masonic strategy.

Dagobert I, one of the last rulers of the Merovingian dynasty whose descendants purportedly have been protected for centuries by the secret Priory of Sion to preserve Jesus's bloodline.

Although Dan Brown denied having used *The Holy Blood and the Holy Grail* as a source for *The Da Vinci Code*, the similarities between the two volumes led Baigent and Leigh to sue over plagiarism. The plaintiffs pointed to the fact that one of Brown's characters was called Leigh, and another's rather unusual name, Teabing, was an anagram of Baigent. However, they lost their case on the grounds that, as "history," their book's findings were available to be freely reinterpreted. Nonetheless, the book's sales soared, which had presumably been part of the plan anyway.

Meanwhile, Plantard had died in penury in 2000, knowing that his ultimately unremunerative Priory of Sion had become a cause célèbre but blissfully unaware that a book based on his cynical confabulation would soon sell 80 million copies. As for the Priory of Sion itself, in its short history it had never boasted more than a dozen members.

POLITICAL LIES

O n February 15, 1898, the U.S. armored cruiser *Maine*, sent to Cuba to protect perceived national interests during the island's revolt against imperial Spain, mysteriously exploded and sank in Havana harbor. Two hundred and fifty-three lives—three-quarters of her crew—were lost. On February 17, William Randolph Hearst's *New York Journal* loudly insinuated that the ship had been sunk by a Spanish torpedo, indirectly bringing about the Spanish-American War.

On the morning of February 15, 1898, only twisted parts of the USS *Maine*'s huge superstructure could be seen protruding above the water in Havana's harbor. In the short war with Spain that followed the cruiser's sinking, far more Americans died from typhoid, yellow fever, and malaria—roughly 4,000—than were killed in battle—about 400.

In August 1964, the USS *Maddox,* patrolling in the Gulf of Tonkin, reported being fired upon by three Vietnamese torpedo boats, seen in the distance in this night photograph. A second incident was reported two days later. This supposed attack became the basis for the Gulf of Tonkin Resolution that authorized escalation of U.S. military involvement in Vietnam. A 2005 National Security Agency study concluded that the attack may not have occurred at all. Years after the incident, President Johnson commented, "For all I know, our navy was shooting at whales out there."

Nobody has ever proved that the Spanish were involved in the *Maine* incident; but then, Hearst was the publisher who, when disappointingly informed by a photographer that little was happening in Cuba, sent him a telegram reading: "Please remain. You furnish the pictures and I'll furnish the war." Hearst knew what the public wanted, and he supplied it—and they believed it—regardless of the truth.

Politicians are evidently no better than publishers. On August 4, 1964, the U.S. destroyer *Maddox* was apparently involved in a skirmish with North Vietnamese navy ships while cruising in the Gulf of Tonkin. Two days later, a second similar incident was reported by the National Security Agency, and was promulgated by the administration of President Lyndon Baines Johnson as intolerable aggression. It served as the basis for the Gulf of Tonkin Resolution, which gave the Johnson government the green light to begin open warfare against North Vietnam—and got the United States bogged down for a decade in a costly, scarring, morally questionable, and ultimately unwinnable war. Only problem? All sides now agree that the second incident never happened.

In March 2003, in the wake of the World Trade Center atrocity eighteen months earlier, the United States (and a miscellaneous "coalition" of lackey states) invaded Saddam Hussein's Iraq under the pretext that the latter was developing "weapons of mass destruction" and directly threatening the United States. No matter that the United Nations was not allowed to complete its investigation of these allegations, or that no WMDs were ever found, or that no two human beings in the world were less likely to be in cahoots than the secular dictator Saddam Hussein and the religious zealot Osama bin Laden. Evidently the George W. Bush administration simply wanted to lash out at someone, regardless of the consequences. As indeed, a substantial proportion of the American public also did, if it is permissible to judge by the actions of their elected representatives: the Senate voted by a shocking 77 to 23 to authorize military action.

All three of these hugely consequential political and military initiatives were based on outright lies, or at best on untruths that could have easily been discounted by dispassionate analysis. And action based on those lies led to self-destructive behavior on increasingly epic scales. The clear lesson of history is "look before you leap"— preferably twice. So why did we believe such things in the past—and why do we continue to believe them now? Evidently, experience has failed to teach us to evaluate what politicians tell us as closely as we should.

At first glance this appears a little odd. But look closer, and it may not seem quite so strange. As far as we can tell—and that is a big caveat, since it is really tough to know, for example, just what is going on in a dolphin's clearly complex brain—we human beings are cognitively different from all other organisms in living in a world that we reconstruct in our minds. Even such highly intelligent close relatives as chimpanzees basically live in the world that nature presents to them. They may react to what happens in that world in very sophisticated ways, but they don't mentally transcend or transform it. They cannot imagine that it could be a different place.

We human beings, on the other hand, can do just that. We routinely mentally deconstruct our experience into a vocabulary of elements, and refashion the world around us— or imagine the one we would like to live in—by recombining those elements in new ways. We can tell ourselves, and each other, stories about what we are experiencing, and how convincing those stories are will often be more dependent on our storytelling skills than on the actual facts at issue.

Believing forged documents alleging that Saddam Hussein had acquired yellow cake uranium from Niger, Secretary of State Colin Powell claimed in his February 5, 2003, speech at the United Nations that Iraq posed an imminent nuclear threat.

Now put yourself in the shoes of the skilled storyteller that every politician must be. You may have the purest of motives and the highest of ideals, but to do anything with them you have to get elected first, and that clearly involves telling your voters—and your potential allies—what they want to hear. That will probably not be the unvarnished truth; and of course, the very same thing applies even if your motives are base and all you want to do is to rip society off.

The basic problem here is that the truth is often unpalatable, and for a human being whose cognitive system just happens to give him or her the option, ignoring an inconvenient truth—or going for an alternative interpretation of the facts—is often preferable to facing reality, at least in the short term.

What is more, there is research out there suggesting that once you have convinced yourself of something, your belief in it will actually be reinforced by evidence to the contrary. As indeed it will be, if you hear that evidence repeated over and over again. It seems that we subliminally assume that lies will not last, so if a statement shows any staying power we will begin to assume it is the truth.

This puts a huge onus on every member of a democracy. For although we instinctively want to see the world in simple terms, nothing exists outside a context. And contexts are often complex and nuanced, the very reverse of the slogans, simplifications, and often downright lies that are the stuff of politics. In political messages, the signal-to-noise ratio is often abysmally low, because the candidates and their political consultants are all too well aware that human nature is far from entirely rational. The best advice for the voter is thus that which is routinely offered to the purchasers of any other product: *caveat emptor*, let the buyer beware.

THE DREYFUS AFFAIR

With its German-inflected dialect, Alsace, a remnant of the rather untidy breakup of Charlemagne's empire in the early ninth century, has always been a little bit of an anomaly in France. Indeed, from the end of the Franco-Prussian War in 1871 through World War I the province was actually under German control. So, as a Jewish officer from Alsace serving in the armed forces of France, a country in which an undercurrent of anti-Semitism flowed quite strongly, Alfred Dreyfus already had two strikes against him.

The third strike came in 1894, when a Parisian cleaning lady discovered the fragments of a handwritten document in a wastebasket in the German embassy and turned them over to the army intelligence service. This document—the *bordereau*—had been written by a French officer offering to sell French military secrets to the Germans, who at the time were in league with the Italians and Austrians and at best very uneasily at peace with France.

The humiliation of Alfred Dreyfus, January 5, 1895, in the courtyard of the Paris Military School. Drums rolled, Dreyfus's badges were ripped from his jacket, and his sword was broken in two. This illustration is from the front page of *Le Petit Journal* with the headline LE TRAITRE (THE TRAITOR).

The contents of the bordereau indicated that its anonymous author was both an artillery officer and a member of the General Staff. This narrowed down the potential field of authors to a small group including Dreyfus, upon whom suspicion immediately fell for no better reason than his Jewish background. The scripts on the bordereau and on a text obtained from Dreyfus by subterfuge were submitted to a handwriting expert for comparison. Although the expert found the writing on the two documents to be different he also, incredibly, declared that this difference was the result of "self-forgery." The writing on the bordereau, he declared, represented a deliberate attempt by Dreyfus to disguise his own handwriting.

By this time Dreyfus was already under arrest, and a court-martial swiftly followed. The supposedly incriminating handwriting evidence was supplemented by a scandalous letter (withheld from Dreyfus's lawyer in the interests of "national security") written by the Italian military attaché to his counterpart (and lover) at the German embassy—the man in whose wastebasket the bordereau had been discovered—that mentioned "this scoundrel D" who had "offered plans of Nice." The "D" concerned was probably another lover; but on this thinnest of evidence the eminently respectable Alfred Dreyfus was convicted, in closed trial, of treason.

At the trial's end Dreyfus was publicly humiliated in the courtyard of the École Militaire in Paris, amid cries of "Jew!" and "Judas!" His medals were stripped from him, his ceremonial sword was broken, and he was sent to the remote and horrible penal colony popularly known as Devil's Island, off the coast of French Guiana.

Throughout, Dreyfus maintained his innocence; but public reaction, urged on by the press and particularly by the overtly anti-Semitic newspaper editor Édouard Drumont, was hysterical. Dreyfus had become the most despised man in France, and a symbol of Jewishness in an atmosphere of mounting insecurity, hostility, and mistrust.

A year later, in March 1896, another letter to the German embassy was intercepted by the French authorities. It was in the handwriting of the author of the bordereau, and this time it was signed: by Major Ferdinand Walsin Esterhazy, a heavily indebted descendant of Hungarian royalty who was deeply disaffected with the French Army he served.

The new intelligence chief, another Alsatian, brought this new evidence bearing on the bordereau's authorship to the attention of the army's chief of staff. At first he was ignored, later he was reassigned to a war in Tunisia, and ultimately he found himself imprisoned. The Dreyfus affair was an embarrassment to be covered up as its distant victim rotted away, and accordingly, even as the already flimsy evidence against

OPPOSITE: A photograph of the unsigned and undated letter addressed to the German military attaché, offering to sell French military secrets.

[...] ...

[...] ... ... indiqué que vous
désirez me voir, je vous adresse cependant
... ... renseignements intéressants:

1° ... une note ... le frein hydraulique
du 120 et la manière dont ... est conduit
... cette pièce ...

2° une note sur les troupes de couverture.
(quelques modifications seront apportées par
le nouveau plan).

3° une note sur une modification aux
formations de l'artillerie.

4° une note relative à Madagascar.

5° le projet de manuel de tir de
l'artillerie de campagne (14 mars 1894.)

Ce dernier document est extrêmement
difficile à se procurer et je ne puis
l'avoir à ma disposition que très-peu
de jours. Le ministère de la guerre

An 1898 cartoon of the novelist Émile Zola famously accusing the French Army of scapegoating Alfred Dreyfus.

Dreyfus frayed further, a branch of the General Staff began forging more incriminating documents in pursuit of this aim. These included a letter purporting to be from the Italian to the German embassy that specifically identified Dreyfus as a seller of military secrets.

Late 1897 saw an incredibly tortuous series of events. First, Esterhazy was retired from the army. The handwriting of the bordereau was then publicly revealed to be his, and his disaffection with France was subsequently confirmed by his equally disaffected mistress. Early in 1898, just after a court-martial had acquitted Esterhazy despite all this, the novelist Émile Zola published his famous *"J'accuse!"* open letter to the president of France, declaring Dreyfus innocent and declaring the truth to be "terrifying."

Zola's accusation of fraud went beyond the General Staff, to three handwriting experts it had hired to bolster its case; and he promptly found himself on trial for defamation. After a sensational trial Zola was convicted; on appeal he was convicted again. He fled to England, while the government ordered a sale of his property to pay his fine and rescinded his *légion d'honneur*.

The next year, 1899, was equally eventful. Early on, the sitting French president died, to be replaced by someone more sympathetic to Dreyfus. At midyear, Esterhazy admitted to the press that he had written the bordereau—although, he claimed, he had done so by order of his superiors. He died many years later, in exile.

Following Esterhazy's admission, Dreyfus was recalled from Devil's Island for a retrial—and, unbelievably, was found guilty again, albeit with "extenuating circumstances"! Uproar followed, and within ten days the case was formally closed when the new president issued Dreyfus a pardon, while legislators granted amnesty to all involved in his persecution.

Dreyfus himself continued to campaign for total exoneration, and succeeded in 1906, when he was formally found innocent by a civilian court. Later that year, he received his own *légion d'honneur* decoration in the very courtyard in which he had been stripped of his rank and honors twelve years earlier. To the ironic shouts of "Long live Dreyfus!" he replied, "No!…Long live France!"

The controversy deeply divided the country. For the anti-Dreyfus forces, to question the guilty verdicts was to impugn the honor of the army and, by extension, of the nation itself: an attitude that presaged Stalin's show trials of the 1930s, in which innocent defendants were pressured to plead guilty "for the good of the party." For the supporters of Dreyfus, the affair exposed deep flaws in French justice and even its democratic system. And despite everything, a reluctance to recognize those flaws continues to resonate in France: as recently as 1994, the director of the Historical Section of the French Army was still asserting that Alfred Dreyfus's innocence was merely "a thesis generally admitted by historians."

The Dreyfus affair thus lives in memory for very good reason; and it is much more than simply an object lesson in the evils of the anti-Semitism that was later to expand into the Holocaust. As Louis Begley points out in his book *Why the Dreyfus Affair Matters*, the case dramatically shows us just what can happen when unreasoning panic grips a nation, as it was poised to do in France in that apprehensive time between two wars with Germany.

Alarmingly, the frenzied French response to the entirely trumped-up charges that Dreyfus faced has its equivalents in our own time; Begley explicitly suggests a parallel with those Guantánamo Bay internees who have never been brought to trial. But clearly, even due process is sometimes not by itself enough. Alfred Dreyfus had all the due process in the world, but he was still the defrauded victim of a terrible miscarriage of justice.

SYNDICATE MILLER GUILTY

Jury Convicts Him of the Crime of Grand Larceny.

TO BE SENTENCED NEXT WEEK

The "Sapho" Case Cited as a Precedent for Acquittal by Counsel for the Defense.

The jury in the case of William F. Miller, the "manager" of the "Franklin Syndicate; returns to investors 520 per cent. a week," rendered a verdict at 8:30 o'clock last evening that Miller was guilty of the crime of grand larceny, with which he was charged. The jury had been out about five hours, including the dinner hour.

The defendant's lawyers had the jury polled, and spoke bravely to reporters about what their next steps will be, but the hard fact remains that "Syndicate" Miller is convicted of stealing the sum of $1,000 from Mrs. Moesar, an investor in the concern that misused the name of a great American, and that the convict will be sentenced by Judge Hurd a week from next Friday.

Miller did not even have the consolation of being a kind of "popular hero" on the last day of his trial. Judging from the interest that was shown in his fate in and around the Brooklyn Court House, he might have been on trial for stealing a mutton.

Ex-District Attorney James W. Ridgway, counsel for Miller, made the announcement that no witnesses would be called for the defense. He made this announcement with the air and the words of a man who felt that there was really nothing to defend. He took the position that the case against Miller was so flimsy that the defense did not feel justified in calling witnesses to take up time.

"On what count of the indictment do you proceed?" queried Mr. Ridgway of District Attorney Clarke.

"On the second count—the common law count," replied the District Attorney.

Mr. Ridgway strove to bring the atten-

THE SCAMMER SCAMMED

The technique may bear the name of the headline-grabbing Charles Ponzi, Charles Dickens may have described its principles in novels such as *Martin Chuzzlewit* and *Little Dorrit*, and in terms of sheer scale the laurels may rest with the infamous Bernie Madoff, but the modern practice of defrauding investors by paying old ones with new deposits actually originated with an obscure tea company bookkeeper named William Miller.

In March 1899, at age twenty-one, the impecunious Miller was president of a Bible class at a church in Brooklyn, New York. An unsuccessful investor in the as-yet barely regulated stock market, he was nonetheless able to persuade three fellow Bible students to invest in a fund he was creating, promising them a juicy return of 10 percent a week (520 percent annually, hence his soon-to-be nickname, "Mr. 520 Percent").

Miller's initial approach to recruiting investors showed an instinctive mastery of what has come to be known as affinity fraud. Trusting him as a church leader and teacher, his victims willingly turned over their money to someone they viewed as one of their own, much as Southern Baptists more recently did to the fraudsters Allen Stanford and Ephren Taylor, and social elites in Florida, New York, and Israel did to Bernie Madoff, who eventually took in some $65 billion, only $11 billion of which has been recovered.

When his crooked lawyer advised "Mr. 520 Percent" to retrieve these incriminating Franklin Syndicate receipts he had given customers, Miller offered to exchange them for equally worthless Franklin Syndicate stock certificates.

Indeed, almost any community you can think of has attracted its own scammers; although religious groups appear to be particularly vulnerable, for obvious reasons of authority and trust. Moreover, as the *Economist* recently pointed out, "Mistrust of mainstream finance helps the scammers. The big guys on Wall Street have shown they can't be trusted, they say; better to go with someone you know."

In Miller's case the scheme took off like wildfire and rapidly extended beyond its local religious base to policemen, firemen, and small businessmen throughout New York City and well beyond. With an associate named Edward Schlessinger, Miller rapidly formed the Franklin Syndicate, from which investors received receipts bearing the likeness of the eponymous founding father, increasing confidence yet further.

Miller fanned the flames by advertising in newspapers nationwide, and with his declaration that his intention was to make "the Franklin Syndicate one of the largest and strongest syndicates operating in Wall Street, which will enable us to manipulate stocks, putting them up and down as we desire....We also guarantee you against loss…as we depend entirely on inside information."

Today a statement like that would be tantamount to surrendering yourself to the attorney general. But in those robber-baron days, anything went on Wall Street. And by one account, "So great was the crush on the stoop of the house on Floyd Street" where Miller had his office, that it was "broken by the people anxious to invest their money."

There was only one problem. Which was, of course, that Miller was paying those of his investors who asked for their weekly 10 percent with the money he was taking in from new ones. Nothing was going into any legitimate investment. Oddly enough, for a long time Miller himself didn't seem to care much where the scheme was ultimately headed. But Schlessinger was smarter: he demanded one-third of receipts in cash each day, and eventually fled to Europe with a significant cut of the takings.

In October 1899, as Miller's activities were beginning to attract unwanted press and bureaucratic attention despite the crush of new investors, he took on board a legal partner, a shyster named Colonel Robert Ammon. Ammon usefully figured out a way of calling back Miller's receipts and replacing them with stock certificates in a new corporation, a swap made more attractive by the promise of huge capital gains in addition to the 520 percent interest. But he also had a deeper motive.

As debts mounted, cash flow was squeezed, and the authorities and the press moved in closer. In late November, Miller asked Ammon for advice. Ammon pointed out that Miller was directly liable to his creditors, but that as his attorney he, Ammon, was protected by privilege. Logically, then, to safeguard his ill-gotten loot and avoid entanglement with the law, Miller should deposit it with Ammon and abscond to Canada.

The pair duly took a suitcase full of cash to Ammon's bank, and a number of other transfers to Ammon's bank account basically wiped out everything Miller had gained from his scam, which had reportedly grossed something in the region of a million dollars.

The very next day word reached Miller that he was under indictment, and Ammon had him smuggled to Montreal, where police soon found him. Miller returned to Brooklyn to face trial, remaining silent about Ammon's involvement in the scam in return for Ammon's promise to pay Miller's wife and daughter maintenance of five dollars a week. In May 1900 Miller was convicted of grand larceny and sentenced to serve ten years in Sing Sing prison.

Charles Ponzi working in his Boston office in 1920. When located and interviewed by a reporter fifteen years after his release from prison, Miller remarked, "I may be rather dense, but I can't understand how Ponzi made so much money in so short a time in foreign exchange."

Even with all of Miller's cash in hand, Ammon proved reluctant to pay his client's wife and daughter. So by the time the state attorney charged Ammon with theft of $30,500 from the syndicate, Miller was eager to testify against him. Ammon was convicted and sentenced to four years, and thereafter presumably went into a comfortable retirement. What happened to Miller, stricken with tuberculosis by the time of his release, is less certain; one story has him opening a grocery, another has him going back to the tea company where he started.

What emerges from this very first Ponzi scheme is that no such scam can last forever, and that the chickens tend to come home to roost sooner rather than later. Indeed, given mounting experience, it is as remarkable that the fraudsters don't tend to bolt sooner, as it is that so many people fall for their siren songs.

But apparently human nature doesn't change, and neither does the desire to believe in those things that are too good to be true. As one woman told the *New York Times* back in 1899, "Mr. Miller has never failed us....I put in $100 six weeks ago and have taken $60 out. It is these newspapers and bankers that are causing this trouble. Nobody believes the papers. It's envy. They'd like to make the money themselves."

PILTDOWN

Today we know that the early ancestors of humankind were small-bodied, broad-hipped, long-armed, and short-legged bipeds that possessed brains not much bigger than those of chimpanzees—which is to say, only around a third the size of our own. But in the early years of the twentieth century, fossil knowledge of those ancient relatives still lay far in the future.

Charles Darwin and Alfred Russel Wallace had gone public with their theory of natural selection half a century earlier, so by the early twentieth century scientists were already comfortable thinking in evolutionary terms. But most human fossils available at the time to document the human evolutionary story belonged to *Homo neanderthalensis*, a recently extinct continental European human species with a curiously built skull but a brain of modern size, which was known to have existed alongside *Homo sapiens*. The only others belonged to an earlier but poorly known form from distant Java called *Pithecanthropus* (now *Homo*) *erectus*, whose discoverer had failed to convince all

Reconstruction of the Piltdown skull. The fossil human remains of "Eoanthropus dawsoni" were found from 1912–1915 at Piltdown, Sussex, and were thought to hold the key to our evolutionary past until proven fakes in 1952.

Excavations at Piltdown in 1913. Charles Dawson is seen second from left, wearing a boater, and Sir Arthur Smith Woodward is at extreme right. The goose was named Chipper.

his colleagues that the smallish skullcap he had found was properly associated with some thigh bones that looked a lot like our own.

Meanwhile England, in 1912 still at the center of an enormous empire, had no human fossil record at all. So imagine the joy in the English press when scientists from the Natural History branch of the British Museum proclaimed the discovery at Piltdown, near the country's southern coast, of a set of homegrown hominid fossils boasting that most prized of human attributes, a big brain.

The fossils in question had been discovered in 1908 by a local antiquarian named Charles Dawson, and comprised fragments of a thick but humanlike skull and a rather apelike jaw that was missing the area where the diagnostic human chin would have been. Dawson took these fragments to the paleontologist Arthur Smith Woodward at the British Museum, and together the two announced to the world in 1912 that, back in the Pliocene epoch (nobody yet knew how long ago that was exactly, but it was well before the Neanderthals), an early human relative living at Piltdown had possessed a brain of moderate size and a somewhat apelike jaw. A new reconstruction soon caused revision of this description to that of a large-brained human with an apelike jaw that had apparently possessed a chin.

Awkwardly missing was a canine tooth, which Smith Woodward's original reconstruction had assumed to be rather bigger (and hence more apelike) than its diminutive modern counterpart. And at Piltdown a canine duly showed up. It was rather thick at its base, but it was short like its modern equivalent and apparently proved the accuracy of the second (humanlike) reconstruction. It was actually found by the Jesuit mystic and paleontologist Pierre Teilhard de Chardin, who had joined the field investigation and was the first person other than Dawson to find a hominid at Piltdown.

By 1916, when Dawson died, the site (and a neighboring locality) had yielded a miscellany of alleged finds including fossils of extinct mammal species that proved the great apparent age of the hominid, and a curious bone object that vaguely resembled a cricket bat, the very symbol of Englishness.

From the start, some observers had had their doubts about the alleged Piltdown hominid. As early as 1913, the King's College London biologist David Waterston published his conclusion that the "fossil" consisted of cranial parts from a modern human and the jaw of an ape; and others, including the Smithsonian's Gerrit Miller, soon concurred in various ways. Whether or not the combination was fortuitous was tactfully left in abeyance by most observers, although in 1923 the German anatomist Franz Weidenreich came close to suggesting that deliberate forgery was involved.

As the human fossil record enlarged, most paleoanthropologists eventually came to write off the Piltdown-derived "brain first" view of human evolution, in favor of the idea that upright locomotion had preceded the expansion of the brain. But the fraudulent nature of the specimen was not proved until 1953.

The infamous "Piltdown cricket bat." An elephant bone, bottom, shaped to look like a hand tool, this was perhaps the most ludicrous deception in the whole scandal.

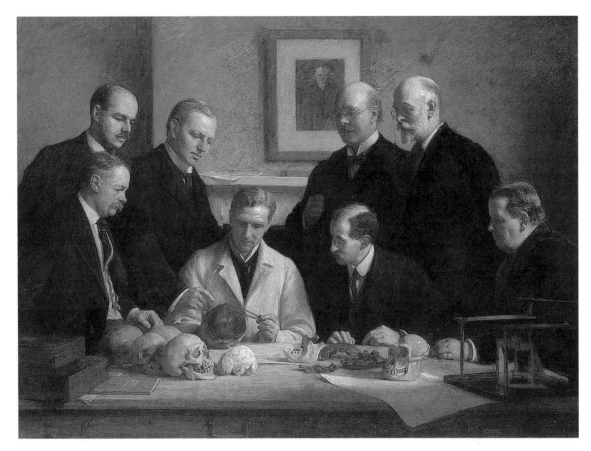

An imagined group portrait of the Piltdown skull being examined. BACK ROW (FROM LEFT): F. O. Barlow, G. Elliot Smith, Charles Dawson, Arthur Smith Woodward. FRONT ROW: A. S. Underwood, Arthur Keith, W. P. Pycraft, and Ray Lankester. Note the portrait of Charles Darwin on the wall.

In that year, the cranial and mandibular fossils were shown by chemical testing to be of different origins, and to have been stained to look similar. The cranial bits were identified as those of a modern human; the jaw was that of an orangutan, artfully broken to disguise its origin; and the ape canine tooth had been filed down to resemble that of a human. This concatenation of specimens at the same site was very clearly no coincidence.

Looked at in retrospect, the Piltdown fraud appears a crude one. And it certainly could never be repeated in similar form today. But in one important respect it was extremely sophisticated indeed. The deception had succeeded because, like all successful con jobs, it had fed directly into the desires and preconceptions of those at whom it was aimed—in this case the British paleoanthropological establishment. Clearly the fraudster(s) had both a very considerable animus toward those scientists and a very detailed knowledge of the milieu in which they worked.

Nobody now doubts that Dawson was an important player in the hoax—and indeed, it has turned out that he was an inveterate faker, having been involved in a host of other fraudulent "discoveries." But it is possible—although the latest study concludes otherwise—that he was working with a co-conspirator, even one within paleoanthropology itself.

Numerous candidates have been put forward for this role, including such names as Teilhard de Chardin; Martin Hinton, a colleague of Smith Woodward's at the museum; Smith Woodward's rival, anatomist Arthur Keith; and even the novelist Arthur Conan Doyle, who played golf nearby and often gave the scientists a ride to the dig from the local train station. Smith Woodward himself has even been implicated, although this strains credulity beyond the breaking point, given how completely this episode eventually blighted his career.

Whether or not Dawson acted alone, it seems that he (or they) may have gotten cold feet as the fraud succeeded beyond his wildest dreams: the "cricket bat" may have been a final effort to persuade the scam's victims to realize just how cruelly they were being taken in.

ROBERT PEARY

In the early years of the twentieth century the race for the poles, South and North, gripped the public imagination in very much the same way as the race to the moon would fifty years later. Of course, reaching the two poles required altogether different strategies. Getting to the South Pole (a feat first accomplished by the Norwegian explorer Roald Amundsen in 1911) involved crossing a vast rocky continent covered by a thick permanent ice sheet, whereas the geographical North Pole was under almost fourteen thousand feet of ocean water that supported an ever-moving skin of pack ice.

Robert Peary and his team purportedly at the North Pole. Actually, they were at least eighty miles shy of it. From left: Ooqueah, Ootah, Henson, Egingwah, and Seeglo.

In 1893 the Norwegian explorer Fridtjof Nansen allowed his ship to freeze into the Arctic ice pack, in the hope that it would drift with the ice toward the North Pole. But, alas, the ice drifted the wrong way and the attempt fizzled. Four years later an equally brave and ingenious Swede, Salomon Andrée, tried to fly from Svalbard (then known by its Dutch name Spitsbergen) to the North Pole in a hydrogen balloon. He and his companions perished after ice formed atop their balloon and brought their journey to an end. The sea and the air routes both having disappointed, only one viable option remained—dogsledding over the sea ice.

The foremost proponent of this approach was Robert E. Peary, a civil engineer from Pennsylvania who eventually joined the U.S. Navy. The child of an overbearing mother

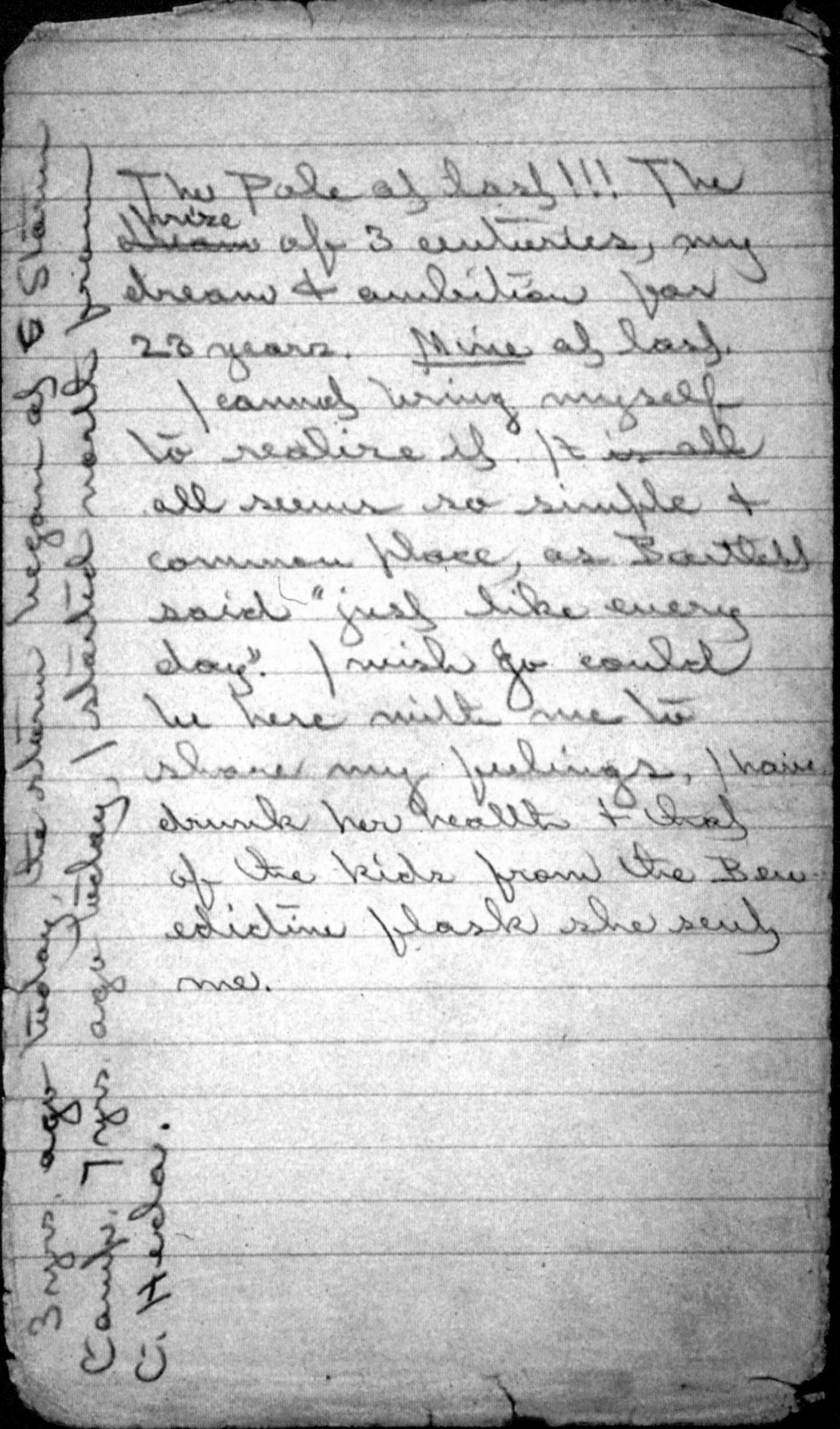

The Pole at last!!!! The
Prize of 3 centuries, my
dream & ambition for
23 years. Mine at last.
I cannot bring myself
to realize it. It is all
all seems so simple &
commonplace, as Bartlett
said "just like every
day". I wish Jo could
be here with me to
share my feelings, I have
drunk her health & that
of the kids from the Ben-
edictine flask she sent
me.

3 m.p.h. ago today, the storms began at 6 Start... / Camp 7 m.p.h. ago today, I started north from / C. Heckla.

The April 6, 1909, page from Peary's diary, in which he writes, "The Pole at last!" Peary's navigational records have been the subject of considerable skepticism.

from whom he was still doubtless anxious to escape even as he approached his forties, Peary worked throughout the 1890s on his sledding techniques and logistics in remote Arctic regions, preparing for an onslaught on the North Pole. In 1906 he reached 87°06' N, the closest anyone had yet come; he was predictably annoyed the next year to learn that his former collaborator Frederick Cook was planning to attack the pole via "his" route through northern Greenland and Ellesmere Island.

The rival explorers independently converged on the pole in 1908–09. Cook traveled light, with just two Inuit for company. Peary began his trek with several sleds and a sizable team of companions. The Peary group arrived in Greenland to learn that Cook had long since headed north, but they remained confident that their larger operation had the edge.

By March 1909, Peary's expedition had seen considerable attrition, and the two remaining sleds were moving more slowly toward the pole than expected, at not much more than ten miles a day. Still, progress was being made when, on reaching 87°47' N—a new northerly record, about 133 miles from the pole—Peary sent the leading sled back to the mother ship the SS *Roosevelt*, anchored far south at Ellesmere Island. The colleagues who returned with the sled included his navigator, Robert Bartlett.

That left Peary, his longtime personal assistant Matthew Henson, and four Inuit without navigational experience to carry on. According to Peary, at this point daily travel increased significantly because the party was traveling lighter, until on April 6 he recorded a latitude of 89°57' N, virtually at the pole itself.

Circling around to make sure he'd hit the spot, Peary lingered briefly and then rapidly returned south, rejoining his ship on April 26, only a couple of days after the other sled. Soon he learned that Cook and his Inuit companions had returned from the pole some time earlier, minus dogs and sleds but still alive.

Matthew Henson accompanied Peary on six Arctic expeditions over a space of twenty years. He mastered the Avanersuaq Inuit dialect, and was remembered as the only non-Inuit who became skilled in driving dogsleds.

The stage was thus set for an epic and long-drawn-out dispute over who had first arrived at the North Pole, one in which both protagonists proved extremely reluctant to produce detailed evidence for their claimed feat.

The two great Arctic rivals, Robert Peary (left) and Roald Amundsen (right), not quite wanting to shake hands. Amundsen was unquestionably the first man to reach both the South Pole (by dogsled) and the North Pole (by airship).

First out of the gate, Cook had initially led the field, but when he could produce only typewritten transcriptions rather than actual field records, suspicions that he hadn't actually reached the pole began to mount—especially when the public was reminded by Peary advocates of his widely dismissed claim to have summited Mount McKinley in the previous year. Things did not improve when, allegedly paid off by those same Peary supporters, Cook's only Mount McKinley climbing companion denied that the pair had attained the peak, and by the end of 1909, Cook's polar claim had been formally rejected by a committee of the University of Copenhagen.

Then Peary's extensive network of connections kicked in. In 1910 a committee of the National Geographic Society (which had sponsored his expedition) verified his polar feat, and this success emboldened Peary the next year to petition Congress to certify his achievement and to promote him to vice admiral in the navy. A bill approving both items passed the Senate and ultimately—though not without some pointed questioning—the House. Peary duly retired from the military, to die nine years later laden with honors.

And yet…and yet. Nagging questions remained about the amazing speed of his last dash to the pole and back. Up to the time he inexplicably dismissed most of his remaining companions, he had covered less than ten miles a day. But over that final stretch he allegedly traveled an amazing twenty-six miles daily; and the British geographer J. Gordon Hayes calculated in 1934 that if Peary had actually returned from the pole to the fateful parting point in the time claimed, he would have to have covered an unimaginable and unprecedented fifty-three miles a day. In his book *Cook and Peary* the author Robert Bryce put it this way: Peary "was a man with big secrets to hide."

The simplest explanation for sending his expert navigator Bob Bartlett back at the last minute was that Peary knew by then that he was not going to reach the pole; and numerous subsequent analyses confirm that, in reality, he had at best come no closer than about one hundred miles to his goal. Even his sponsor, the National Geographic Society, which for a century supported his claims, eventually conceded that "Peary was actually 30 to 60 miles…short of the Pole."

What is more, according to the loyal Henson, when he congratulated Peary on arrival at their final camp, purportedly only six miles from the Pole, the evasive response was "I do not suppose we can swear that we are exactly at the Pole." And that was just the beginning. Henson later recalled: "From the time we knew we were at the Pole Commander [Peary] scarcely spoke to me. Probably he did not speak to me four times on the whole return journey to the ship.…After twenty-two years of close companionship he refused even to say goodbye when we separated in New York…Nearly ten years before we had carried Peary nearly 200 miles with his feet frozen, traveling days and hunting nights for food to keep him and ourselves alive!"

What about Peary himself? Despite his evident reservations at the time, and his rather guilty behavior toward Henson, did he eventually convince himself that he had actually reached the North Pole? That is something we are unlikely ever to know for certain.

Still, chances are that at some level Peary remained aware. By 1909 his strength and endurance were waning. He had already lost most of his toes to frostbite, and he knew, at the age of fifty-three, that this would be his last chance to reach the pole. Blindly, he took it; and then his human capacity to rationalize seems to have taken over. Maybe what went on in his mind was aptly characterized by Frank Bruni of the *New York Times*, who once wrote, "Of all the abilities that human beings possess, perhaps none is as mysterious as our talent for compartmentalization.…It's because there are so many chambers inside [the mind], and a few are more hidden from others, even from the person himself."

In September 1924, *Scientific American* published the results of an extensive investigation into Albert Abrams's treatment methods and concluded they were "without value." Abrams had died eight months before, leaving a $2 million estate, amassed chiefly by leasing out his Electronic Reaction equipment.

RADIONICS

A s long as there has been disease, there have been both hope and denial. Over the last century and a half the grounds for hope have grown by leaps and bounds as clinical medicine has co-opted the methods of science to design and test the efficacy of potential treatments for almost every imaginable condition that threatens our health. This has led to immeasurably better outcomes, and at the very least to more realistic perspectives on our prospects for cure. But it was not ever thus.

In a very real sense, modern medicine was ultimately born of what we would have to call quackery: from the attempt to provide treatments for a disease in the absence of any knowledge of what caused the particular condition or of how its symptoms might be effectively ameliorated. Since time immemorial, the ingestion of noxious—and sometimes fatal—substances has been indiscriminately used in the attempt to alleviate disease, along with cutting holes into the skull, bleeding, leeches, and a host of other gambits.

Nothing but blind faith (probably originally born of desperation), and later the weight of tradition, supported the efficacy of such approaches; and indeed, many such "treatments" did a great deal more damage than good—which was, of course, the reason for the main principle of the physicians' Hippocratic Oath, initially promulgated in the fifth century BC: "First, do no harm."

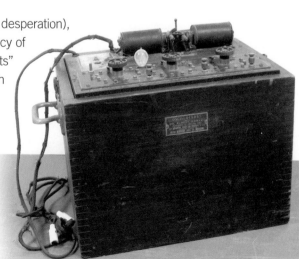

The Dynomizer looked something like a radio. Abrams claimed it could diagnose any known disease from a single drop of blood, or even from the subject's handwriting.

All that began to change as the nineteenth century progressed and advances in scientific knowledge and its technological application began to impact the daily lives of ordinary citizens. Suddenly, technology began to promise people a degree of control over their health that they had never before thought possible.

But ironically, just as the new high-tech capabilities began to signal the emergence of mainstream medicine from its origins in quackery, the resulting faith in "miracle" technologies, especially those using electricity, began to open up the field to the con artists. The sky became the limit for almost any bogus medical claim, especially when promoted by individuals with impressive medical credentials.

One of the shrewdest exploiters of this new realm of possibility was Albert Abrams, a Californian physician who attended medical college in San Francisco and subsequently, in 1882, graduated from the Faculty of Medicine at the University of Heidelberg, Germany. An imposing figure who exuded authority, Abrams seemed set on a hugely successful career in conventional medicine, having by 1893 become president of the San Francisco Medical-Surgical Society at the tender age of thirty. Yet before the twentieth century was a decade old, he had already veered off into the nether regions of the radically unconventional—and the sensationally lucrative.

Anticipating the remote diagnostics that the Internet was to make possible a century later, during World War I Abrams came up with a diagnostic device he called the "Dynomizer." Using what its inventor self-promotingly called the "Electronic Reactions of Abrams" (ERA), the machine was purportedly able to diagnose any malady from a

A drop of a patient's blood was placed inside a Dynomizer. Abrams would then tap on the abdomen of the patient who was stripped to the waist and always facing west. By listening to the sounds emitted by the Dynomizer, he claimed he was able to diagnose the patient's ills.

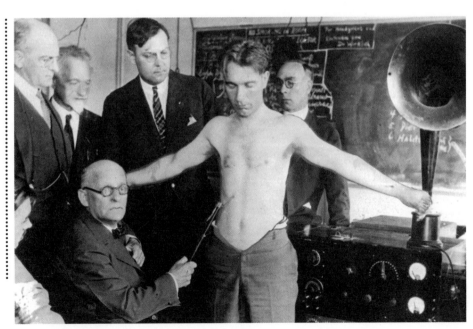

single drop of blood, fresh or otherwise, making it possible to identify diseases through the mail. And it tended to come up with some pretty alarming diagnoses, including cancer, diabetes, and syphilis. Even more remarkably, Abrams found it could do the same thing just from handwriting samples, thereby discovering that the literary luminaries Samuel Johnson, Edgar Allan Poe, and Oscar Wilde had all suffered from syphilis.

Technology with capabilities such as these was bound to be in demand, though why so few questions seem to have been asked about just how it worked remains a mystery. Abrams leaped at the burgeoning market, training Dynomizer operators at $200 a pop (over $3,000 in today's money) and leasing out his machines at a further $200 plus a monthly fee—with the provision that they never be opened, allegedly to protect the delicate innards.

Soon the Dynomizer had been joined by another machine called the Oscilloclast. This was designed to treat the diseases the Dynomizer had diagnosed by directing at patients electrical pulses that allegedly had the same "vibratory rates" as their diseases. By 1921 there were allegedly 3,500 "Radionics" practitioners around the country, "treating" tens of thousands of patients.

No science supported any of this; but major complaint nonetheless waited until 1923, when an elderly patient with terminal cancer went to an Abrams practitioner who assured him of a complete cure. A month later the patient died, to the outrage of his family. At about the same time, a group of scientists examined the interior of an Oscilloclast, only to find a meaningless tangle of wires and parts.

All hell broke loose, but by the time the full hue and cry had developed, Abrams himself had conveniently died of pneumonia, leaving an estate worth millions of dollars. By that time several fraud suits were in court, and *Scientific American* had launched an exhaustive investigation, the damning results of which were published shortly after Abrams's death. After revealing in March 1924 that an ERA practitioner had been unable to correctly identify any of six samples submitted, the magazine delivered the coup de grace: "No less an authority than Professor Millikan, probably America's greatest physicist in the field of the electron, investigated the Abrams apparatus and stated that it did not rest on any sort of scientific foundation whatsoever....The E.R.A. claims are the height of absurdity."

But even then, voices were raised in support of Abrams and his vile contraptions. In the 1926 edition of *The Book of Life*, published long after the fraud had been comprehensively outed, the muckraking novelist Upton Sinclair, a man with as good a nose for a scandal as anyone, went out of his way to defend the late fraudster. Why? The reasons are as mysterious as the human psyche itself. Some things are manifestly too good to believe. But others are evidently too good not to believe.

Authorities inspecting the recovered *Mona Lisa* in Florence.

THE SIX MONA LISAS

Leonardo da Vinci's *Mona Lisa* is, by a wide margin, the world's best-known Renaissance painting. The pride of Paris's Louvre museum, it is hard nowadays for a visitor to get a good look at. Not only do heavy stanchions and a substantial velvet rope keep art lovers at bay, but a jostling horde of phone-pointing tourists typically accomplishes the same thing even more effectively. While you can expect to scrutinize Leonardo's nearby *Virgin and Child with Saint Anne* up close and in reasonable tranquility, you are lucky to catch more than a glimpse of the *Mona Lisa* over the heads of the heaving crowd. And that's just getting to admire the painting: with elaborate electronic protection and constantly circulating guards, stealing the iconic piece is pretty much unthinkable.

At a time when the standards of security were considerably more lax, around noon on Tuesday, August 22, 1911, horrified museum staff reported that the *Mona Lisa* was missing from her place on the gallery wall. The Louvre was immediately closed down and minutely searched (the picture's empty frame was found on a staircase), and the ports and eastern land borders of France were closed until all departing traffic could be examined. To no avail. After a frantic investigation that temporarily implicated both the poet Guillaume Apollinaire and the then-aspiring young artist Pablo Picasso, all that was left was wild rumor: the smiling lady was in Russia, in the Bronx, even in the home of the banker J. P. Morgan.

Two years later the painting was recovered after a Florentine art dealer contacted the Louvre saying that it had been offered to him by the thief. The latter turned out to have been Vincenzo Peruggia, an Italian artist who had worked at the Louvre on a program to protect many of the museum's masterworks under glass.

Peruggia reportedly told police that, early on the Monday morning before the theft was discovered—a day on which the museum was closed to the public—he had entered the Louvre dressed as a workman. Once inside, he had headed for the *Mona Lisa*, taken her off the wall and out of her frame, wrapped her up in his workman's smock,

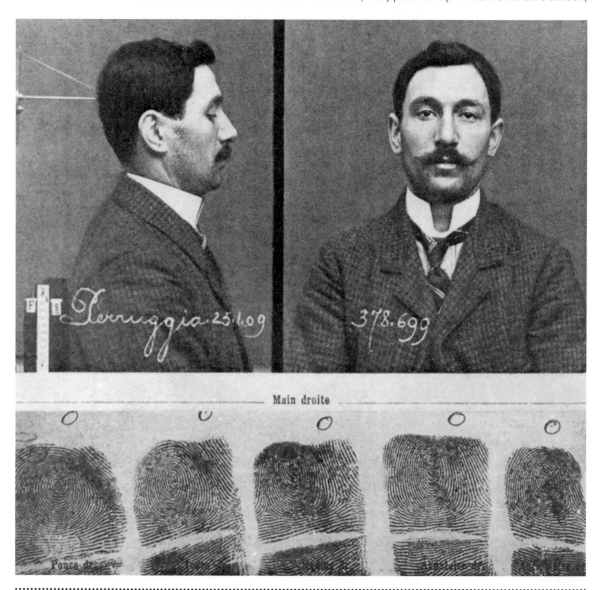

Main droite

After Vincenzo Peruggia walked out of Paris's Louvre museum with the *Mona Lisa* tucked under his arm, a massive police dragnet was launched. Pablo Picasso was a suspect at one point. Two years later, Peruggia walked into Florence's Uffizi Gallery with the painting, expecting to be acclaimed a national hero. Instead he was arrested and sentenced to a year in jail, but only served seven months.

and carried her out under his arm. Another version has Peruggia hiding in a museum closet overnight, but in any event the heist itself was clearly a pretty simple and straightforward affair.

Peruggia's motivations appear to have been a little more confused. The story he told the police was that he had wanted to return the *Mona Lisa* to Italy, his and its country of origin, in the belief that the painting had been plundered by Napoleon—whose armies had indeed committed many similar trespasses in the many countries they invaded.

But even if he believed his story, Peruggia had his history entirely wrong. For it had been Leonardo himself who had brought the unfinished painting to France, when he became court painter to King François I in 1503. After Leonardo died in a Loire Valley château in 1519, the *Mona Lisa* was legitimately purchased for the royal collections.

So it didn't seem so far-fetched when, in a 1932 *Saturday Evening Post* article, the journalist Karl Decker gave a significantly different account of the affair. According to Decker, an Argentinian con man calling himself Eduardo, Marqués de Valfierno, had told him that it was he who had masterminded Peruggia's theft of the *Mona Lisa*. And that he had sold the painting six times!

Valfierno's plan had been a pretty elaborate one, and it had involved employing the services of a skilled forger who could exactly replicate any stolen painting—in the *Mona Lisa*'s case, right down to the many layers of surface glaze its creator had used. By Decker's account, Valfierno not only sold such fakes on multiple occasions, but used them to increase the confidence of potential buyers, ahead of the heist, that they would be getting the real thing after the theft.

The fraudster would take a victim to a public art gallery and invite him to make a surreptitious mark on the back of a painting that he had scheduled to be stolen. Later Valfierno would present him with the marked canvas, which had allegedly been stolen and replaced with a copy.

This trick was actually accomplished by secretly placing the copy behind the real painting, and removing it after the buyer had applied his mark. According to Valfierno, this was an amazingly effective sales ploy: so effective, indeed, that by his account he managed to presell the scheduled-to-be-stolen *Mona Lisa* to six different United States buyers, all of whom actually received copies.

Those copies had been smuggled into America prior to the heist at the Louvre, when nobody was on the lookout for them, and the well-publicized theft itself served to validate their apparent authenticity when they were delivered to the marks in return for hefty sums in cash.

Why and How the Mona Lisa Was Stolen

By KARL DECKER

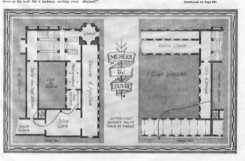

According to Valfierno, the major problem in all this turned out to be Peruggia, who stole the stolen *Mona Lisa* from him and took it back to Italy. Still, when he was caught trying to dispose of the painting there, Peruggia could not implicate Valfierno without compromising his own story of being a patriotic thief, so the true scheme remained secret. Similarly, when the original *Mona Lisa* was returned to the Louvre, Valfierno's buyers could assume that it was a copy—and in any case, they would hardly have been in a position to complain.

Decker's story of Valfierno's extraordinary machinations caused a sensation, and it rapidly became accepted as the truth behind the *Mona Lisa*'s disappearance. Perhaps this is hardly surprising because, after all, Peruggia's rather prosaic account somehow seems a little too mundane for such an icon of Renaissance artistic achievement. The more flamboyant Valfierno version was widely believed, and is still repeated over and over again, including in two recent books.

Yet there are numerous problems with Decker's *Saturday Evening Post* account, including the fact that nobody has ever been able to show for certain that Valfierno actually existed (though you can Google a picture of him). Only Peruggia's role in the disappearance of the *Mona Lisa* seems to be reasonably clear-cut. Still, although it remains up in the air whether Valfierno faked his account, or whether Decker fabricated both him and his report, the *Mona Lisa* that hangs in the Louvre today is probably the original.

FRITZ KREISLER

M usic is almost certainly as old as humankind itself. A vulture-bone flute made more than forty thousand years ago is known from an Ice Age cave in Germany, but it's just the earliest proof we currently have that people were making music back in the Old Stone Age. It's a safe bet that the roots of music itself run much deeper in time.

For most of that long history, music presented rather strictly limited opportunities for fraud—although "faking it" as a musician's technique certainly has a respectable history. But particularly once individual composers and performers had gained mass audiences through recordings and video, the calculation changed.

....

Fritz Kreisler is regarded as one of the greatest violin masters of all time. Known for his mellifluous tones and nuanced phrasing, he produced a sound that was immediately recognizable as his own. His 1920s performances of the Beethoven, Mendelssohn, and Brahms violin concertos with the Berlin State Opera Orchestra are considered his finest. The two most popular compositions he wrote under his own name are "Liebesfreud" ("Love's Joy") and its companion "Liebesleid" ("Love's Sorrow").

In 1990, the pop group Milli Vanilli was stripped of its Grammy award after it was revealed that frontmen Fab Morvan (left) and Rob Pilatus (right) had not sung on their hit album. On the eve of a 1998 comeback tour, Pilatus was found dead in a Frankfurt hotel room of a suspected alcohol and prescription drug overdose.

Musical frauds have been many and varied, though most have been of only parochial consequence. In the early nineteenth century, the Anglo-Polish musician Isaac Nathan published a series of traditional synagogue melodies that he improbably claimed to have been the same music that had been played in Solomon's Temple in ancient Jerusalem. So convincingly did he argue this fraudulent attribution that the poet Lord Byron actually wrote English words to accompany Nathan's music. Nathan himself went on to fight a duel over Byron's mistress Lady Caroline Lamb, and ultimately emigrated to Australia, where he wrote and produced the first indigenous opera, performed in Sydney in 1847.

The most publicized musical fraud of recent years, if not necessarily the most noteworthy, was perpetrated by the German hip-hop funk duo Milli Vanilli, who turned out not to have actually sung any of the vocals on their hit debut album, allegedly at the insistence of their manager. When this relatively harmless deception came to light, the album's Grammy was withdrawn, and the affair ended in tragedy when one of the musicians died of a drug overdose on the eve of a planned comeback tour.

On the classical front, a large number of recordings allegedly by an obscure and long-retired English pianist called Joyce Hatto famously appeared, to much critical acclaim, between 2003 and her death in 2008 at age seventy-seven. Eventually, these turned out to be digitally altered versions of recordings by other artists; and although Hatto's husband insisted that she herself had not been knowingly complicit in the fraud, doubts persist.

As musicians themselves have become hugely commercially valuable properties, so have the instruments they play. In 2012 an Austrian court sentenced the well-known instrument dealer Dietmar Machold, formerly nicknamed "Mr. Stradivarius," to six years in prison. Not only had Machold sold several inferior violins at vastly inflated prices as the products of the genius eighteenth-century Italian luthier Antonio Stradivari, but he had secured numerous large bank loans on instruments that belonged to clients, or that turned out not to be the work of the master.

Since Stradivari instruments have sold for close to $10 million (and up to $45 million has been asked for them at auction) it is hardly surprising that Machold is only the most recent of many Stradivarius forgers: while some 650 documented Stradivarius instruments of all kinds survive (violins, violas, cellos, and the occasional harp), there are many thousands of instruments out there that bear the Stradivari name.

But unquestionably the most genial deception in the history of music—or indeed, of practically anything else—was perpetrated in the early twentieth century by the Austrian virtuoso violinist Fritz Kreisler. Kreisler was a youthful prodigy who fizzled out on his first visit to the United States and almost became a painter instead. But music eventually won out, and in 1899 he made a triumphant reappearance on the American classical music scene. Audiences loved him, and, unusually, so did both the critics and his musical colleagues.

Still, the young violinist yearned not only to play but to compose as well. The problem was that, at the time, it was considered inappropriate for young performers to play their own pieces. Accordingly, after 1913 he began to "discover," and then perform, lost masterpieces by famous composers such as Mendelssohn, Paganini, Vivaldi, and Couperin. These he had allegedly obtained by combing the ancient monastery libraries of Europe to unearth a continuous stream of forgotten and dusty old musical manuscripts by earlier masters.

Kreisler's apparent luck in this quest was truly phenomenal, but for years nobody saw fit to question the authenticity of any of these discoveries. Partly this was because the music itself was so well written, and so much in character with the other output of those who had ostensibly written it. And partly it was because in the hands of Kreisler the music sounded wonderful. For although Kreisler had actually written all of those pieces himself, he was truly both a composer and a performer of distinction. The public was enthralled by the combined result, and Kreisler went on to be the most highly paid violinist of his day, commanding up to $3,000 for a single appearance.

A string of serendipitous discoveries of this kind was bound eventually to raise suspicion. In 1935, the *New York Times* music critic Olin Downes duly contrived to locate one of Kreisler's original manuscripts, and it became obvious that the jig was up. Kreisler readily confessed, and a predictable scandal ensued. But it was a pretty good-natured scandal. Shock there might have been, but no horror. Nobody really wanted to see Kreisler brought down, both because he was so engaging personally and because his music was simply so good.

So good, indeed, that many of his pieces—both his forgeries, which usually appear in hyphenated form (e.g., "Dittersdorf-Kreisler, Scherzo") and works that appeared under his own name—survive today in the repertoires of prominent contemporary violinists. Listen to them.

Praeludium and Allegro

in the style of G. Pugnani

for violin and piano

F. Kreisler (1875-1962)

So great were Kreisler's fame and the affection in which he was held that he easily weathered the controversy that erupted when in 1935 he admitted that the pieces he had performed as rediscovered works by earlier composers were, in fact, his own. As Kreisler remarked, "The name changes, the value remains."

FLAT AND HOLLOW EARTHS

H ad you been an early twentieth-century stroller passing through the town of Zion, Illinois, on a Sunday, and felt like whistling, you would have done well to think again. As indeed it would have been wise to reconsider smoking, or drinking alcohol, or eating pork there on any day of the week. For you would not have been guaranteed a good time at the hands of the Zion police, in a city run with an iron fist by the Evangelical fundamentalist Wilbur Glenn Voliva.

An eighth-century BC Babylonian clay tablet map of the world depicting a flat Earth. By the sixth century BC the Greek philosophers Pythagoras of Samos and Parmenides of Elea are reported to have described Earth as a globe. In the third century BC the Greek mathematician and geographer Eratosthenes of Cyrene calculated Earth's circumference as 24,900 miles, an error of only a shade over 40 miles from the currently accepted polar circumference of Earth.

Evangelical fundamentalist Wilbur Glenn Voliva based his belief in a flat Earth on what he considered a literal interpretation of the Bible. He and others of the same ilk were particularly impressed with Isaiah 11:12 and Revelation 7:1, which refer to "the four corners of the Earth."

If, on the other hand, your aim was to win $5,000, this was perhaps the place to be. All you had to do to pocket that tidy sum was to prove to the city's eccentric mayor that the world was not flat: something that Aristotle had already done to most people's satisfaction some 2,500 years earlier. Aristotle pointed out that as a ship sailed over the horizon, its masts would gradually disappear from view; that the stars appeared differently at different latitudes; and that Earth cast a curved shadow on the moon during an eclipse. Surely this was all the evidence a normal person would want that Earth was a sphere.

Well, no. Sadly, none of this would have been good enough. The problem was that you couldn't start from the proposition that the world was a globe; and without that assumption, it was tough to prove that the world was not, as Voliva claimed, a flat disk walled by ice to keep sailors from falling off its edge. After all, the mayor argued, on a spherical Earth the compass of a ship at the South Pole would have to point to the planet's center: something that doesn't happen. Of course, the South Pole is dry land; but in Voliva's flat world, a ship could indisputably follow a constant compass direction and still wind up where it started, not even needing the protection of that wall of ice unless it strayed off course.

In 1931 a correspondent for the magazine *Modern Mechanics and Inventions* thoroughly investigated the Voliva claims and their possible refutations, and concluded that the Voliva prize would "probably remain uncollected unless some future space traveler…anchors his ship a few thousand miles out in space and takes a movie of a

The seventeenth-century German polymath Athanasius Kircher concluded that the tides were caused by water moving to and fro in a subterranean ocean. His geological investigations culminated in his lavishly illustrated *Mundus Subterraneus*. Pictured here is Kircher's model of Earth's internal fires.

globular world turning on its axis." Fortunately this has now been done—but alas, too late to collect the prize, whose potential awarder died, bankrupt, in 1942.

Still, even this hasn't convinced everyone. In 2016 the *Guardian* newspaper reported that the rapper B.o.B had tweeted far and wide that Earth is flat. Even though he hadn't initially wanted to believe it, he claimed, "There's no way u can see all the evidence and not know." Still, he was assured by our colleague the astrophysicist Neil deGrasse Tyson that "being five centuries regressed in your reasoning doesn't mean we all can't still like your music."

Although we are not aware of any recent polls, the *Guardian* claims that the flat-Earth movement "has been gaining ground in the US as of late." Let us hope that the same cannot be said for modern hollow-Earth theorists, who actually have more respectable antecedents than the flat-Earth folks do.

Modern geologists tell us that our planet is a sphere structured a bit like an onion, with concentric layers. At the center is a solid core of mostly iron and nickel, some 750 miles across. Next is a more fluid outer core of generally similar composition, some 1,400 miles thick. On top of that is the semimolten mantle, in two layers totaling around 1,800 miles in thickness, and on the outside is the rocky crust, which is around 20 miles deep under the continents, thinner under the ocean basins.

But back in the seventeenth century the astronomer Edmond Halley (for whom the comet is named; also see chapter 11, *Fraudulent Ethnicity*) observed that Earth's magnetic field fluctuates a bit unpredictably, shifting a little from one year to the next—due, it is now thought, to the flow of molten iron in the planet's interior. Not knowing this, Halley deduced that the crust of Earth is actually the outermost of four concentric shells whose magnetic fields interfere with one another as they spin, all held neatly in place by gravity.

Halley wasn't the first to think of this general idea, but he was the first to deduce it from the principles recently enunciated by his friend and colleague Sir Isaac Newton. And at least he got the idea of the layering of the planet beneath our feet right, although he was surely wrong in surmising that the "subterranean orbs [are] capable of being inhabited."

Others have been yet more fanciful. Not only is there a substantial science fiction literature based on the premise that Earth is hollow, with a lot of stuff going on inside, but the Greek idea of the underworld was exactly that—a world of the dead, beneath the planet's surface. Closer to our own times, the American John Cleves Symmes Jr. suggested in 1818 that beneath an eight-hundred-mile thick crust the globe was hollow, with giant openings at each pole. An official expedition to the

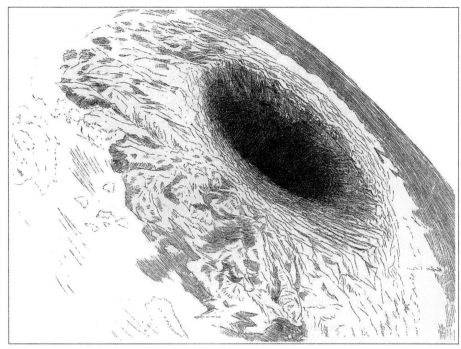

SYMMES'S HOLE, AS IT WOULD APPEAR TO A LUNARIAN WITH A TELESCOPE.

John Cleves Symmes Jr. postulated that polar openings connected Earth's surface to an inner Earth. In 1823 he lobbied the U.S. Congress to fund an expedition to the North Pole to locate the opening there, only to have newly elected Andrew Jackson kill the project.

North Pole was planned, but it was abandoned when Andrew Jackson assumed the presidency and canceled the funding for it.

Later in the same century, a latter-day alchemist called Cyrus Teed had a vision that we are living on the *inside* of the hollow Earth, while the sun, the other planets, and all the rest of the objects we see in the sky are yet farther inside. Teed (who, probably not coincidentally, considered himself a messiah) founded a cult (the Koreshans) to pursue this bizarre proposition, which, using a bit of pseudomathematics, can be made practically irrefutable in principle.

The twentieth century saw a number of revivals of the hollow-Earth notion, though they mostly resulted in the publication of sensationalist books rather than in the establishment of entire new towns to house cult adherents, as Teed did in 1894 at Estero, near Fort Myers in Florida. We are still awaiting a significant revival of the hollow-Earth theory in the twenty-first century; but there will probably be one before too long because, if there is one lesson to be learned here, it is that if it's possible to think it, someone out there believes it.

TRIBUTE OR EXPLOITATION?

When Dutch art forger Han van Meegeren unveiled this "Vermeer," *The Supper at Emmaus*, **it was touted as one of the greatest art discoveries of the century.**

Although the *Mona Lisa* hanging in the Louvre is probably the real thing (see chapter 31, *Mythogenesis*), it is highly likely that thousands of fake paintings hang proudly on the walls of museums around the world. And indeed, if fakery of art objects is not the world's oldest profession, it is certainly one of the oldest. Roman sculptors made copies of earlier Greek statues, while artists from all periods of post-classical history paid similar tribute to them (see chapter 10, *Renaissance Reprobates*). Not all fakes have been made to deceive, of course; and in fact, as far as the law is concerned it is no crime to paint in the style of another artist. What shows criminal intent is forging a painting's signature, or making some other form of documentary misrepresentation.

OPPOSITE: A fake Amedeo Modigliani nude by Elmyr de Hory. Paintings by the artists de Hory faked go for tens, on occasion hundreds, of millions of dollars; de Hory fakes can currently be found at auction for up to $20,000—and now there are fake de Hory fakes on the market.

By the nature of things, the greatest art forgers are the anonymous ones: skilled artists who never got caught, and whose paintings still adorn those museum walls, labeled as the work of someone else. But some truly great art forgers have been identified, and have even achieved fame as such, not because their art is significantly distinguishable from that of the artists they forged (though sometimes it is, at least in retrospect—which by itself raises a host of questions), but for entirely unrelated reasons.

One of the most celebrated such cases was that of the Dutch painter Han van Meegeren. Having started his career pretty conventionally in the 1910s at the Royal Academy of Art in the Hague, van Meegeren initially won recognition as a portraitist who borrowed liberally from the techniques of the seventeenth-century masters. But eventually this kind of art went out of fashion, and in the 1930s he turned his technical skills to producing paintings in the styles of specific Dutch Old Masters, beginning with Frans Hals and ultimately coming to specialize in Vermeer.

Assiduously replicating old materials and methods, and applying his hand-ground paints to genuine seventeenth-century canvases, van Meegeren aimed to outdo those he emulated. Eventually he painted a supposed Vermeer, entitled *The Supper at Emmaus,* which upon its "discovery" was hailed by at least one leading expert as the master's finest work.

Van Meegeren's downfall came only following the German occupation of Holland in the early 1940s, during which one of his forgeries had fallen into the hands of Hermann Göring. After the war the painting was traced back to van Meegeren, who was promptly imprisoned on the charge of having sold the national patrimony to the enemy. The painter extricated himself from the worst consequences of this charge only by confessing the fraud, and painting another "Vermeer" in front of a panel of court-appointed witnesses. Had he not been forced to do this, who knows how his forgeries would be regarded today?

Another of the twentieth century's great art forgers faked not only paintings but his own identity. Born to a middle-class Budapest family in 1906, Elemér Albert Hoffmann spent most of his life as Elmyr de Hory, alleged scion of an aristocratic Hungarian banking family that, he claimed, had an extensive private art collection that it had become necessary to sell.

De Hory trained as a classical figurative painter at a time when the market was shifting toward less-traditional artistic expressions, and to earn a better living he soon began to paint and draw in the style of established artists, beginning with Picasso. He later insisted that he had never fraudulently signed any of these pieces; but he certainly worked with a series of unscrupulous dealers who did. He moved around the world producing and selling works in the manner of Picasso, Modigliani, Matisse, and Renoir until, in the late 1940s, his fraud was unmasked and attracted the attention of the FBI.

As more of his forgeries were gradually revealed, de Hory developed something of an underground reputation. Eventually, he collaborated with Clifford Irving on a biography titled *Fake! The Story of Elmyr de Hory, the Greatest Art Forger of Our Time*, published in 1969. Ironically, Irving himself would soon thereafter gain fame as the fabricator of a supposed "autobiography" of Howard Hughes.

By 1976 de Hory was living in Ibiza, where he was actively painting when he was tipped off that he was about to be extradited to France to face fraud charges. He then overdosed on sleeping pills and died, although Irving later charged that he had faked even his own death.

Throughout his career de Hory was frustrated by the thought that he, a creative artist in his own right, could profitably sell his work only under the banner of others. (Even nowadays with the faker's considerable notoriety, a de Hory Modigliani fetches $20,000, while a real one has sold for $170 million). But he consoled himself with the thought, "If my work hangs in a museum long enough, it becomes real."

And that rumination raises some real imponderables. For, if even experts can't tell a forgery from the real thing (though unfeeling modern scientific instruments might), what is the essential difference? Well, oddly enough, the answer to this question seems to reside less in the intrinsic nature of the artwork itself than in our innate sense of fairness.

That inchoate sense of equity is so deeply ingrained in our biological heritage that we share it not only with our close relatives the great apes, but with capuchin monkeys as well. Intuitively, we *know* that it isn't fair to misrepresent something, and we will therefore reject something we know to be fake regardless of its actual attributes—just as a capuchin will reject a piece of cucumber it would normally happily devour, for no better reason than that its neighbor has—unfairly—been given a tastier grape.

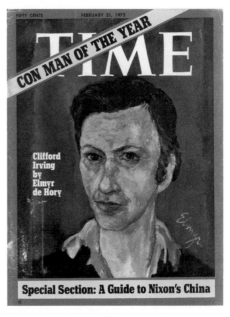

Elmyr de Hory's forgeries garnered much celebrity from Clifford Irving's best-selling biography, *Fake! The Story of Elmyr de Hory, the Greatest Art Forger of Our Time.* Subsequently, Irving forged a purported autobiography by the reclusive Howard Hughes. When the fraud was exposed, Irving was convicted and sentenced to two and a half years in prison. *The Hoax*, Irving's account of this escapade, was made into a film starring Richard Gere.

Hence the wise reflection of Mark Jones, a former director of London's Victoria and Albert Museum: "It is the misfortune of fakes that they are almost always defined by what they are not, instead of being valued for what they are."

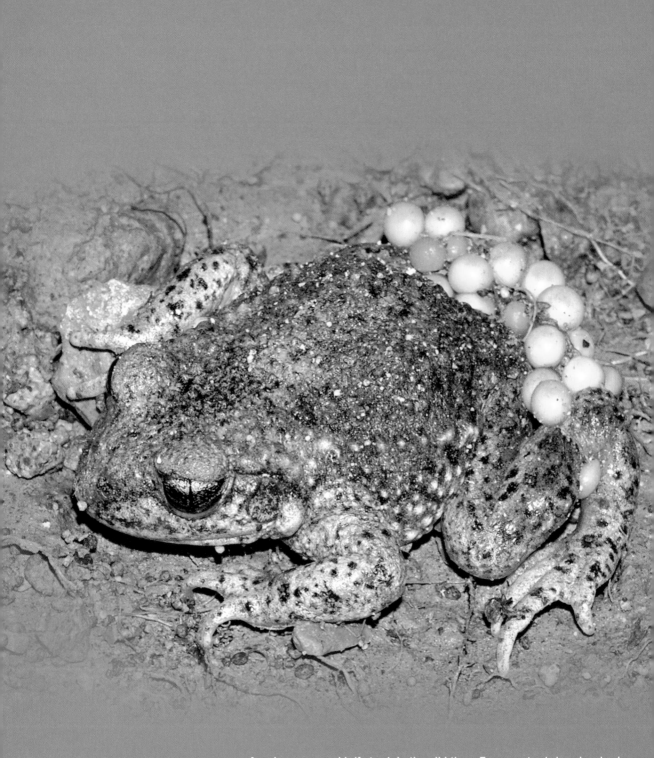

A male common midwife toad. In the wild these European toads breed on land. In his lab the Viennese biologist Paul Kammerer, who advocated the notion that organisms may pass to their offspring characteristics acquired in their lifetimes, induced them to breed in water. He claimed that after only two generations, his male toads had developed black "nuptial pads" on their hind limbs.

LYSENKOISM AND ITS CONSEQUENCES

Evolutionary thinking began to emerge at the beginning of the nineteenth century, with the realization that the fossil record contains compelling evidence that life has changed over time. The very first scientist to articulate this recognition in a coherent way was Jean Baptiste Lamarck, in France. To account for the evolutionary changes he saw in the fossils he studied, in his 1809 *Philosophie Zoologique* Lamarck adopted the then-uncontroversial idea that individuals could pass along to their offspring characteristics that had been acquired over their lifetimes. For example, the theory went that giraffes had acquired their dominant feature gradually, as each generation stretched their necks out farther, striving to feed ever higher in the trees.

Although Lamarck was broadly right about evolutionary change, he was dead wrong about the mechanism that underlay it. Still, progress in the modern science of inheritance had to await a rebirth in 1900, when three groups of investigators independently "rediscovered" the rules of genetics that had been first articulated in an obscure journal by the Czech monk Gregor Mendel thirty-four years earlier.

Mendel's main message had been that parental characteristics do not "blend" in the offspring. Instead, they are consistently transmitted in "particulate" form from one generation to the next. The grand discovery of the early twentieth century was that intergenerational changes came in the form of "mutations" that occurred randomly—

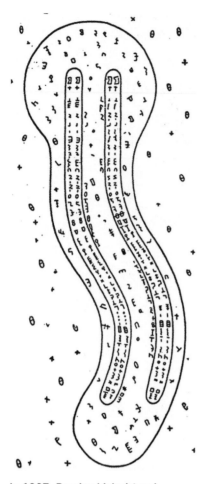

In 1927, Russian biologist and pioneer of modern genetics Nikolai Koltsov proposed that inherited traits are transmitted via a "giant hereditary molecule...made up of two mirror strands," as pictured here. This prescient observation was confirmed more than twenty-five years later when James Watson and Francis Crick published their model of a double-stranded DNA helix. In 1939 Lysenko and his supporters condemned Koltsov for spreading "racial theories of fascists." Koltsov died the next year, allegedly poisoned by the NKVD.

as we now know, because of spontaneous changes that occur in the DNA. This view of heredity was eventually co-opted into the "new evolutionary synthesis," which in the mid-twentieth century came to underpin our modern views of how evolution occurs.

Meanwhile, though, an extremely unhappy episode in early genetics unfolded between 1905 and 1910, in the laboratory of the geneticist Paul Kammerer at the University of Vienna. Kammerer induced the common midwife toad, which usually bred on land, to breed in water. He then reported that, after a mere two generations, his male toads had developed black "nuptial pads" on their hind limbs, the better to grip their slippery mates. This innovation, he suggested, supported the Lamarckian view of change as the accumulation of novelties acquired during the lifetimes of individuals.

When the American Museum of Natural History's G. Kingsley Noble showed in 1926 that the appearance of nuptial pads had been simulated by the injection of India ink, Kammerer shot himself. Whether he was the faker or, as he claimed, the unwitting victim of a hoax, still remains unclear.

But while Kammerer's fate is the stuff of tragedy, it pales in comparison with what occurred in Russia between 1925 and 1965. Russia was an early center of innovation in the nascent science of genetics; indeed, as early as 1934, one Russian scientist, Nikolai Koltsov, had already speculated that traits were inherited via a "giant hereditary molecule" that was "made up of two mirror strands that would replicate...using each strand as a template." He thereby anticipated by almost two decades the genomics revolution that was inaugurated in the early 1950s by the Watson-Crick discovery of the structure of DNA.

Science thrives on pluralist views, and in Russian genetics there was lively debate during the 1920s and 1930s between those who supported Mendelian ideas and those who clung to Lamarckism. Sadly, into this arena strode Trofim Lysenko, a plant breeder of humble origins who (falsely) claimed credit for developing a "cold treatment" whereby the time between the planting and harvesting of wheat could be reduced. This technique had been of particular value to politicians who were otherwise engaged in dramatically reducing the efficiency of the Soviet agricultural machine through collectivization, and it gave Lysenko huge political credibility. And, disastrously, Lysenko was a fervent advocate of something like Lamarckian heredity.

Trofim Lysenko (left) speaking at the Kremlin in 1935, with Josef Stalin (far right) who was the first to stand and shout, "Bravo, Comrade Lysenko. Bravo." Center from left to right are Soviet Politburo members Stanislav Kosior, Anastas Mikoyan, and Andrey Andreyev. Forced collectivization under Kosior was the principal cause of the Ukrainian famine of 1932 to 1933. He was executed by Stalin's order in the Great Purge of 1939. At the time, Kosior was first secretary of the Communist Party of Ukraine. He was succeeded by Stalin's successor Nikita Khrushchev, who eventually became the Soviet leader and was overthrown in 1964 partly due to his continued support of Lysenko.

By 1938 the wily and charismatic Lysenko had risen to the presidency of the powerful Lenin All-Union Academy of Agricultural Sciences; soon he also replaced the distinguished Nikolai Vavilov as director of the USSR Academy of Sciences' Institute of Genetics. Lysenko's rise to power was sponsored by Josef Stalin, who was obsessed with Lamarckianism. It was said that toward the end of his life Stalin's only physical exercise came from trying to alter plants in greenhouses he had erected adjacent to his country dachas. When he failed to grow lemon trees in the Crimea, with its killing frosts, he unsuccessfully tried propagating oaks and other deciduous trees in the arid and salty steppes near the Caspian Sea, in the hopeless belief that they would adapt.

Lysenko never developed a scientifically coherent view of inheritance himself, but he nevertheless supervised the systematic suppression of mainstream (non-Lamarckian) genetic research in Russia. Numerous geneticists and evolutionists were incarcerated, or executed, or simply disappeared, while their work vanished from official records and textbooks. Koltsov was a particular target and mysteriously died in 1940, poisoned, it was rumored, by the secret police. Vavilov, renowned for his dedication to ending famine, and founder of the world's most significant seed bank, starved to death in prison in 1943.

Backed by Stalin, and later by Nikita Khrushchev, Lysenko continued to wreak havoc on Soviet science until Khrushchev fell in 1964, following which he continued to live peacefully at his Gorki Leninskiye experimental farm until his natural death in 1976. But the most damning contemporary indictment of his career had already been published three decades earlier, penned by the distinguished American geneticist Hermann J. Muller. In an article baldly titled "The Destruction of Science in the USSR," Muller wrote that "to a scientist, Lysenko's writings are the merest drivel."

And indeed, Lysenko could never have survived in a pluralist scientific environment in which ideas competed on merit. His success was entirely due to the backing of politicians who neither knew nor cared what made science tick, but who encouraged him to do irreparable damage to Russian science. This is something we would do well to remember in our own day, when science risks becoming something of a political football, and scientists themselves often find it easier to go to their congressman or senator for federal support than to risk the judgment of their peers in the national competition for funding.

Meanwhile, perhaps ironically, recent discoveries have brought to light natural mechanisms that might explain results of the general kind that Kammerer reported (though not, of course, the India ink). Water fleas, for example, may develop spiky (and hard-to-swallow) heads in the presence of a predator. Resulting from chemical signals emitted by the predator, this spiky feature may be passed to offspring because it is caused by alterations to the DNA that are stimulated by contact with the enemy.

Alterations of this kind are known as *epigenetic*, and they have nothing to do with the mechanism envisaged by Lamarck. Nor do they shed any doubt on the established principles of heredity. Yet, as Loren Graham points out in his 2016 book *Lysenko's Ghost*, they have recently been seized on by scientifically illiterate Russian nationalists as evidence that the great Russian scientist Trofim Lysenko had been arbitrarily silenced by the power of Western propaganda. Once again, it appears, Russian science is under threat from politicians with agendas of their own. Today, Russia. Tomorrow, where else?

"THE MAN WHO NEVER WAS"

P erhaps the most famous instance of deploying human ingenuity in the cause of misleading the enemy is the case of *The Man Who Never Was*, to cite the memorable title of Ewen Montagu's 1953 book and the 1956 movie based on this remarkable feat of deception.

At the beginning of 1943 the outcome of World War II still hung in the balance. The campaign in North Africa had not yet been won, but Allied strategic planners were already beginning to contemplate an invasion of southern Europe from Africa to squeeze the Germans, whose resources were already spread thin from northern Europe to Russia.

The Germans were, of course, keenly aware of this possibility, and the Allies' most obvious route into continental Europe was through Sicily, then nominally in the hands of Mussolini's Fascists but occupied by German troops. As Winston Churchill reportedly said at the time, "Anybody but a bloody fool would know it's Sicily."

But the invasion of well-defended Sicily would be a costly undertaking. Was there any way of convincing

For his elaborate deception, Ewen Montagu manufactured an entire life history and even a living fiancée for his mythical young serviceman, whose body was actually that of a homeless Welshman who had died from eating rat poison.

the Germans to divert resources from the target area by making them believe that the expected invasion would be centered somewhere else? An incident the year before suggested one possibility.

An Allied aircraft had crashed off Spain, and the body of an English courier carrying secret documents had washed ashore there. Spain was nominally neutral in the war, but it was infested by German spies. The Spanish authorities had eventually returned the corpse, documents and all, to the English authorities, but it was suspected that the papers had been read by unfriendly eyes. Which raised the question: What if they had been, and the information they contained was misleading?

The corpse of Glyndwr Michael used in Operation Mincemeat.

The need to distract German attention from Sicily became more urgent in the buildup to the planned invasion. The British intelligence service, through its "Twenty" (XX, double cross) Committee, instructed the former lawyer Ewen Montagu and the Royal Air Force officer Charles Cholmondeley (both of whom possessed what Churchill called "corkscrew minds") to develop a plan to use the remains of an apparent aircraft crash victim to get false information about the invasion to the Germans.

The information concerned had a brilliant twist to it. Consisting principally of a top-secret letter purportedly from the British High Command to a top commander in North Africa, it portrayed the real targets of the forthcoming invasion as Sardinia and Greece, while representing the preparations for the invasion of Sicily (which the Germans could hardly miss) as purely diversionary. It even stated baldly, "We have a very good chance of making [the Germans] think we will go for Sicily."

The unfortunately named "Operation Mincemeat" first faced the problem of obtaining an un-autopsied cadaver nobody would miss. Not an easy job, but it was done well. For years, the body Montagu and Cholmondeley eventually procured was believed to have belonged to a victim of a German attack on a British navy ship. But research by the historian Denis Smyth now suggests that it had belonged to a homeless Welsh alcoholic named Glyndwr Michael, who had swallowed rat poison and died in an abandoned warehouse at age thirty-four. Supplied by a London coroner, his unclaimed corpse was kept on ice until needed.

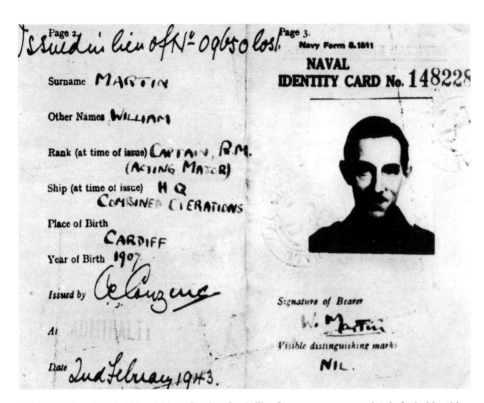

Issued in lieu of № 09650 lost.

Navy Form S.1511

NAVAL
IDENTITY CARD No. 148228

Surname MARTIN

Other Names WILLIAM

Rank (at time of issue) CAPTAIN, R.M.
(ACTING MAJOR)

Ship (at time of issue) H Q
COMBINED OPERATIONS

Place of Birth
CARDIFF

Year of Birth 1907

Issued by *[signature]*

At

Date 2nd February 1943.

Signature of Bearer
W. Martin

Visible distinguishing marks
NIL.

"Major William Martin" Naval Identification Card. The Germans were completely fooled by this and other false documents Montagu planted on the corpse. Deciphered Enigma encrypts made it clear that the false battle plans suggesting Sicily was not the British's primary target went all the way to Hitler's headquarters.

If this is correct, Montagu and Cholmondeley must have known that they were taking a huge risk: Michael's cadaver would not have shown telltale signs of either drowning or of the trauma that might have been incurred in an emergency landing at sea. But they evidently trusted in the reluctance of the Catholic Spanish authorities—demonstrated in the earlier incident—to conduct an autopsy on a floater, especially one in a fairly advanced stage of decomposition.

In contrast to this initial nonchalance, they dedicated enormous care to constructing a convincing identity for the subject. Released off the Spanish coast by a British submarine in April 1943, the body, wearing British Marines battle dress, bore the papers of a "Major William Martin," a navy officer with plausibly defective credentials (he had apparently forgotten to renew his pass to Combined Operations HQ). His wallet bore "litter" that included not only proof of a complicated social and financial life, but indications that he had stayed at London's Naval and Military Club just days before he was expected to wash ashore in Spain. No false identity was ever more complete than Major Martin's, and to complete the illusion, his death was announced in the London *Times* of June 4.

The documents were packed in a briefcase chained to the cadaver's belt, and the body was committed to the sea a mile offshore from Huelva in southern Spain, a rubber life raft nearby. It was rapidly recovered by a sardine fisherman, and the remains were eventually released to the British naval attaché after a cursory examination concluded death had been by drowning. The documentation was returned, too, but not before it had been seen by the Germans, copies eventually making their way up the entire chain of command to Adolf Hitler.

Not everyone was convinced by the false documents, but Hitler was. When the British attacked Sicily on July 9, the Wehrmacht had already diverted forces to Sardinia and Greece, and was unable to redeploy them in time to repel the invaders. Sicily fell with modest casualties, giving rise to a chain of events that ended in Mussolini's overthrow later in the month (though Hitler later reinstated him).

But the story didn't stop there. For the affair of *The Man Who Never Was* turned out in the end to be not a double, but a triple bluff. Just after the D-Day landings in Normandy in June 1944, an abandoned Allied landing craft washed ashore bearing genuine secret plans for future military operations in the region. Believing these were part of another "Mincemeat"-style operation, Hitler ignored them.

KORLA PANDIT

ife wasn't easy for young black American musicians in the years during and after World War II. After all, this was a time when Sammy Davis Jr. could headline at the Frontier casino in Las Vegas but was excluded from the glittering hotels of the famous Strip, rooming instead at a dilapidated boardinghouse on the city's outskirts. How much worse if you weren't a member of the Rat Pack?

Such was the situation that faced John Roland Redd, born in 1921 to the descendants of slaves in St. Louis, Missouri (home of the original Dred Scott case that led to the 1857 Supreme Court decision that persons of African descent, free or slave, could not hold American citizenship). A year later, his family moved to Hannibal, Missouri, and thence to Columbia, Missouri. A hugely talented keyboard player, the young John Redd clearly felt very early on that his race (see chapter 41, *Human Variation*) was limiting his chances of advancement in his musical career; and, soon after relocating to Los Angeles in 1939, he changed his professional name to Juan Rolando. As an ostensibly Mexican musician, he now had access to the all-white Musician's Union, which he duly joined.

Oddly enough, at about the same time, the newly minted Juan started wearing a turban similar to the one worn by the lead character in the 1939 all-black-cast movie *Midnight Shadow*, in which his sister Frances had performed. This headgear became

Korla Pandit was a con man in that he wasn't who he said he was. Yet he wasn't trying to cheat his audience out of anything. Quite the opposite; he was offering them the gift of music, "The Universal Language of Love."

HE SPENT HIS EARLY LIFE IN NEW DELHI, INDIA, HIS MOTHER WAS A SINGER WHICH ACCOUNTED FOR HIS SHOWING MUSICAL TALENT AT A VERY EARLY AGE; HIS FATHER, A MEMBER OF ONE OF INDIA'S FIRST FAMILIES, REALIZED HIS NATURAL ABILITY AND THAT LATER ON HE WOULD SEND HIS BOY TO ENGLAND FOR FORMAL TUTORING.

KORLA PANDIT
KTTV CHANNEL 11

YOUNG PANDIT STUDIED IN ENGLAND BEFORE COMING TO AMERICA WHERE HE CONTINUED HIS EDUCATION AT THE UNIV. OF CHICAGO; FROM THE TIME HE BEGAN STUDYING MUSIC HE HAS APPEARED IN CONCERTS THROUGHOUT THE BRITISH ISLES, EUROPE AND THE U.S. AT ONE TIME HE HAD INTENDED JOINING THE GOV'T. SERVICE IN INDIA, BUT HIS MUSICAL ABILITIES, HOWEVER, OUTGAINED HIS POLITICAL INTERESTS. .

AGE: KORLA MAINTAINS THAT AGE IS DETERMINED BY ONE'S MENTAL OUTLOOK; PROFESSES HIS TO BE THAT OF A YOUNG MAN OF 22.

WHILE ATTENDING COLLEGE, HE MASTERED THE ORGAN IN AN EXCEPTIONALLY SHORT TIME; LATER CAME TO HOLLYWOOD WHERE HE ESTABLISHED HIMSELF IN RADIO AND TV. AS STAFF ORGANIST WITH NBC, LED TO HIS OWN PROGRAM. IN 1948 CONTRACTED FOR BACKGROUND MUSIC FOR "CHANDU, THE MAGICIAN"; CO-STARRED WITH LINA ROMAY; FOR 2½ YRS MUSICAL DIRECTOR FOR "TIME FOR BEANY"; ON JULY 6, 1952, JOINED STAFF OF KTTV. LOVES TO WRITE MUSIC, IS AN AMATEUR PHOTOGRAPHER; MARRIED, HAS A SON, SHARI, AGE 4.

a trademark for the rest of his career, and it may well have made life easier for the supposed Mexican during the Los Angeles "Zoot Suit Riots" of 1943, during which gangs of white servicemen awaiting transfer to the Pacific Theater randomly attacked supposedly unpatriotic Latinos, some of whom favored wearing the baggy outfits.

By this time Juan was working as staff organist for the Bakersfield radio station KPMC, while moonlighting for NBC in Hollywood and releasing his first recording in 1942 as an individual artist, a shellac disc called *Right as the Rain*. In 1944 he married his sister's onetime roommate, the Euro-American Disney animator Beryl DeBeeson, who worked in the effects department of the Walt Disney Studio. Since interracial marriage was still illegal in California at the time, the ceremony was performed in Tijuana, Mexico.

It seems to have been his new wife's idea that John/Juan should change his identity yet again. But this time, far from merely Hispanicizing his own name, he assumed an entirely different ethnic persona, and Korla Pandit was born. His name may have been inspired by that of Vijaya Lakshmi Pandit, a well-known politician of the time who was the sister of India's first prime minister and who had recently completed a highly publicized lecture tour in the United States. Korla Pandit's biography gradually took shape as that of a piano prodigy born in New Delhi, India, to a French opera singer and a Brahmin father. As a child he had been sent to England to be educated, and then he had continued across the Atlantic to the University of Chicago, where he had trained as a classical musician and become acquainted with the pipe organ.

The identity makeover worked miraculously well. In 1948–49 Korla played Eastern-inflected organ music for an adventure-detective radio show called *Chandu the Magician*, and later that year he was offered a fifteen-minute daily television show of his own on KTLA, in which he did not speak but instead played the Hammond organ and a grand piano—often both at the same time—as he soulfully gazed into the camera.

Whether or not his silence was due to the difficulty of reproducing an Indian accent, the formula worked magnificently. Five days a week, the turbaned prodigy is said to have mesmerized a huge audience of mostly white housewives with that sensual gaze and spectacular keyboard playing. In all, some nine hundred episodes went out—a feat rarely matched in the years since. It is sad that very few of those live performances were recorded.

During the early 1950s Korla occasionally recorded with the Sons of the Pioneers, Roy Rogers's original band, and began to release albums with Vita Records. This house

••

OPPOSITE: Elmyr de Hory claimed that when one of his fakes hung in a museum long enough, it became real. Pandit's audiences thought he was really a musical prodigy from New Delhi, India. After so many years of playing the part, did there come a time in his own consciousness when he was no longer John Redd from Missouri?

was known as a "black artist" label, but Korla maintained his Indian identity and ultimately established his own label, India Records, moving later on to Fantasy Records.

By 1951 Korla had also begun working with Louis B. Snader, an entrepreneur who pioneered "telescriptions," video recordings that were leased to TV stations nationwide as fill material, and that gave huge exposure to the artists who made them. In 1954 Snader signed him up for a series of fifty-two half-hour TV shows, but the terms of the contract were so onerous that Korla pulled out after having played the minimum number of performances. He was replaced by an unknown piano player who took over Korla's set, piano, and decorations. The new pianist had only one name: Liberace. And at least part of the Liberace persona that emerged had already been preformed by Korla.

As time progressed, Korla's style of music went out of fashion, although he experienced a brief revival in the 1990s with the reappearance of the tiki bar phenomenon. His last performance came in 1997, at the LunaPark club in Los Angeles, when his health was already in decline.

Korla Pandit with his wife, Beryl, and two sons, Shari and Khris Koram.

John Roland Redd's whole life was spent as a performer. But maybe his most amazing performance of all took place behind the scenes: he maintained a close relationship with his family even as he became Juan Rolando and later Korla Pandit. This was unusual because, for fear of being outed, in the 1950s most light-skinned black performers who successfully "passed" did so at the cost of cutting ties to their family and their background.

Korla never abandoned his family, and, as the *San Francisco Chronicle* reporter Jessica Zack once mused, "living a lie on a daily basis must have been very difficult." As she pointed out, "This wasn't an act that occurred on stage for an hour or two, this was 24/7, all through his life. Korla put on this persona and couldn't take it off." Inevitably, all through this long saga plenty of insiders knew the true story. But out of respect for the extraordinary person that Korla was, *nobody* talked.

Of course, the exotic identity was only a small part of the tale. The main reason why the silent, hypnotic, and entirely invented Korla Pandit succeeded in being one of the most broadcast musical stars of all time was the most straightforward one of all. Like Psalmanazar (see chapter 11, *Fraudulent Ethnicity*) he was supremely good at what he did.

A LION IN WINTER

He was the world's most famous paleoanthropologist, a weather-beaten fossil prospector famous for having discovered the world's earliest artifacts and human fossils in his native Africa. Fifteen years his junior, she was a lively, ambitious archaeologist from western North America, a continent that almost all authorities still agree was uncontaminated by human beings until at most thirty thousand years before the present.

Excited by what she had found in the Calico Mountains region of California's Mojave Desert, Ruth DeEtte "Dee" Simpson flew to England in 1959 to meet Louis Leakey, then visiting at London's Natural History Museum. Clutched in her hand were some pieces of broken stone that she believed were tools that had been flaked by early Americans as much as 100,000 years ago. They looked unremarkable. But then, the very early artifacts that Leakey had found at Olduvai Gorge in what was then Tanganyika hadn't looked like much, either.

Louis Leakey and Ruth DeEtte Simpson at the Calico Mountain site. Simpson reminisced that during Leakey's first visit, while the two were climbing a hillside, he stopped and told her, "You will dig here."

Born in Kenya in 1903 to missionary parents, Louis Leakey had always plowed his own scientific furrow. He studied anthropology at Cambridge and soon began looking for ancient human fossils in his native East Africa, where he was convinced humankind had initially evolved. This conclusion ran directly counter to the prevailing scientific belief that Eurasia was the home continent of the hominid family; indeed, right around the time Leakey graduated, the anatomist Raymond Dart was running into firm establishment opposition to his announcement of the earliest "ape-man" fossil from his adopted country of South Africa.

A messy divorce soon put paid to Leakey's prospects for advancement at Cambridge, and he became an independent Kenya-based operator for the remainder of his career. After exploring western Kenya for ancient ape fossils, Leakey and his new wife, Mary, had begun working seriously at Olduvai Gorge. There they found an abundance of early stone tools. These included large teardrop-shaped "handaxes," like those long known from Europe; and in earlier deposits they found both simple stone flakes and the fist-size cobbles from which they had been knocked with a stone hammer.

Mary's meticulous work convinced archaeologists that the unprepossessing flaked cobbles were indeed the earliest deliberately made stone tools. Since the existence of a tool implies a maker, the search was also on for the ancient hominids who had manufactured them. It took years, but in 1959 the Leakeys' perseverance paid off with the discovery of the famous "Nutcracker Man" skull at Olduvai. Soon thereafter, Louis announced that his team had also found the more lightly built hominid fossils that he

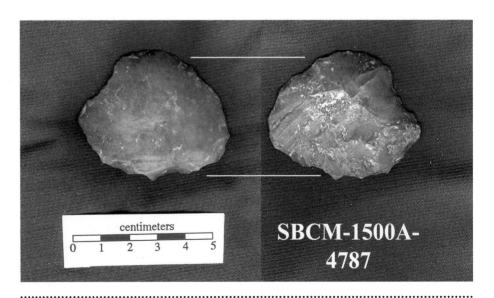

SBCM-1500A-4787

The controversy over the rock fragments unearthed in the Calico Mountains centered on whether they are artifacts (shaped by humans) or geofacts (naturally occurring). The overwhelming consensus among American archaeologists nowadays is that they are the latter.

triumphantly named *Homo habilis* ("handy man"): the very earliest species of our own human genus, dated to about 1.8 million years ago.

These discoveries made the Leakeys instant scientific celebrities, and vindicated Louis's longstanding faith in Africa as the cradle of humankind. They also evidently enhanced his conviction that what was important was to discover the "earliest" of everything. But his newfound fame also allowed Louis to promote his longtime interest in the study of living primates, which he saw as indispensable models for understanding the behavior of early humans. Notably, he was instrumental in making it possible—in a blaze of publicity—for three young women, Jane Goodall, Dian Fossey, and Biruté Galdikas, to begin their studies of chimpanzees, gorillas, and orangutans, respectively.

Leakey's weakness for attractive young ladies was hardly a secret, and when Dee Simpson appeared on the scene in 1959, the two instantly bonded over those stones from Calico. What's more, back in 1929 Leakey had declared, in a Cambridge lecture, that people had settled in the New World at least 15,000 years ago. This was far earlier than was then believed, and he was not taken seriously; but now, thirty years later, he saw the chance to vindicate his pronouncement.

Much to the disgust of Mary, who was by now the preeminent authority on primitive stone tools and who harbored huge doubts about the geology of the site, Louis raised money for an archaeological prospection of the Calico Mountains. The National Geographic Society, which provided those funds to its superstar du jour, did so against the advice of Vance Haynes, its distinguished archaeological consultant.

Little wonder, then, that excavations started, in 1964, in an atmosphere of general skepticism. Nevertheless, in 1968 Leakey and Simpson published a paper in the prestigious journal *Science* claiming that numerous stone flakes they had excavated at a new Calico Mountains site had been deliberately made by people, and were at least 50,000 years old (privately, Leakey guessed a lot more).

Almost nobody believed them then, and almost nobody believes them now. The most authoritative analysis of the Calico Hills "artifacts," published by Vance Haynes in 1973, concluded that these alleged tools are actually ordinary stones that were fractured by being bashed together in a riverbed. In which case, the time at which they were deposited at the site—which still remains uncertain—is irrelevant to the early peopling of the Americas.

His long involvement in the Calico Mountains fiasco cost the ailing and aging Leakey much of his professional credibility, as well as his relationship with his wife, who had already begun to lead an increasingly separate life. As Mary tartly summarized the matter, Calico was "catastrophic" to Louis's career, and "was largely responsible for our parting of the ways." Dee Simpson, on the other hand, parlayed the Calico dig into a curatorship at the San Bernardino County Museum, where she remained until she retired in 1982, a decade after Louis's death at the age of sixty-nine.

Louis Leakey was a powerfully instinctual man whose instincts had finally let him down, just as a lifetime of rugged tropical fieldwork had begun to take a serious toll on his body. Indeed, Mary strongly implied in her memoirs that his judgment was impaired by the physical pain of which he was rarely free after 1966. And that makes it even sadder to reflect that, had Louis stuck to his original intuition, he might be hailed today as mightily prescient. For at a time when most authorities reckoned the Americas had been colonized only around 2,000 years ago, Louis's estimate of 15,000 years was remarkably close to the 13,000 years to which the Clovis, the earliest widespread and well-documented human culture in the Americas, is nowadays dated. Though there are now yet earlier contenders…

In 1972 the Calico Mountains site was placed on the National Register of Historic Places. It is open to the public, with a visitor center, a gift shop, and guided tours.

THE **SAD SAGA** OF DONALD CROWHURST

Who hasn't wanted to sail around the globe single-handed, and faster than anyone else? Well, actually, not us; but in the years since the lone master mariner Joshua Slocum sailed his sloop *Spray* out of Boston Harbor and around the world (with many stops) from 1895 to 1898, many have yearned mightily to pull off this increasingly demanding feat. Indeed, since 1989 a formal round-the-world solo sail race has been held every four years. Known as the Vendée Globe, this epic adventure has regularly attracted as many as two dozen hardy souls in the attempt to make the fastest nonstop circumnavigation.

Today Vendée Globe entrants compete in yachts equipped with radar, transponders, GPS positioning equipment, and all the other paraphernalia of modern navigation. They can be tracked every mile of their route, and their sailors know where they are with incredible accuracy. But when the *Sunday Times* of London sponsored the very first around-the-world single-handed race some fifty years ago, everything was much more primitive. The sea was a very lonely place, and a crackling shortwave radio was the major means of communicating with the shore.

Yet despite (or just as likely because of) all the hazards involved, in 1968 enthusiasm for extreme yachting was at its height. Nowhere was this truer than in England, where the *Sunday Times*–sponsored seafarer Francis Chichester had recently returned to

Donald Crowhurst aboard the *Teignmouth Electron* shortly before he set off on his ill-fated attempt to compete in a solo round-the-world yacht race. His radio reports suggested he would make the fastest time of the race, until its closing stages, when he disappeared, never to be seen again.

Plymouth from the first one-stop single-handed circumnavigation, to be knighted by Queen Elizabeth on the quayside next to his plucky yawl *Gipsy Moth IV*. Still, whether a nonstop circumnavigation was even possible, no one yet knew.

Little wonder, then, that the *Times*'s Golden Globe first-and-fastest-around-the-world race attracted an amazing assortment of competitors, from vastly experienced seamen to celebrities with negligible knowledge of sailing. As unusual as any was a late entrant of whom nobody in the extreme sailing community had ever heard: Donald Crowhurst. And more oddly yet, at one point in the proceedings it was Crowhurst who appeared to be winning the race. Based on sparse radio reports of his position, by early December 1968 newspapers around the world were avidly predicting that the obscure sailor's time would be the Golden Globe's fastest. Then the tragedy began to unfold.

Donald Crowhurst was an electronics engineer who ran a small business manufacturing navigational equipment and sailed strictly for amusement. As his business faltered, his eye fell on the £5,000 offered by the Golden Globe for the fastest round-the-world time. Scenting both money and good publicity, and seeing potential in the fast but then-unproven trimaran design, he anticipated salvation in the race.

But he was broke and had to turn for sponsorship in the race to one of his investors, who drove a hard bargain. In the end, Crowhurst ended up mortgaging not only his business but his home to enter the race in the *Teignmouth Electron*, a forty-foot-long trimaran built hurriedly to meet the race's departure deadline of October 31, 1968.

Ominously, there were problems from the very beginning. And even when construction of Crowhurst's vessel was complete, the planned three-day trip from the boatyard to the race's starting point in Devon actually took two weeks, leaving scant time for provisioning and last-minute fixes. Accordingly, Crowhurst left on his fateful voyage at the last possible moment, and hopelessly unprepared. Eight competitors had already left since the first allowable date of June 1, but by the time of his departure three of them had already retired, with more soon to follow.

By early December only four competitors remained in the race, and one, well placed to win, would later abandon it for philosophical reasons. That left only Crowhurst and the former naval officers Robin Knox-Johnston, in a conventional ketch, and Nigel Tetley, in another trimaran. Both Knox-Johnston and Tetley had already long rounded the Cape of Good Hope and headed east while Crowhurst was still far behind in the north Atlantic, in a rapidly deteriorating vessel that he was beginning to realize would never withstand the rough waters of the Southern Ocean.

At about this time, Crowhurst's reported speed mysteriously picked up, and at Christmas he radioed his wife that he was "off Cape Town." In fact, he was off southern

Brazil, having evidently decided that he had no hope of winning. He thereafter maintained as much radio silence as the newspapers would allow, but began falsifying his logs to record nonexistent progress. In March he snuck ashore in Brazil for supplies; and then he dawdled around in the Atlantic, while reporting on the radio that he was approaching Cape Horn from the west.

Clearly the game plan was to wait in the Atlantic until he could plausibly rejoin the race and claim the prize ahead of the leader—much as the runner Rosie Ruiz would later famously do in the 1980 Boston Marathon. Tetley, then in the lead but believing that Crowhurst was hard on his heels, piled on sail and overstressed his own fragile trimaran, which eventually sank a mere 1,300 miles short of its goal.

Tetley was rescued, and Knox-Johnston duly won the trophy for the first single-handed nonstop circumnavigation on April 22, 1969. Since he had left after Knox-Johnston, Crowhurst was still at that point in the running for the prize for the fastest circumnavigation, but it evidently dawned on him that if he did win the money, his log and other records would come under closer scrutiny than they could withstand. This, combined with a barrage of press interest and promises of a celebrity reception back in England, evidently made the pressure and guilt unbearable.

The last entry in Crowhurst's increasingly rambling diary, dated July 1, 1969, includes the words "It is finished…I will resign the game." A mere nine days later, the mail boat

***Teignmouth Electron* was found adrift and abandoned on July 10, 1969, by a passing freighter. She was subsequently sold several times, and today lies decayed and battered on a beach on Cayman Brac.**

At home in Seaton, Devon, Donald Crowhurst's widow, Clare, reminisced: "I definitely think about Donald every single day...I genuinely feel that that's it—there really is nothing left."

Picardy encountered an empty *Teignmouth Electron* drifting in the mid-Atlantic. On hearing the news, a grieving nation made Crowhurst a national hero, and Knox-Johnston donated his prize money to Crowhurst's family. But the lionizing was brief. As Crowhurst himself had known all too well, his falsified logs, shortly to be published, told the true story.

That story hardly made him an ideal role model. Yet since his presumed death by drowning, Donald Crowhurst has become a counterculture icon. His dubious Atlantic exploits have inspired books, movies, documentaries, videos, songs, stage performances, and poetry. With its mixture of hubris, deceit, and tragedy, the Crowhurst story appeals to what one can only characterize as humankind's deep attachment to ambiguity, moral and otherwise. You simply have to feel for this desperate man, alone in a vast ocean and caught between his ambition, his conscience, and his sense of impending doom.

Yet even all this is somehow not quite enough to explain just how Crowhurst has managed, posthumously, to capture the imagination of a generation. Exactly what is it about the flawed antihero that we can't seem to resist?

Due to anomalies perceived in NASA photographs, transmissions, and data, and to supposed mechanical and environmental contradictions, the six manned U.S. moon landings between 1969 and 1972 are sometimes claimed to be a hoax as depicted by this phony photo.

CONSPIRACY
THEORIES

Following the first moon landing in 1969, the conspiracy theorists immediately leaped out of the closet: the landing had been staged in a Hollywood film studio by the U.S. government in an attempt to one-up the Russians in the Space Race. A huge number of supposedly rational "proofs" of governmental fraudulence were put forward: in NASA photographs the flag planted on the moon by Neil Armstrong and Buzz Aldrin was fluttering in a nonexistent breeze; there is no blast crater to mark the lunar module's landing; the scene appears inappropriately lit by multiple light sources; in one image (see photo on opposite page) a mysterious object might be a studio spotlight; and on and on. All these allegations were rapidly and comprehensively refuted by NASA scientists.

Somewhat later, a totally contradictory story emerged: Armstrong and Aldrin actually had been on the moon—and, while there, had discovered a human skeleton wearing a plaid shirt and blue jeans, with barefoot prints nearby. The astronauts' pictures of these bizarre finds were allegedly sequestered by NASA until one came into the possession of a Chinese astrophysicist named Kang Mao-pang, who claimed a giant cover-up because "the Americans apparently feel that nobody else in the world is privileged enough to share the information."

The story of the skeleton seems to have originated in the supermarket tabloid the *Weekly World News*, hardly the most credible of sources. But it spread across the

According to Chinese astrophysicist Kang Mao-pang, a human skeleton was discovered on the moon in 1969 during the Apollo 11 mission. Kang claimed to have received, from "an unimpeachable U.S. source," photographs of the skeleton that were so secret even the astronauts didn't know they existed.

Internet like wildfire, as it was posted and reposted, many years after the event, again and again. That it bore repeating at all ought in principle to be hard to believe—though of course, to weary observers of the human scene it isn't at all—but even more amazing about this bizarre episode is the finding by sociologists that if you believed one story (astronauts never went to the moon) you were very likely also to believe the other (they found a skeleton there). This is cognitive dissonance—the ability to simultaneously entertain two entirely contradictory ideas—taken to an unusual extreme. So what was going on?

Well, one of the great myths of our time is that evolution is a process of fine-tuning by which living organisms become optimized to their environments. In fact, as evolutionary theory has itself evolved, it has become ever clearer that evolutionary change results from all sorts of different influences, some of them completely random with respect to adaptation. Accordingly, human beings have not been optimized by nature to any specific condition; the human brain is a case in point.

Human beings are sharply distinguished from all other animals in being able to reduce the inputs from their senses into a vocabulary of mental symbols, among which they can make complex associations. This ability to make associations is the basis of our vaunted rational abilities. Yet it is one that was quite recently grafted onto a much more ancient ancestral brain, gradually accreted over literally hundreds of millions of years of vertebrate evolution, that functions in a more intuitive and emotional manner.

It is the presence of this ancient brain lurking beneath the more recent rational veneer that ensures that we are not all Spocks—cold, calculating machines. Thank God for that; but this odd combination of ancient intuitive and newer rational mechanisms also means that our brains sometimes express themselves in irrational ways, occasionally defaulting, for example, to conspiracy theories where no conspiracy exists. Perhaps the nastiest recent example of this human deficit followed the mass murder of schoolchildren at Sandy Hook Elementary School in Newtown, Connecticut, where grieving parents were assailed by threats from mainly anonymous zealots, some of whom apparently believed that the event had never taken place and was instead a political stunt by gun-control advocates.

Even the sanest among us are prey to this kind of thing: not long ago, a survey showed that 63 percent of registered voters in the United States currently believe in at least one political conspiracy theory. And rather than being fixed, this tendency appears to be highly responsive to external circumstances. In good times, people tend to be more complacent and contented. But when they feel helpless and unempowered, they are much more liable to believe in conspiracies (see also chapter 2, *Apocalypticism*).

Most likely this is because feeling that you know the explanation for some important event (and perhaps especially when you think that others don't) confers a sense of agency and control. And it is fear of losing that control that apparently explains the "backfire effect" whereby, in the words of political scientists Brendan Nyhan and Jason Reifler, "efforts to debunk inaccurate political information can leave people *more* convinced that false information is true than would have been otherwise" (emphasis ours).

The underlying feeling of control is entirely our subjective creation. But no matter: for better or for worse, we live as much of the time in the worlds that we create in our heads as we do in the real one.

THE FALLACY OF RACE

No term in our language is more divisive and misunderstood than the word *race*, or more redolent of a truly dark period in American history. But while many scientists nowadays argue that "race doesn't exist," the continued use of this tricky and ultimately unhelpful concept is constantly reinforced by a well-meaning government, every time a citizen is asked to classify him- or herself by ticking a box on a form.

Of course, the "race doesn't exist" argument is, on the face of it, a highly counterintuitive one. Anyone walking down a street in a large American city will be instantly aware of just how heterogeneous the human population is. And that heterogeneity does indeed seem to be organized along

A typical street scene of the sort encountered in many large urban areas of North America, Europe, and Australia.

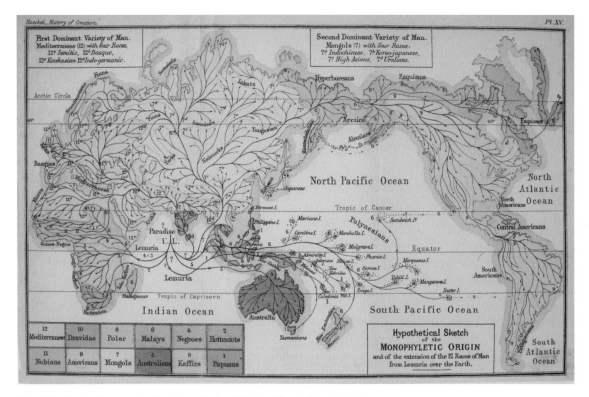

Ernst Haeckel, who promoted and popularized Charles Darwin's work in Germany, hypothesized a lost continent of Lemuria from which the various human races dispersed.

broadly geographical lines: it is often not too difficult to guess if a some part of an individual's ancestry lies in Africa, or in Europe, or in eastern Asia. This is because to the—very variable—extent to which such guesses are accurate, the perception of "race" does carry a historical echo.

Homo sapiens is a young species, born around 200,000 years ago. And it was less than 100,000 years ago that this species first left its African continent of origin and rapidly took over the entire world, displacing resident human species such as *Homo neanderthalensis* in the process. What this very recent origin and exodus clearly mean—and what the burgeoning science of genomics has equally eloquently demonstrated—is that the genetic variation we see among human beings today is very recent and very superficial indeed. There is greater genetic diversity found in three populations of central African chimpanzees than among humans worldwide.

While our newly born species was spreading across the globe, its members were itinerant hunters and gatherers. They moved, in small numbers, across vast tracts of landscape. In such demographic circumstances minor diversifications among local populations are highly likely to occur, whatever the species. And it was at this early stage of human history that people in different parts of the world acquired the minor physical features that tip us off today to geographical origin.

Some of those differentiating features had significant consequences: for example the ability, typical of cow-herding peoples, to tolerate lactose as adults and thus to subsist on dairy products. Others—probably most—were simply random variations, without much if any functional significance. Because evolution is not, as is often assumed, a process of single-minded adaptation and optimization, chance has played a large role in our coming to be as we are.

But even after people had become established in all the habitable zones of the world, the human population continued to grow. And that growth really took off after the origin of settled existence and agriculture (independently in several different places around the world) about ten thousand years ago.

Hunter-gatherers do not live in great density, but farmers need labor to till the fields, and sedentary mothers can cope with more children at once. The new settled way of life changed the entire human demographic dynamic, initiating a population explosion in the course of which, instead of acquiring their own minor local peculiarities, the expanding local populations began reproducing and blending with their neighbors, blurring genetic and physical differentiations.

What we see today, in a world of unparalleled individual and population mobility, is the result of a long and ongoing process of blending and blurring that has ensured the absence of any fixed lines to be drawn, anywhere within the human population. This is why many scientists maintain that races don't exist, because you cannot define an entity that has no discernible boundaries.

In 1972 the Harvard geneticist Richard Lewontin looked at the genetic variation seen in human populations from around the world and concluded that some 85 percent of that variation existed within local populations, and only some 15 percent between them. In other words, the heterogeneity *within* local groups—even groups you might in some way view as "racial"—is hugely larger than the genetic differentiation *among* them. The general pattern of differentiation that Lewontin saw has held up well as vast amounts of genomic information have poured in from all over the world, shedding yet more doubt on the utility—or even the possibility—of recognizing "races."

The human genome is a fantastically complicated thing, containing 3 billion different bits of information. All these data encode a lot of historical information about each individual, and about the movement of people around the globe from which each of us has ultimately resulted. And analyzing the genomes of people in different countries has produced some very unexpected results. The supposedly homogeneous people of

A map of the four major geographic groups of *Homo sapiens*. Africans are represented by yellow, Australians by red, and Europeans by green. Asians, in blue, exhibit some similarities with Europeans on one side (a light yellowish green tinge in the middle of Siberia) and with Australians on the other side. The extensive gradients due to admixture between Africans and Europeans in both North America and North Africa, and between Europeans and Asians in Central Asia, are clearly visible.

Iceland have turned out to have a suspicious amount of Scottish in their ancestry, for instance; and rarely does anyone submit a DNA sample to the Genographic Project or to the ancestry company 23andMe without getting at least a minor surprise.

So what we are genetically, and what family tradition tells us we are, are often quite different. Maybe that's not too surprising, because genes are biologically measurable entities, while identities are matters of human belief. And it is this reality that underlies the most important thing of all about the notion of race: that (to the extent to which it is useful at all) it should never be confused with cultural identity. Because from whatever background he or she comes, each new human is born into this world with the potential to absorb any language, or any set of cultural beliefs, that humanity has yet devised.

On the other hand, by the time they are six years old—maybe earlier—participants in different human cultures have already absorbed preconceptions and values that may mean they are living in perceptually different worlds from their peers raised elsewhere. And on a rapidly globalizing planet this is, of course, a major source of potential—and actual—conflict. Whatever our geographical origins, it is our cultures that most fundamentally determine our identities. Today we are, above all, who we think we are.

THE **FROZEN SELF**

n the basement of New York City's American Museum of Natural History is a spotlessly clean room packed with large stainless steel vats. Open one and a freezing cloud of liquid nitrogen rises to greet you. Inside you will find, carefully packaged and identified, tissue samples taken from individuals belonging to a huge array of animal species. Most importantly, they harbor the DNA of each species represented; and since it has become possible to rapidly and inexpensively sequence the long DNA molecule, DNA has become a vital tool in scientists' quest to figure out exactly where each species stands in the great tree of life to which we all belong.

The Ambrose Monell Collection is an innovative expression of biological cryogenics, a field that seeks to preserve living tissues through maintaining them at extremely low temperatures. Other biological uses of cryogenic technology include the freezing of sperm, ova, and embryos for future reproduction, and various applications in transplant surgery and emergency medicine.

One extraordinary natural experiment in biological cryogenics occurred in 1986 when a Salt Lake City toddler named Michelle Funk fell into a freezing mountain stream, in which she lay submerged for more than an hour. Although she didn't have a pulse and was not breathing when she was found and rushed to a hospital, doctors using a heart-lung bypass machine were able to warm her body; and once her internal temperature had risen to about 77°F, her heart spontaneously began pumping and she started to breathe again.

Within a couple of years, Michelle was once more a normally developing child. Her physicians surmised that her brain had been cooled so rapidly that it had immediately lost its need for oxygen; and during the entire sixty-six minutes of her immersion her bodily functions had apparently halted completely, obviating brain and other tissue damage.

By the time this incident occurred, the notion of preserving the human body through freezing was already well established in some circles. In 1962 the physicist Robert Ettinger had published a book called *The Prospect of Immortality*, the founding document of a field that has come to be known as cryonics.

Impressed by rapid advances in medical technology, but worried that by the time he died science would not yet have found a cure for the disease that would carry him away, Ettinger imagined being deep-frozen after his death and revived when a cure for his malady (and freezing) had been found.

"Dewar" tanks are used to store cryopreserved bodies using liquid nitrogen. At room temperature, nitrogen is a transparent, odorless gas that makes up about 78 percent of Earth's atmosphere. At −320° F it becomes a clear colorless liquid that is used by biologists to preserve blood, reproductive cells (eggs and sperm), and tissues, and by the cryonics industry to preserve clinically dead human bodies for possible future revival.

The fallacy was obvious: freezing tissues (as opposed to cooling them) causes irreversible changes, and restoring a frozen body—especially a dead one—to normal function is something nobody has the slightest idea how to do yet. No matter; Ettinger established a company to carry out his vision. And such is some people's faith in the march of technology that in 1967 he deep-froze his first client, a University of California psychologist named James Bedford, in a vat of liquid nitrogen (from which he was moved to more state-of-the-art accommodations in 1991).

One of the issues here, of course, is that you cannot be frozen until you are legally dead. And death is, well, final. But the cryonics experts get around this by defining death as a process, rather than as an event: a process that is complete only when all the information encoded in the brain has been lost.

What is more, it turned out on further thought that, since personhood and all that goes along with it is the emergent product of each individual's brain, all you really need to confer immortality to the person is to preserve the brain itself, usually conveniently housed within a head. And heads, of course, take up a lot less room in cryogenic "dewar" tanks than whole bodies do.

As to the technology itself, normal freezing tends to damage tissues through ice crystal formation in the water lying between the cells. Cryonics technicians who acoustically monitored heads as they were cooled apparently detected sounds that they attributed to microfracturing of the tissues; and although the investigators concluded that this microfracturing does not happen at the favored temperature of –140°C, this temperature is considerably above that of liquid nitrogen, the cheapest extreme coolant, making the necessary equipment—and the procedure—much more complicated and expensive.

But "cryopreservation" doesn't stop there. "Cryoprotectant" chemicals can also be used to prevent mechanical cell damage, although returning tissues to proper function after they have been stabilized in this way is another story. The latest wrinkle is "vitrification," whereby infusion of the tissues with special cryoprotectants (aka "antifreeze"), combined with slow cooling, converts the organ or body involved to a stable "glass-like" state. A rabbit brain was recently vitrified in this way, and its tissues reportedly looked entirely normal when thawed and examined microscopically. How well it would have worked if restored to its original owner is, of course, something else entirely.

Plan on spending a large chunk of change if you are considering any of this. Three commercial outfits offer the service in the United States, and one in Russia; charges vary. The all-in luxury model will set you back over $200,000, with annual maintenance charges extra; some clients have elected to finance these fees through life insurance (with the cryonics folks as beneficiaries, of course). A bare-bones procedure, if you'll excuse the expression, is $35,000, on top of which you'll have to pay for your own

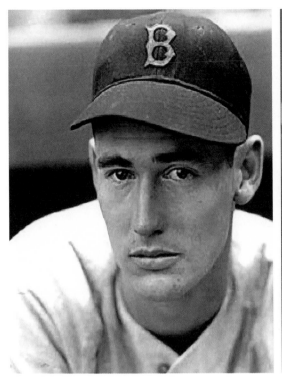

expensive transportation to the preservation site. If you elect to have just your brain preserved, a leading facility is currently quoting around $80,000.

To date, nearly three hundred people have been cryopreserved in the United States. The most famous of these is the baseball player Ted Williams (contrary to rumor, Walt Disney was not frozen). Timothy Leary almost signed up but begged off, saying that the cryonics people "have no sense of humor." Nonetheless, some 1,500 other hopefuls have apparently already ponied up for the service, and are waiting in the wings.

Exactly how and under what circumstances the thawing of human bodies would be done remains conjectural, and for the moment the chances it could ever be done successfully look pretty dim at best. And whether the world you or your shade wake up in will be one you could in any way relate to is, of course, just as uncertain. Guaranteed, though, you'd have a tougher time than Woody Allen in *Sleeper*.

Finally, the mainstream Cryogenic Society of America, obviously embarrassed by its similarity in name to something it considers entirely disreputable, makes a point of saying this about cryonics on its website: "We do NOT endorse this belief, and indeed find it untenable." Better to spend your money on something you know will make you happy while you know you can enjoy it.

When in 2002 baseball Hall-of-Famer Ted Williams died, his head was cryopreserved. In the years that followed his frozen head became the subject of acrimonious legal disputes between his son John Henry and other members of the family, including claims that it allegedly had been mistreated by the company preserving the head.

ALTERIVS NON SIT QVI SVVS ESSE POTEST.

REOLVS PHILIPPVS
AB HOHENHEIM.

THEOPHRASTVS BOMBAST,
DICTVS PARACELSVS

AVR. PHILIP. THEOPH.

PARACELSI

BOMBAST AB HOHENHEIM,
MEDICI ET PHILOSOPHI CELEBERRIMI,
Chemicorúmque PRINCIPIS.

OPERA OMNIA

MEDICO~CHEMICO~CHIRVRGICA,
TRIBVS VOLVMINIBVS COMPREHENSA.

EDITIO NOVISSIMA ET EMENDATISSIMA, AD GERMANICA
& Latina exemplaria accuratissimè collata: Variis tractatibus & opusculis summâ
hinc inde diligentiâ conquisitis, vt in Voluminis Primi Praefatione
indicatur, locupletata: Indicibúsque exactissimis instructa.

VOLVMEN PRIMVM,

Opera Medica complectens.

QVOD TIBI
FIERI NON
VIS, ALTERI
NE FECERIS.

GENEVÆ,
Sumptibus Ioan. Antonij, & Samuelis De Tournes.

M. DC. LIIX.
CVM PRIVILEGIO.

Paracelsus was an early Renaissance philosopher, physician, botanist, astrologer, and occultist. While most of his theoretical work has been discounted by modern scientific thought, his insights laid the foundation for a more dynamic approach to the medical sciences.

THE MEMORY OF WATER

Homeopathic medicine has a long pedigree. Some trace it all the way back to the fifth-century BC physician Hippocrates, who is said to have prescribed small doses of mandrake root to cure psychoses resembling those caused by larger doses of the stuff. Others look to the sixteenth-century physician and alchemist Paracelsus, who believed that "what makes a man ill also cures him." But in its modern form homeopathy emerged around the turn of the nineteenth century, when it was promoted by the German physician Samuel Hahnemann as an alternative to the (admittedly rather barbaric) mainstream medical practices of his time. It has since become a multibillion-dollar business.

Practitioners who followed Paracelsus and his "like cures like" formula (give extract of onion for curing colds' running noses, for example) rapidly discovered that many of the supposedly healing animal, vegetal, and mineral substances they prescribed their patients were actually toxic in large doses. It therefore became customary to dilute such substances with water.

Hahnemann's contribution was to systematize that dilution process, and to test its application in the treatment of numerous different conditions—with results that have since been widely disputed. The dilution was typically accomplished by violently shaking the solution and by knocking its container against a hard surface—a part of the process that came to be regarded as of particular importance.

Samuel Hahnemann, the creator of homeopathy. The term stems from the Greek roots for "alike" and "suffering."

Kalium bichromicum (bichromate of potash) is a homeopathic remedy recommended for treatment of maladies of the mucous membranes. It is usually prescribed at 30C, which means the compound has been diluted to the equivalent of one molecule in all the oceans of the world combined. The FTC has recently mandated that marketing claims made for over-the-counter homeopathic drugs must meet the same standards as those for other medicines.

Today, following Hahnemann's precedent, the accepted unit of dilution is known as C (one unit in a hundred), and the dilution is typically done repeatedly. One drop in one hundred, diluted six times, gives you the equivalent of one drop in a couple of Olympic-size swimming pools; twelve repeats corresponds to one drop in the entire Atlantic Ocean. Any higher than 12C, and the probability is negligible that even one molecule of the supposedly curative substance will remain in a sample of any reasonable size. Yet 30C—far less than one drop in all the oceans of the world—is not unusual in modern homeopathic preparations.

No wonder, then, that modern scientists are skeptical of homeopathic medicine. For if the chances are that there is not even one molecule of the supposedly curative substance present in it, how can the medicine possibly work?

One obvious possibility is the placebo effect, whereby patients' belief that they are being treated with something effective actually has a beneficial effect on their condition. When tested in clinical trials against bona fide medicines that looked identical, placebos—sugar pills are the favorite—have been shown to have some effect.

What's more, the more powerful the belief, the more powerful is the apparent effect—which is why large colored pills are more efficacious than small white ones. Exactly how the placebo effect works is not fully understood, though one plausible suggestion is that a psychogenic reduction of stress hormones leads to a general improvement in patients' health.

But with none of the supposedly curative agent present, there was no known way in which any homeopathic medicine could by itself have any effect, aside from whatever might have been derived purely from patients' belief in it. So imagine scientists' surprise in 1988, when a team led by the French biologist Jacques Benveniste published a paper in the prestigious journal *Nature* that claimed to have demonstrated the efficacy of a homeopathic preparation.

In that article Benveniste and colleagues claimed that the human white blood cells known as basophils changed their properties when exposed to *vigorously shaken* dilutes of antibodies that, by their own calculation, could have contained *none* of the original molecules. The diluting fluid itself apparently somehow retained a "memory" of the product that was no longer present.

Because of the controversial nature of this conclusion, *Nature* sent a team to Benveniste's lab to investigate. The investigators included the magician and professional skeptic

James Randi, and they came away unimpressed by the lab's sample control. They concluded that the Benveniste group's findings had been affected by "unintentional bias," and labeled its results a "delusion."

Undeterred, in 1997 Benveniste further boggled the minds of his fellow biologists by claiming that the effects of water memory—caused by an "electromagnetic imprint" in the fluid—could be transmitted over phone lines (the Internet was later added). This upset a lot of physicists (though one radical Nobelist rallied to his support), even as biologists in other labs were unable to reproduce his results.

In 1999 the pharmacologist Madeleine Ennis and several colleagues reported experiments showing that super-dilute histamines did inhibit basophil activity, and the fuss started afresh. Randi promptly offered a prize of $1 million to anyone who could replicate Ennis's findings, and the gauntlet was picked up by the BBC TV program *Horizon*, which gathered an all-star team of scientists to replicate the Ennis experiments under the auspices of the august Royal Society.

With Randi in attendance, two separate laboratories followed an elaborate double-blind procedure in which the effects on basophils of extreme histamine dilutions were compared with those of samples of pure water. Only after the end of the trial did any of the participants know which samples were dilutes and which were controls. To cut a long story short, in the end Randi kept his million dollars. No replicable effects could be demonstrated, and variations among the samples in their effect on the basophils were no greater than would be expected by pure chance.

Even after all this, for some observers the case for water memory was not definitively closed. As recently as 2010 Ennis wrote—in a homeopathy journal—that to clarify the (inevitable) slight variations to be expected in smaller-scale experiments, an expensive and rigorously designed "multi-centre trial" was still required. Water memory has no known physical basis, but apparently it is a hard idea for some folks to let go of. And given the complexities of human belief mechanisms, there is little doubt that, as Ennis herself put it, this will be a "never-ending story."

But maybe it shouldn't be. In 2015 the National Health and Medical Research Council of Australia published a comprehensive report in which more than 1,800 studies on homeopathy were scrutinized. Of these, it found that a paltry 225 were rigorous enough to be worth a closer look. And when it examined those better studies in detail, it discovered "no good quality evidence to support the claim that homeopathy is effective in treating health conditions." Even more emphatically, the report's authors recommend that "homeopathy should *not* be used to treat health conditions that are chronic, serious, or could become serious" (emphasis ours). Apparently, water does forget.

"ARCHAEORAPTOR"

lthough we can determine beyond reasonable doubt how all organisms on the planet are related by common descent just by analyzing the diversity of animals in the living world, we can find out the details of their evolution only by looking at fossils. Most vertebrate fossils, the remains of the major group to which we humans belong, are the mineralized bones and teeth of ancient animals that were preserved after their death in accumulating sedimentary rocks and later exposed by erosion.

Due to the vagaries of this process, the vast majority of the fossils that paleontologists find as they prowl over ancient landscapes are isolated teeth, bits of jaw with a few teeth, or broken bones of the body skeleton. Only comparatively rarely will a fossil seeker discover a complete skull, and much more seldom yet an even semicomplete skeleton. Full skeletons, which encode disproportionately large amounts of information about extinct animals, are scarcer yet and are the vertebrate paleontologist's Holy Grail.

Over the past several decades, China has become an important source of new vertebrate fossils—especially full skeletons preserved, flattened, in fine-grained sediments—that have filled in former gaps in our knowledge of the evolution of many groups. Recognizing the scientific importance of these fossils, the Chinese government long ago banned their export, declaring them a national resource.

However, most of the rocky exposures in China that yield such fossils occur on land farmed by impecunious peasants, who find selling fossils on the—regrettably large— black market a more lucrative source of income than raising the crops they have traditionally grown. In some places, bootlegging fossils has become a mini industry, even though such activities deprive science of the information those fossils contain, and crude excavation techniques lead to broken specimens and poor provenance data.

In the summer of 1997, while hacking away at early Cretaceous (~120 million-year-old) rocks in a shale quarry, a farmer in China's northeastern Liaoning Province discovered, and accidentally fractured into numerous pieces, several fossil-bearing slabs of rock. He took his findings home, eventually gluing together many of the bits to make a commercially valuable semicomplete skeleton. A local dealer, the full extent of whose complicity is not known, obtained a fraudulent permit for the glued-together specimen and exported it to the United States, where it sold for $80,000 at a gem and mineral show.

The buyer was Stephen Czerkas, director of a small dinosaur museum in Utah. Czerkas immediately recognized that the creature in the slab was unlike anything else yet discovered. Its upper body and thorax, replete with the impressions of wing feathers, looked like those of a very primitive toothed

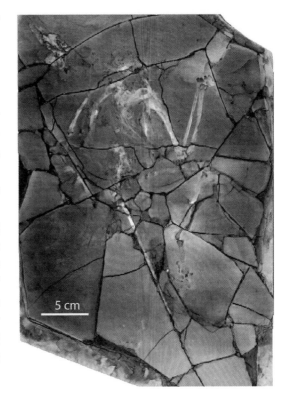

....

TOP: The details are murky, but supposedly a farmer in the northeastern Chinese province of Liaoning found a rare fossil of a toothed bird. Smuggled out of China and sold to a private dinosaur museum, the fossil became the subject of a major announcement in *National Geographic* magazine. The specimen turned out to be a composite.

BOTTOM: When the fossil that had been christened *Archaeoraptor liaoningensis* was examined using high-resolution X-ray computed tomography (CT) scans, it was found to comprise eighty-eight separate pieces cobbled together from at least two, and possibly up to five, different individuals.

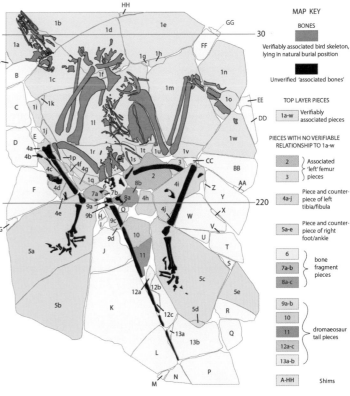

bird resembling the famous *Archaeopteryx* in shoulder structure, while its long, stiff tail was typical of a group of predatory dinosaurs known as dromaeosaurs.

In quick succession Czerkas contacted the Canadian dinosaur expert Phil Currie and *National Geographic,* and in the November 1999 issue, with great fanfare but apparently not much deliberation, the magazine published an article by its reporter Christopher Sloan that called the specimen *Archaeoraptor liaoningensis* and lauded it as a "true missing link" between dinosaurs and birds.

By this time, though, the specimen had been sent to Tim Rowe at the University of Texas for high-resolution CT scanning. Rowe soon realized that the top of the slab, the part bearing the fossil bone, was a composite of many broken pieces. Some of these were originally from different slabs, and all had been grouted onto a single piece of shale below, to give the appearance of a single skeleton. In particular, the creature's tail did not match with its abdomen, and the two legs were actually part-counterpart (squashed specimens like this one have top and bottom impressions) of the same single leg.

Both Currie and Czerkas showed up for the scanning, but for reasons that are unclear *National Geographic* did not immediately get wind of Rowe's conclusion (independently backed up by the testimony of a preparator who had examined the fossil), and went ahead with its sensational article. The find was immediately picked up by the national media, with great fanfare.

The sequence in which the *Archaeoraptor* forgery was fabricated.

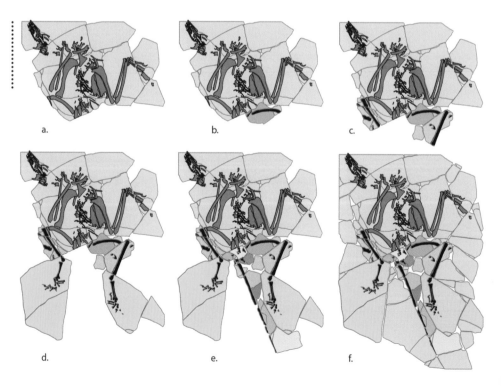

a.

b.

c.

d.

e.

f.

The publication was immediately criticized by the Smithsonian's Storrs Olson; but the major blow came in March 2000, when *National Geographic* inconspicuously published a brief letter from the Chinese expert Xu Xing, who had been brought in earlier to study the new specimen (which by then was destined to return to China, where it resides now).

Back home in China, Xu had been shown the counterpart impression of the *Archaeoraptor* tail (this time joined to a dromaeosaur body), and he immediately realized that "*Archaeoraptor* is a composite…a dromaeosaur tail and a bird body." Originally Xu's letter had said "fake" rather than "composite," but eventually he diluted his statement. In the same month, the science journal *Nature*, originally intended as a vehicle for publishing the no-longer-missing "link," carried instead an account of the deception, with Rowe, Xu, and Currie among its authors.

Finally, in October 2000, a deeply embarrassed *National Geographic* published an article it had commissioned from an independent investigator. This detailed a lamentable story of negligence, denial, and finger-pointing by most of those concerned—except for the original finder/fabricator(s), who remained anonymous. The report drew a definitive line under the story of "*Archaeoraptor*"—although not under the specimens concerned, which turned out to be important as representatives of new species of early bird and dromaeosaur, respectively.

Few come out of this unhappy story of scientific fraud with any credit, although despite some nefarious motives it is hard to demonstrate much malice such as that clearly involved in the earlier Piltdown forgery (see chapter 28, *Fake Paleoanthropology*). The dirt-poor finder probably wanted merely to maximize the market value of his illicit fossils, as doubtless did the dealer who sold the composite under the table; for the most part, the scientists showed negligence rather than bad faith, and while *National Geographic* was clearly not anxious to let the facts get in the way of a good story, once alerted to the fraud it acted quickly.

Of course, China emerges as a hotbed of local corruption, and as a source of fakes extending far beyond Vuitton handbags and Rolex watches. And in America there were inevitably those who cynically used the story to their own advantage: Richard Nixon's onetime Watergate co-conspirator Charles Colson announced in his radio commentary that it was an "elaborate and deliberate hoax," designed to hide a lack of "transitional forms" in the fossil record.

Ironically, though, it is science itself that emerges best, having in this instance corrected itself very quickly—thanks partly to very recently developed technologies, although Xu's intervention showed the enduring value of good old-fashioned brain work. The speed with which *Archaeoraptor* was dispatched contrasted gratifyingly with the fifty years it had taken to expose its Piltdown precursor.

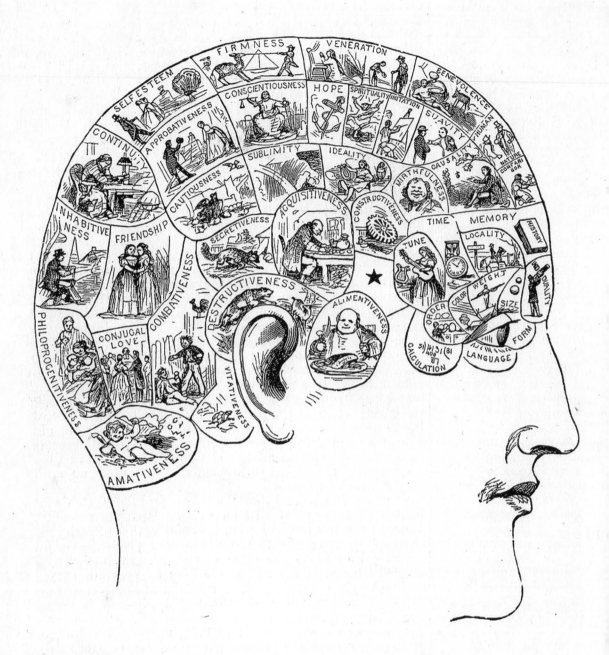

Memories aren't permanently
stored in our brains like folders in
a file cabinet. Research has shown
that memory is fungible. Each time
a memory is retrieved, it is altered.
Sometimes the alteration is subtle,
almost unnoticed; sometimes,
depending on circumstances, it is
changed drastically.

FAKE MEMOIRS

Just where does nonfiction end and fiction begin? Although this question has been the subject of endless debate, many consider the distinction an entirely artificial one. After all, human memory is famously unreliable. Eyewitness testimony, once the gold standard for evidence in courts throughout the nation, has turned out to be hugely fickle, and scientists have figured out that every time you take a recollection out of your mental memory bank and dust it off, you risk returning it to storage in slightly altered form. And there is, of course, even a well-established genre of fictionalized nonfiction, of which Truman Capote's "nonfiction novel" *In Cold Blood* is probably the most widely known example.

Still, when it comes to writing a personal memoir, it might seem reasonable to expect a certain degree of accuracy, plus or minus the vagaries of recollection. But even though truth may be stranger than fiction, some memoirists have evidently thought it desirable to deliberately embellish the one with the other. Indeed, some have seen fit to make up the entire thing.

Margaret B. Jones, here wearing a black hoodie and flashing a Bloods gang bandanna, described the tattoo of a large, weeping pit bull on her back that memorialized a friend's scheduled execution as "the most ghetto thing on my body." Her memoir, *Love and Consequences*, was an intimate, visceral portrait of a mixed-race white and Native American foster child growing up in drug-infested South Central Los Angeles. It was a complete fabrication.

···

One of the most extreme recent cases of this kind was "Margaret B. Jones" (real name Margaret Seltzer), who wrote *Love and Consequences: A Memoir of Hope and Survival* as an allegedly truthful account of growing up as a racially mixed foster child on the mean and gang-infested streets of South Central Los Angeles, when she was actually raised in a comfortable middle-class white family in affluent Sherman Oaks. As a total fabrication, this 2000 memoir—withdrawn by the publisher in short order when the deception was exposed—ranks with Misha Defonseca's "autobiographical" 1997 *Misha: A Mémoire of the Holocaust Years*, which spun a fantastical yarn about a child who, at the age of six, lost her parents to deportation, and subsequently wandered around occupied Europe in search of them, at one point under the protection of friendly wolves and at another killing a menacing German soldier.

The Holocaust genre has actually attracted more than its fair share of fabrications, although more commonly in the context of accounts based on some degree of actual personal experience. This seems to have been the case with Herman Rosenblat's 2003 *Angel at the Fence: The True Story of a Love That Survived*. Rosenblat had actually been imprisoned in the Buchenwald concentration camp, but his central account of having been thrown apples over the fence by a young farm girl—whom he later married following a chance meeting in Coney Island after the war—was clearly made up, since given the documented layout of the camp it was logistically impossible. After suspicions were raised and the book was pulled from the market before publication, Rosenblat confessed all on *The Oprah Winfrey Show*. But he still insisted that he retained his "dream" image of the apple drama.

One of the most aggressive and widely publicized literary scandals of recent times involved the writer James Frey, whose 2003 memoir, *A Million Little Pieces*, brought Oprah to public tears and which—largely thanks to the publicity this incident gave it—sold well over 3 million copies. It told a gut-wrenching and vomit-filled story of a criminal drug addict with a drinking problem and horrific prison experience, and it was packed with frequently violent incidents that, the Smoking Gun website later alleged, had at the very least been richly

In James Frey's harrowing memoir, *A Million Little Pieces*, describing his years as an alcoholic, drug addict, and criminal, he claimed he had been repeatedly arrested and incarcerated for months at a time. In fact, the closest Frey ever came to a jail cell was the few hours he once spent in a small Ohio police headquarters waiting for a buddy to post a $733 cash bond (The Smoking Gun).

embroidered. In the end, the publishers added a disclaimer to future editions of the book and offered to give any customers who felt duped their money back. Surprisingly, or maybe not, few took up this offer; and Frey himself continues to flourish as a media producer.

Sometimes even the author himself turns out to be entirely fictitious. The Albanian playwright Jiri Kajane labored precariously in isolated Tirana under the tyrannical rule of Enver Hoxha, achieving a single performance of his play *Neser Perdite* ("Tomorrow Every Day") before it was banned by the culture ministry. Subsequently he wrote a string of short stories which, even after Hoxha's death in 1985, he felt it too dangerous to publish in his home country: many of them featured a character known as the Deputy Minister of Slogans, a clear dig at the regime.

Editors in the West eagerly published Kajane's work, however, and one story was featured in a prestigious American anthology alongside such literary luminaries as Ian McEwan, Joyce Carol Oates, Patricia Highsmith, Graham Greene, and Ernest Hemingway. One magazine declared him to be "Albania's second greatest living writer," trailing only the prizewinning author Ismail Kadare.

Only it turned out that Kajane didn't actually exist. He was the fictitious creation of the FBI agent Kevin Phelan (who had posed as Kajane's translator) and Bill U'Ren, at one time a psychological coach to the San Diego Padres. The pair had met in a creative writing class at UCLA and had discovered that their stories were more salable set in Albania and submitted under Kajane's name than they were set in the United States and submitted under their own. Now you can buy the entertaining book *Winter in Tirane* credited to the real authors, with Kajane as "narrator."

You might expect other writers to be particularly censorious about these and many other fraudulent episodes. After all, it is the veracity of their profession that is at stake. But despite the odd lawsuit, writerly attitudes to the exposure of literary hoaxes have actually been pretty relaxed in recent years. And the issue is indeed not a straightforward one. Were the intrinsic literary merits (such as they might have been) of any of these works diminished by their outing as frauds? And is there really a bright line to be drawn between admitted fiction and the (sometimes) inevitable fictive elements of nonfiction?

Phelan asked a good question when he wondered out loud why, if readers had liked the stories when they thought an Albanian had written them, they should like them any less when they knew their true authorship (see also chapter 34, *Fake Art*). And Professor Sue Vice, now of the University of Sheffield, has been among those urging thinking before condemning: "If memoirs include even a small amount of fictional or reconstructed material, they may be judged as wholly worthless, even though they may have value in literary or psychological terms that exceeds their truth value."

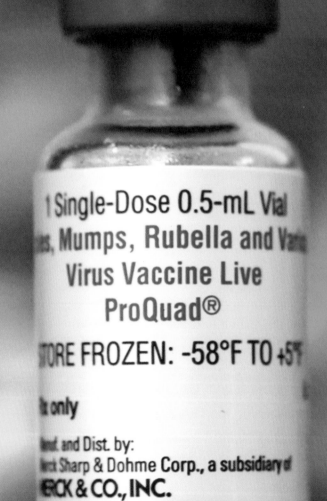

1 Single-Dose 0.5-mL Vial

...es, Mumps, Rubella and Var...

Virus Vaccine Live
ProQuad®

...TORE FROZEN: -58°F TO +5°...

Rx only

...ed. and Dist. by:

...erck Sharp & Dohme Corp., a subsidiary of

...ERCK & CO., INC.

...tehouse Station, NJ 08889, USA

The MMR vaccine acts against measles, mumps, and rubella (German measles). Before the widespread application of a vaccine against measles, the incidence of the disease was so high that it was felt to be "as inevitable as death and taxes." Mumps acquired by postpubescent males can lead in some cases to sterility, while significant congenital defects are possible if a woman contracts rubella during pregnancy. The combined MMR vaccine was introduced to induce immunity less painfully than three separate injections.

VACCINES AND AUTISM

n 1971 a three-in-one vaccine was introduced in the United States for measles, mumps, and rubella (MMR), all diseases that made both of us authors extremely unhappy—and our parents desperately worried—decades ago. Administered to children at twelve months to fifteen months of age, the new combination vaccine represented a huge leap forward in the control of childhood diseases, and in 1988, after years of successful use in America, it was introduced into the UK. It is particularly crucial to control childhood infectious diseases via vaccination, since kids' natural immune systems are still immature and underdeveloped; and so effective was the new MMR vaccine that, by the early 1990s, measles and rubella had been almost eradicated in the United States and most countries of western Europe.

But early in 1992 JABS (Justice, Awareness and Basic Support), a group of antivaccine enthusiasts in northern England, began to allege that the MMR vaccination caused brain damage to the children who received it. Soon the group's lawyer had secretly retained the services of Andrew Wakefield, a researcher at London's Royal Free Hospital School of Medicine, to amass evidence in anticipation of legal action against the manufacturers of the MMR vaccine. The hourly fee for Wakefield's services was outlandish, and the aim was to associate the vaccine with a "new syndrome" that could form the basis of a mutually lucrative class action suit. What's more, Wakefield soon filed for a patent on a "safer" stand-alone measles vaccine that would only ever have stood any chance of commercial success if the MMR vaccine were to drop out of the market.

In February 1998, the well-known English medical journal *Lancet* published a peer-reviewed article by Wakefield and a dozen collaborators that claimed the MMR vaccine was associated with the sudden onset of not only an inflammatory disease of the bowel, but also a particularly disturbing form of "regressive autism," in which self-injury was seen along with other deficits that included language impairment. The authors noted that the "intestinal and behavioral pathologies may have occurred together by chance," but went on to dismiss this possibility.

Though couched in impeccably impenetrable jargon, the whole paper reads as curiously anecdotal, and its findings were based on a sample of only a dozen children—five of whom, it later turned out, had developmental delays that had been noted before MMR vaccination.

On its own dubious merits the article might have just been ignored, but its findings were announced to the press with great fanfare, and the British tabloids seized it with glee as Wakefield spun their reporters a tale whereby the triple whammy of the three vaccines altered the youthful immune system in such a fashion that measles virus penetrated the intestines, releasing proteins that in turn impacted neurons in the brain. This was pure fantasy, but nobody loves a good story more than the press and presumably its readers.

Even the British prime minister became involved when it was reported that his son had not been vaccinated, a claim that was curiously tardily denied. With the tabloids in full cry, the rate of MMR vaccination plummeted, and by January 2003 the number of English kids vaccinated had plunged to well below the 92 percent needed to assure the "herd immunity" required for a successful vaccination campaign. The occurrence of measles began to spike.

As early as December 1999, Wakefield ran into problems at the Royal Free Hospital, when he was asked to replicate his study. Having failed to do so, he was asked in 2001 to leave; two years later another research group published an exhaustive study that failed to substantiate his findings. By 2003, funding for the lawsuit had been withdrawn for lack of evidence, and it was soon revealed that, amazingly, many of Wakefield's autistic subjects had actually been litigants in the case.

By March 2004, the findings of the *Lancet* paper had been disavowed by a majority of its authors, and eventually a *Sunday Times* investigation revealed the full scale of the fraud. In May 2010, Wakefield was struck off the medical register.

But meanwhile he had become a media star. In November 2001, he appeared on CBS's *60 Minutes* program to condemn an "epidemic of autism." Not content to inculpate just the MMR vaccine, his supporters, who included the actress and former *Playboy* model Jenny McCarthy, went on to blame all vaccines.

In January 2011, well after his fall from scientific and medical grace, Wakefield addressed a capacity crowd at a church in Tomball, Texas (his adopted home state).

According to the *New York Times*, which reported the event, his audience (mainly the parents of autistic children) "stood and applauded wildly." And the organizer sternly told the *Times* writer, "Be nice to him, or we will hurt you." In the same story, the head of an antivaccination group is reported to have said of Wakefield: "He is Nelson Mandela and Jesus Christ rolled up into one."

Between them, investigations published in the late 1990s in the London *Sunday Times* and the *British Medical Journal* by the reporter Brian Deer will leave no doubt in rational observers' minds that the MMR/autism connection was entirely specious. And a 2012 systematic review of dozens of scientific studies involving more than 14.7 million children found no credible evidence of a connection between the MMR vaccines and autism. So why are so many so passionately anxious to believe it?

The problem is not simply a suspicion of high tech, although technology is certainly galloping ahead at a rate with which many people find it hard to cope. People under stress, as the parents of autistic children often are, have a tendency to seek scapegoats; and it seems baked into the human condition to find a cause—any cause will often do—for any unfortunate circumstance (see chapter 40, *Lunacy*). It is apparently easier to live with an undesirable situation if you think you understand it, and in a litigious society that is particularly true if the chosen cause puts you in a position to sue for damages.

But the effect doesn't only exist at the individual level. In late 2014, a nasty measles outbreak at California's Disneyland finally prompted legislators to propose ending exemptions from vaccination requirements for kids attending elementary school and day care (in some places upward of 20 percent of parents had opted out for personal or religious reasons). A tiny but vocal minority leveraged the full power of social media against passage of the new law—as the commentators Renée DiResta and Gilad Lotan pointed out, most antivaccine messages on Twitter came from only a dozen accounts, although they were cleverly structured to pervade the entire Twittersphere.

In 1998, *Lancet*, one of the world's oldest and most prestigious medical journals, published an article on research by Andrew Wakefield and twelve others that claimed a connection between the MMR vaccine and the occurrence of bowel symptoms linked to autism. Twelve years later, after multiple investigations found conflicts of interest and medical misconduct, *Lancet* retracted the paper.

Equally instructively, once the law had passed, the message changed. From making the MMR/autism link, the tweets began to present the matter as one of the freedom to choose. Sound familiar? Evidently, thinking you are right trumps principle every time.

JAN HENDRIK SCHÖN

n a scientist's life there are few things more galling than to submit a brilliant new paper to a prestigious journal only to have it trashed by some ignorant boor of a referee. Along with the referee's insensitive comments will come a letter from the journal's editor, at best demanding that you make major changes to your manuscript, and at worst rejecting it outright.

On a better day, the heavens might smile on you. The editor's letter will tell you the referees liked what you wrote, and that he or she is accepting your manuscript as it is. That is rare indeed. But somewhere in the middle—and almost certainly the best possible outcome of the review process—is an intelligent appraisal that catches errors, suggests specific changes that will definitely improve your manuscript, and maybe even points out implications of your research you'd never thought of.

That's peer review for you. Scientists live and die by their publication records, and there is intense competition to get papers into the top journals in one's field. Those sought-after journals obviously receive many more submissions than they can actually publish, and which ones they go ahead with is in principle determined through appraisal by other scientists—the submitters' peers.

As a form of quality control in scientific publication, peer review has proved to be—well, without peer. But it is still far from perfect. For example, an editor can predetermine the outcome of the review process by sending a manuscript to the author's professional enemies. And even when this isn't done, reviewer objectivity may sometimes be elusive. Occasionally a work will be so specialized that an appropriate referee is hard to find—on one occasion, Louis Leakey (see chapter 38, *Misguided Archaeology*) was asked to examine himself!

What is more, reviewing is an onerous and uncompensated chore. While your paper is out for review, you yourself may be reviewing manuscripts by several different colleagues, and a conscientious appraisal will often take a lot of time. In a busy laboratory setting it is often tempting to save hours, or even days, by doing a cursory job.

As a result, a certain amount of substandard work slips through the peer review net. And maybe some good but unconventional science has never been published at all (though this becomes increasingly unlikely in an age of rapidly proliferating journals, some of them "hoax" titles established to capitalize on the new "author pays" model of Internet open-access publishing).

On the other hand, outright fakery in science is relatively rare, although in recent years such fabricators as the Japanese anesthesiologist Yoshitaka Fujii (who admitted to falsifying data in some 183 scientific papers) and the South Korean stem-cell scientist Hwang Woo-suk (who had been sentenced to two years for embezzlement and bioethical violations before admitting to fraud as well) have received extensive press attention.

Still, in this limited domain it is hard to equal the remarkable if reprehensible achievement of Jan Hendrik Schön. And nobody has gamed the peer-review system quite as well. A high-flying young physicist trained in Germany, Schön was hired in late 1997 by New Jersey's renowned Bell Laboratories, where cutting-edge research was being done on

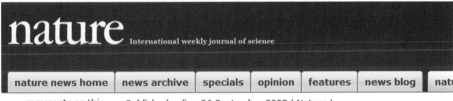

nature
International weekly journal of science

| nature news home | news archive | specials | opinion | features | news blog | natu |

 comments on this story

Published online 26 September 2002 | Nature | doi:10.1038/news020923-9

News

Physicist found guilty of misconduct

Stories by subject

· Physics
· Policy
· Lab life
· Technology

Stories by keywords

· fraud
· misconduct
· nanotechnology
· Bell Labs
· investigation
· nanotechnology

Bell Labs dismisses young nanotechnologist for falsifying data.

An up-and-coming young physicist at Bell Labs in Murray Hill, New Jersey, has been dismissed after being found guilty of 16 counts of scientific misconduct by a review panel charged with investigating his research.

The panel's report, released yesterday, concludes that Jan Hendrik Schön duplicated, falsified and destroyed data. He showed, says the report, "a reckless disregard for the sanctity of data in the value system of science".

Formerly a rising star in the field of nanotechnology, Schön was renowned for creating field-effect transistors, the backbone of modern electronics, out of tiny

Jan Hendrik Schön, formerly a rising star in nanotechnology

© Materials Research Society

This article elsewhere

 Blogs linking to this article

The proportion of scientific research that is retracted due to fraud has increased tenfold since 1997, according to the most comprehensive analysis to date in the *Proceedings of the National Academy of Sciences.*

semiconducting materials in the search for ever-smaller computer circuitry. Immediately, Schön became a sort of innovative mini industry, literally rewriting the book on conventional electronic nanotechnology. He found that ordinarily nonconducting organic materials could be made to superconduct, and to function as lasers and even as single-molecule transistors. This was revolutionary, promising a way of moving beyond silicon-based electronics technology to an organic-based system that could potentially be shrunk much smaller.

Between 2000 and 2002, Schön and his collaborators published paper after paper, most notably in the American *Science* and the English *Nature*, the two most widely circulated and prestigious scientific journals in the world. Normally a scientist might count him- or herself lucky to publish half a dozen papers in those journals in an entire career; in two years Schön published thirteen. Perhaps it helped that at the time both periodicals were trying to branch out from carrying mainly biological articles to a more representative spectrum of science as a whole; but Schön's frequency of appearance in their pages was nonetheless unprecedented. And his overall productivity was stupefying: in November 2001 alone, he produced a staggering seven scientific papers.

Taken together with the radical nature of Schön's claims, this avalanche of publications was bound to raise suspicions—not least at Bell Labs, where he told colleagues who inquired where he was getting his data from that his measurements and observations had all been made on machines back at the University of Konstanz, where he had received his PhD.

Still, suspicions lingered; and colleagues expressed their unease to Lydia Sohn, a physics professor at Princeton who, together with Cornell's Paul McEuen, went through Schön's papers in detail. The pair found much to raise their eyebrows, notably discovering that many of the graphs Schön had published were the same, regardless of the subject of the paper concerned. They informed Bell Labs as well as the editors of *Nature* and *Science*.

Bell thereupon commissioned an inquiry, which began in May 2002. Schön declined to turn over his raw data, saying they had been discarded because of insufficient computer storage space. By September the committee had issued a damning report. Data had been substituted, or had been created out of thin air from standard formulas, yielding results that "contradicted known physics." The wunderkind was out, and his papers were eventually retracted.

Ironically, those papers had actually been made more plausible by the peer review process, as reviewers helpfully told Schön what he would have to do to convince them of his unusual findings. He was only too happy to oblige, and the amended papers duly appeared in print.

Significantly, one of the features that had betrayed Schön's graphs was that they were too good to be true. Every scientist knows that actual measurements never turn out exactly as predicted by theory; and as he represented them Schön's data fit the curves so perfectly that the curves must have been created first and the data fitted to them later. The world is an imperfect place; and in an imperfect world perfection is the enemy not only of the good, but sometimes of the bad, too.

FAKE BOMB
DETECTORS

On July 2, 2016, a truck bomb exploded in Baghdad, Iraq, killing a reported 292 people and injuring 200 others. In the preceding six months, seven other bombing incidents around Iraq had already killed 374 human beings. Bombings are a serious and tragic problem in Iraq, and have been for a long time.

Following the July 2 suicide attack, the Iraqi government declared three days of official mourning. But in practical terms the first response to this atrocity was Prime Minister Haider al-Abadi's weary declaration that he would finally ban the employment of useless ADE 651 bomb detectors at vehicle inspection points on roads leading into the city. These devices had been in use at such checkpoints for several years; and, appallingly, the fact that they were totally ineffective had been known for almost as long.

Indeed, at the time of the Baghdad bombing the man who had sold the phony bomb detectors to the Iraqi government had already been in a UK prison for more than three years, having been convicted on three counts of fraud relating to his "callous confidence trick." Sentencing James McCormick to ten years in prison on May 2, 2013, the judge told him that "the device was useless, the profit outrageous, and your culpability as a fraudster has to be considered to be of the highest order." What's more, the fake bomb detector had already "in all probability materially contributed to causing death and injury to innocent individuals."

The history of the bizarre ADE 651 is almost as odd as the fact that its use was not immediately abandoned when it was shown to be ineffective. The version sold to the

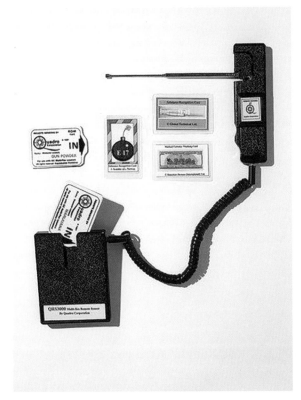
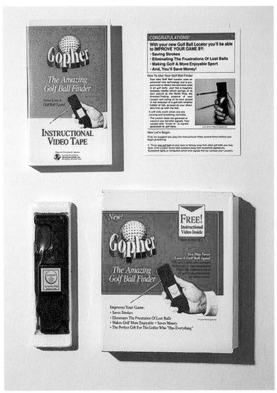

LEFT: The ADE 651 was said to be able to detect the presence of a variety of explosives. A single unit could be sold for as much as $40,000. RIGHT: The Quadro Tracker golf ball finder on which the fake bomb detector was based.

Iraqi authorities ultimately originated in the Quadro Tracker, a device that its inventor, the American treasure hunter Wade Quattlebaum, had initially marketed as a finder of lost golf balls. Later, its purported uses were extended to detecting banned drugs, and well beyond.

It was a really cool idea. A compact handheld unit with a swinging antenna was connected to a belt-worn box allegedly programmed to identify particular "molecular frequencies." The exact frequency was specified by a removable card; this could be changed according to the substance one desired to detect.

Following a 1996 lawsuit, distribution of this curious and ineffective instrument was banned in the United States. But, after jumping bail, one of its promoters moved to England. McCormick, a salesman and former police officer who ran a company called Advanced Tactical Security & Communications, ultimately became involved in the distribution of the gadget, by now known as the Mole Programmable Substance Detector. That version was taken off the market in 2001, when a study by the Sandia National Laboratories conclusively showed it didn't work.

Undeterred, McCormick copied the original Quadro Tracker and started selling it specifically as a bomb detector. After a few tweaks to the design it became the ADE 651, and sales took off in a world rattled by the events of September 11, 2001. The principal buyers were the Iraqi Army and the Iraqi Police Service. Although the devices were said to have cost about $225 each to manufacture, in 2008 McCormick sold eight hundred of them to Iraq for a reported $30 million, followed by a further seven hundred in 2009 (on a single-bid contract) for around $46 million. The unit price was in the region of $7,500, with the rest of the money going to "training," which apparently mainly consisted of showing users how to scuff their feet to generate the static electricity that allegedly powered the apparatus.

Iraq was far from the only market. According to the BBC, the ADE 651 was sold to Georgia, Romania, Niger, Thailand, and Saudi Arabia, and various other countries are rumored to have bought them. But Iraq was the principal client, and it continued to use the device—and to buy more—even though by 2008 the Israelis had specifically tested the ADE 651 model and found it useless.

At a checkpoint in Baghdad in 2010, an Iraqi police officer employs an ADE 651.

At the time, one Israeli explosives specialist told the German magazine *Der Spiegel* that "the thing has absolutely nothing to do with the detection of explosives." A *New York Times* exposé in November 2009 then quoted a spokesman as saying that the U.S. Army had "no confidence that these things work," while one former national security aide described them as "laughable, except someone down the street from you is counting on this to keep bombs off the streets."

McCormick and his malign device were eventually outed to the wider public in January 2010, when the BBC TV *Newsnight* program had one of the removable cards tested at Cambridge University. It proved to contain only a standard supermarket anti-shoplifting tag, and could not have detected anything.

At around the same time, UK and U.S. military personnel in Iraq conveyed their alarm to the English police. Export of the ADE 651 to Iraq and Afghanistan was banned and McCormick was arrested in England on suspicion of fraud. McCormick was convicted in 2013, and the authorities went after his ill-gotten wealth, which included a luxury yacht, a farmhouse in Somerset, and Nicolas Cage's former town house in the elegant resort town of Bath.

But even after an eruption of public outrage in Iraq following the BBC revelation, and the arrest of the fraud's author in the UK, the Iraqi authorities proved reluctant to act. One Interior Ministry spokesman conspiratorially told the journal *Asharq Al-Awsat* that "the reason the director of the company was arrested was not because the device doesn't work, but because he refused to divulge the secret of how it works to the British authorities." Only in early 2011 was the head of the ministry's counterexplosives unit arrested and jailed, on charges of accepting millions of dollars in bribes from McCormick.

Yet even after this action, the Iraqi authorities were still employing the ADE 651—often in lieu of vastly more effective physical inspection—when that truck bomb went off in July 2016. Whether this tragic delay resulted from bureaucratic inertia, from fear of repercussion on the part of complicit officials, or just from a reluctance to admit an unpalatable fact has yet to emerge.

Still, however poor the ADE 651 may have been at detecting explosives, it was an unqualified success in one respect. An associate told *Newsnight* that he had confronted McCormick over the instrument's effectiveness. To which the fraudster had replied: "It does exactly what it is designed to do. It makes money."

"I am the first in the East,
the first in the West,
and the greatest Philosopher
in the Western World;
Affirmed by me,
Timothy Dexter."

Engraved from the Life

by James Akin Newburyport.

The most Noble
Lord Timothy Dexter.

What a piece of work is Man!

how noble in reason! how infinite in faculties! in form & moving, how express & admirable!

Entered according to act of Congress June 1st. 1805 by James Akin. Newburyport. Mass."

AND SOLD BY THOMAS & WHIPPLE.

PSEUDOCIDE

A s if the prospect of one certain death weren't more than enough for most of us to contemplate, some people have seen fit to add an additional voluntary one, in an event that is common enough to have its own name: pseudocide.

Of course, nobody knows exactly how common the faking of one's own demise actually is, because naturally enough successful pseudocides don't make it into the statistics. But one—possibly apocryphal—estimate is that as many as a quarter of the reported leaps from San Francisco's Golden Gate Bridge in which the body is not found represent pseudocides. Certainly, there is enough interest out there that at least one publisher has seen fit to market a book on the subject: *How to Disappear Completely and Never Be Found*. And CNBC's *American Greed: The Fugitives* episode on pseudocides wisely advised that it probably isn't a good idea to use a corpse of the opposite sex, or leave your fingerprints on your own death certificate.

It isn't hard to imagine why an individual might want to wipe the slate clean and start all over again. People have an almost limitless menu of ways in which to mess up their lives, and even in a life that would appear to most observers as entirely satisfactory, something superior may always beckon. The existential dissatisfaction that is evidently so deeply embedded in the human condition seems to result from the fact that, no

....

OPPOSITE: **Timothy Dexter was a New England merchant known both for his eccentricities and for his hard-headed business sense. He exported warming pans (used to heat sheets in the cold New England winters) to the West Indies, and sold them at a profit as ladles for the local molasses industry. He faked his own funeral to find out how his wife and friends would react.**

matter how good things are, we can always imagine that they might be better—even if we can't specify exactly how. A dangerous combination.

What is harder to explain is why anyone would want to escape from their old lives by feigning their own death. After all, there are plenty of ways for those fed up with their old existences simply to move and assume a new identity, without having to go to all the trouble and risk of faking the biological end of the old one. The shelves of bookstores groan with self-help volumes advising you how to go about doing that, and fiction overflows with creative ideas on the subject.

Still, the faking of one's own death remains a popular prelude to beginning a new life, and perhaps it is not surprising that a favored method of departure is via drowning. One famous case combining drowning and fiction is that of John Stonehouse, a British member of Parliament who, in order to escape business woes and start a new life with his mistress in Australia, faked his watery suicide after having gotten the idea from Frederick Forsyth's novel *The Day of the Jackal*.

The great attraction of drowning is that it does not necessarily require a body, which is the hardest thing of all to fake (see chapter 36, *Counterfeit Cadavers*). All you need to do is to create circumstances that would lead to a coroner's verdict of presumed death by drowning; yachting accidents and bridge jumps over fast-moving waters fill the bill particularly nicely. What's more, even though most bodies eventually wash up somewhere, and questions might eventually be raised if yours doesn't, there is also apparently something about water itself: observers have noted the "baptism effect," whereby water is psychologically and spiritually symbolic of cleansing, and thus also of new beginnings.

On January 11, 2009, Marcus Schrenker faked his death in a plane crash when the scams his Indiana investment firms were running started to unravel. Investigators found no body or blood inside the plane. Two days later he was captured hiding in a pup tent in a Florida campground, where he had attempted suicide by slitting his wrists.

There are other motives that relate to the murkier realms of the human psyche. Take the example of "Lord" Timothy Dexter, a difficult and eccentric late eighteenth-century businessman of Newburyport, Massachusetts. Feeling insufficiently adulated by those around him, Dexter decided to pretend to have died to see how much sorrow his family and friends would express. When his wife failed to shed enough tears at his wake he sprang from his casket and beat her, then caroused with the cronies who had been mourning him minutes earlier. Dexter's case may have been an extreme one; but a desire to test the love of family and friends appears not to be an unusual motivation for pseudocide.

More straightforward, and more common, is insurance fraud: load yourself up with life insurance, stage your death, and disappear along with your beneficiary. In 2002 a canoe belonging to John Darwin, a deeply indebted former prison officer, was found empty at sea near his home in northern England. Soon thereafter, disguised as an old man, the thirty-one-year-old returned to live next door to his wife, Anne, whose house he secretly entered through a hole in the shared wall disguised by a cupboard. This subterfuge ultimately gave rise to the immortal headline THE LIE, THE SWITCH, AND THE WARDROBE.

The next year, after Darwin had been declared legally dead and Anne had collected substantial insurance money, the "old man next door" moved in with her. He acquired a false passport, and the pair then traveled quite extensively before buying property in Panama in 2006. In 2007, with an impending change in visa laws threatening to expose his fake passport, Darwin decided to return to England and feign amnesia.

Once home, he discovered the police were reluctant to believe his story that he had no recollection of the past five years, partly because they already knew Anne had been cashing out and was planning to move abroad. And then the *Daily Mirror* ran an exposé, based on a real estate agent's publicity photo of the pair taken in Panama in 2006 that had found its way onto the Internet. The jig was up, and in 2008 both John and Anne were convicted of insurance fraud, serving prison time until 2011.

Pseudocide is also an option for fraudulent financiers. In April 2008, Samuel Israel III was sentenced to twenty years in prison for defrauding investors in his bankrupt Bayou Hedge Fund Group. On June 9, 2008, after he had failed to report to prison, his car was found on the Bear Mountain Bridge, north of New York City. "Suicide is painless"—a tag line from the TV show *M*A*S*H*—was scrawled in the dust covering its hood. The authorities proved reluctant to believe the implication that Israel had jumped off the high bridge, and following their appearance on *America's Most Wanted* Israel and his girlfriend turned themselves in after having spent a month living in a trailer park.

The march of technology is, alas, making pseudocide tougher all the time. Ubiquitous video surveillance, biometrics, DNA, digital databases, and wised-up insurance companies are all making it ever harder and less profitable for us to separate ourselves from our identities. Even the photo that jailed the Darwins turned up when someone simply thought to Google "John, Anne, Panama."

In March 2002, John Darwin disappeared while canoeing near his oceanfront home in County Durham, England. After he was declared dead, his wife collected on a £680,000 insurance policy. Five years later he was spotted very much alive with his wife in Panama, thanks to a photograph posted on a Facebook page.

STEPHEN GLASS, JAYSON BLAIR, AND THEIR LEGACY

Jayson Blair was an American success story. Only the second African American to have edited the University of Maryland's prestigious student newspaper *Diamondback*, by the tender age of twenty-four he had risen from lowly intern to staff writer on the national desk at the *New York Times*. A hugely prolific journalist, he authored hundreds of articles during his nearly four years writing for the *Times*, covering subjects as diverse as the problems faced by wounded veterans, the Washington sniper murders, and scares about anthrax. Although not universally liked by his colleagues, and distrusted by a few, the ambitious and garrulous Blair seemed set for a rapid rise through the ranks at the nation's premier newspaper.

Then the blow fell. In April 2003 the *San Antonio Express-News* notified the *Times* that a story Blair had allegedly filed from Los Fresnos, Texas, had largely been lifted from its pages. That set in motion an inquiry that ultimately revealed a pattern of erratic behavior and inaccurate reporting going back right to his *Diamondback* days. Even then, writing about the university's football team, Blair had embroidered stories with colorful quotes nobody had ever said, and as a manager of the paper he was a disaster, missing production deadlines and causing many of his coeditors to quit. When he himself prematurely stepped down as editor in chief, his successor actually issued an apology for the "speculative" reporting that had been published on Blair's watch.

With a record like this, it seems remarkable in retrospect that Blair was able to get a job as a journalist anywhere, let alone at the nation's leading newspaper. But editors were impressed by his ambition and productivity, and by the *Times*'s own account they accordingly ignored reservations expressed by his reporter colleagues. Still, direct accusations from a sister journal could not be ignored, and within a month of the initial allegation the *Times* publicly admitted that Blair had indeed consistently "misled readers and *Times* colleagues with dispatches that purported to be from Maryland, Texas, and other states, when often he was far away, in New York. He fabricated comments. He concocted scenes. He lifted material from other newspapers and wire services. He selected details from photographs to create the impression he had been somewhere, or seen someone, when he had not." Blair was abruptly out, and disappeared briefly from view.

A NATION AT WAR: MILITARY FAMILIES; Relatives of Missing Soldiers Dread Hearing Worse News

By JAYSON BLAIR MARCH 27, 2003

One of the thirty-six fabricated articles Jayson Blair wrote while a reporter at the *New York Times.*

Blair himself was only one reporter of almost four hundred at the *Times*, and the stories he wrote tended to be of the human interest variety, rather than dealing with significant matters directly affecting public opinion. And the *Times* acted swiftly once the people at the top became aware of the problem. But journalism depends vitally on trust, and the episode severely eroded public trust in the *Times*—and the *Times*'s trust in itself.

Of course, shady journalism was nothing new (see chapter 18, *Aerial Feats*), but public trust in journalists had actually been on particularly shaky ground since the revelation in 1998 that Stephen Glass, an associate editor at the *New Republic*, had fabricated around two-thirds of the articles he had written for the respected magazine. And it was rocked again when, right after the Blair scandal had broken, a team of journalists at *USA Today* "found strong evidence" that Jack Kelley, one of the newspaper's star reporters—and a finalist for the Pulitzer Prize in 2002—had "fabricated substantial portions of at least eight major stories, lifted nearly two dozen quotes or other material from competing publications, lied in speeches he gave for the newspaper and conspired to mislead those investigating his work." This revelation was particularly devastating because, unlike Blair's, Kelley's earlier career had produced no telltale signs for his superiors to ignore. Having developed a sterling reputation, Kelley was able to get away for years with writing about places he did not know, making up quotes by people he had never interviewed, lifting quotes from the work of others, and inventing "informants."

Little wonder, then, that public trust in the journalistic profession—one of the primary guarantors of social and political freedom in our society—has sunk to historic lows in the first part of the twentieth century. In 2015 the polling organization Gallup found

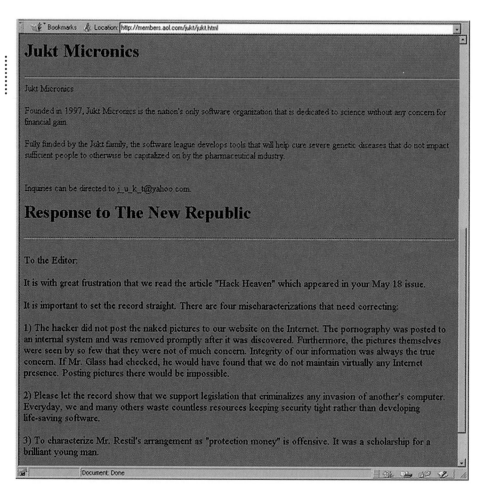

Location: http://members.aol.com/jukt/jukt.html

Jukt Micronics

Jukt Micronics

Founded in 1997, Jukt Micronics is the nation's only software organization that is dedicated to science without any concern for financial gain.

Fully funded by the Jukt family, the software league develops tools that will help cure severe genetic diseases that do not impact sufficient people to otherwise be capitalized on by the pharmaceutical industry.

Inquiries can be directed to j_u_k_t@yahoo.com.

Response to The New Republic

To the Editor:

It is with great frustration that we read the article "Hack Heaven" which appeared in your May 18 issue.

It is important to set the record straight. There are four mischaracterizations that need correcting:

1) The hacker did not post the naked pictures to our website on the Internet. The pornography was posted to an internal system and was removed promptly after it was discovered. Furthermore, the pictures themselves were seen by so few that they were not of much concern. Integrity of our information was always the true concern. If Mr. Glass had checked, he would have found that we do not maintain virtually any Internet presence. Posting pictures there would be impossible.

2) Please let the record show that we support legislation that criminalizes any invasion of another's computer. Everyday, we and many others waste countless resources keeping security tight rather than developing life-saving software.

3) To characterize Mr. Restil's arrangement as "protection money" is offensive. It was a scholarship for a brilliant young man.

Document: Done

that trust in the news media was at one of its lowest points since surveyors had begun asking about respondents' opinions on this subject more than forty years earlier.

And yet, at the same time it seems that the public not only cannot get enough of fake news but is eager to believe it (see chapter 25, *Public Credulity*). The *Weekly World News* flourished for a long time, and the *National Enquirer* is still a staple at supermarket checkouts; both stand as proof of the seductive nature of "infotainment." Nonetheless, the 2016 U.S. presidential election saw an unprecedented proliferation of entirely fictitious "news" reports. These originated mostly on dubious websites, but many of them eventually made it into more mainstream print media as well.

In one small town in the remote and impoverished Republic of Macedonia, a virtual industry of teenage news faking developed, using dozens of bogus websites whose sole aim was to make their untruthful and sensationalist stories go viral. In a society where the average wage is $4,800 per year, one youthful news faker is said to have earned $60,000 from penny-per-click sites targeting American voters during the presidential campaign.

Indeed, the problem of fake news on the Internet has become so acute that in late 2016 both Facebook (through which much of it is disseminated) and Google announced measures to suppress the sites on which it originates. What's more, at around the same time, Indiana University's Network Science Institute announced the availability of a beta version of Hoaxy, a platform that is specifically designed to track the spread of phony news across social media.

This proliferation occurs in some remarkable ways. Take, for example, the apparently widely believed "Pizzagate" story, which had Hillary Clinton and her campaign chairman John Podesta running a pedophilia ring out of a Washington pizzeria. Eventually a (real) gunman showed up at the restaurant and began firing at random. And although he subsequently admitted to the *New York Times* that "the intel on this wasn't 100 percent," that did not prevent a search on Hoaxy for this classic false-news episode from turning up a further twenty fake stories on it!

Ultimately, though, the more important problem lies not on the supply side, but on the demand one. The despised established media are, in fact, pretty vigilant about policing the material they place before us, and every time a member of the public rejects them in favor of believing and propagating phony and often entirely misleading "news" stories on social media or anywhere else, our corporate grip on reality slips a little more.

This slippage is even more alarming when it is led from the top. In an age when the U.S. President with "the biggest inauguration crowd ever" denounces the mainstream media as peddlers of fake news, and excoriates the press indiscriminately as the enemy of the people, it seems that all bets in the domain of public information are off.

On October 30, 2016, a white supremacist Twitter feed claimed there was an international pedophilia ring linked to members of the Democratic Party. Spreading like wildfire on social media, alternative news websites, and talk radio shows, this initial claim quickly morphed into a full-blown conspiracy theory that involved coded messages, satanic rituals, and a Washington D.C. pizza parlor harboring child sex slaves. Five weeks later, a man fired three shots into the restaurant.

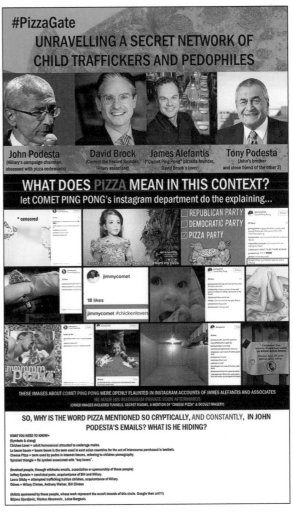

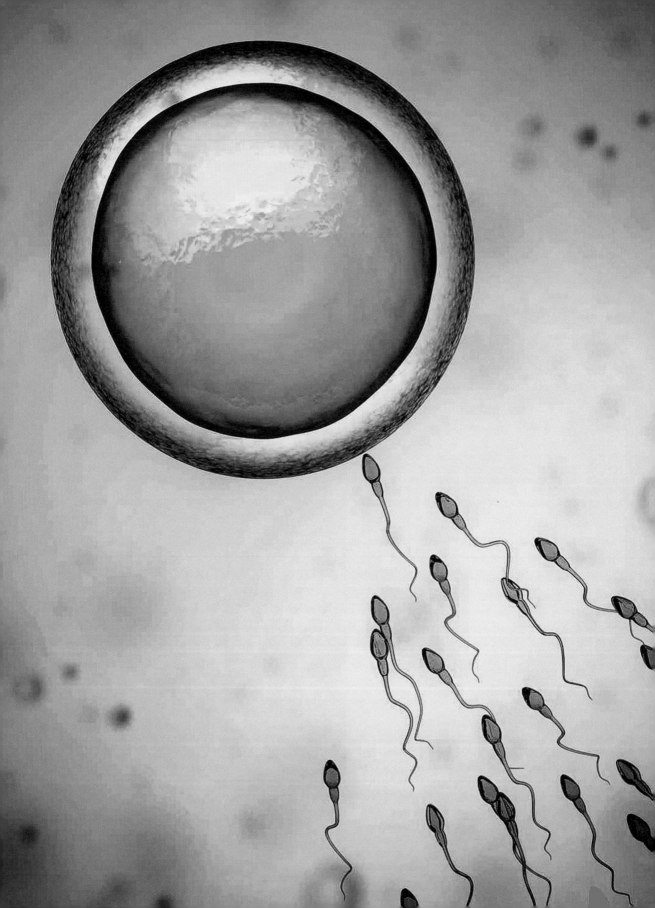

EPILOGUE

After we'd completed our quick canter through the long history of fakery, forgery, and fallacy, we were mildly surprised and gratified—as you may have been—to realize that it has not been one of unrelieved unscrupulousness, venality, gullibility, and self-interest. Indeed, it turns out that this domain of human experience has been as varied, as subtle, as complex, and occasionally as humorous as any other; and the motivations for deceiving one's fellow citizens or believing in the weird are, correspondingly, as diverse as the human psychological tapestry itself. Who could fail to find George Psalmanazar harmlessly and amusingly engaging (see chapter 11, *Fraudulent Ethnicity*), or Fritz Kreisler's virtuosity thrilling (see chapter 32, *Fake Music*)?

Still, the realm of fraudulence is also a vast one, and we must confess to having made our selection here on a relatively capricious basis of variety, or outrageousness, or what we ourselves found particularly interesting. Aside from the everyday white lies everyone tells, the overwhelming majority of the frauds that are committed do indeed have venal motives, and reveal the more appalling and decidedly nonempathic side of human nature. What is more, at some level or another most of us—the potential

....

OPPOSITE: **In 1964, Cecil Byran Jacobson, at the time Chief of the Reproductive Genetics Unit at George Washington University Medical School, claimed that he had impregnated a male baboon by implanting a fertilized egg in its abdominal cavity. This was never proven but brought him notoriety. In 1976, he opened a fertility clinic in Vienna, Virginia, even though he had no specialist training in "in vitro" fertilization. It was later thought that he injected women with hormones that caused a false positive in a pregnancy test. In 1992 he was convicted of using his own sperm to impregnate up to 75 women without their knowledge or consent.**

victims—are perfectly well aware of this. So why does history constantly repeat itself, as we fall for the same scam again and again?

There is a large literature that bears on this question, much of it emanating from the marketing departments of business schools. Many academic studies emphasize how fraud tends to target inherent weaknesses in human nature. Marketers draw on both psychology and empirical investigations of human behavior to determine how best to persuade their fellow citizens to buy a particular product; and, in a sense, virtually all human transactions involve buying or selling something. Humans are social creatures, and in any social setting people have to project an image of themselves, even as they are evaluating the image the other party is presenting to them. Academics have accordingly tried to come up with rules for marketing based on the ways in which humans tend to behave. And of course, these apply equally to fraud.

Eric R. Knowles of the University of Arkansas and Jay A. Linn of Widener University have, for example, come up with what they call the "approach-avoidance model of persuasion." They note that resistance to any sales pitch ("avoidance") "is natural and built-in," and must be overcome using various strategies they outline. At the same time, of course, the salesman or con artist has to emphasize the innately attractive nature of what is on offer (the "approach" part). Knowles and Linn acknowledge that any attempt to persuade is "psychologically complex…engaging multiple and usually conflicting motives." But by speaking to the more suspect aspects of whatever is being sold as well as to the more attractive ones, the con man will make his mark feel like a co-conspirator, and the mark will be less likely to fixate on the possible downsides of the deal.

Maria Konnikova, author of *The Confidence Game*, agrees. She points out that the monstrously sociopathic Gregor MacGregor (chapter 16, *Imaginary Lands*) excelled both at making his marks want to approach the rather farfetched idea of his imaginary land of milk and honey, and at calming fears that might have made them want to avoid it. The approach-avoidance model of persuasion covers both mind-sets and makes it possible to reach a large audience simultaneously, just as MacGregor did through numerous interviews in national newspapers.

Scientific fakery is a rather different kettle of fish. As with most art fraud, success in this domain lies less in grasping the complexities of individual psychology than in understanding the prevailing assumptions of the time. Whether crafting a set of scientific conclusions or a plausible fake art object, the forger has to understand what his or her audience is willing to hear, or wants to possess.

As the MIT physicist and science historian David Kaiser has observed, the Bell Labs physicist Jan Hendrik Schön (see chapter 47, *Peer Review*) "worked with a particular idea of what real or legitimate claims should look like. He sought to make his fakes fit in rather than stand out, massaging his data to better match established predictions." Yet, given the intrinsic nature of science (see chapter 43, *Homeopathy*; chapter 44, *Pseudopaleontology*; and chapter 46, *Irrational Hysteria*) and the constant scrutiny of his peers, Schön could never have rationally expected his published findings to be accepted for long. Indeed, it is hard to imagine that he ever thought he could get away with his fraud in the long run; only extreme self-absorption, and the lust for immediate acclaim, can possibly explain why he even tried.

Trofim Lysenko (see chapter 35, *Dialectical Biology*) took another tack. He used his powers of oratory and his political contacts to persuade an authoritarian and murderous regime to back his false science. Once again, because science is not something that can ever succeed by fiat, Lysenkoism could never have endured over the long term. But it is sobering to recall that Lysenko himself died comfortably at home in bed, while his brilliant rival Nikolai Vavilov perished miserably in prison.

One may reasonably hope that there will never be another Lysenko, but, alas, given that for too many human beings the desire for fame at any price is a powerful motivator, one knows that there will be other Jan Hendrik Schöns.

Fortunately, in the case of science, the fame associated with forgery is usually condemned to be fleeting. In the arts, conversely, successful fabrication usually condemns the forger to anonymity from the get-go—although there are some uplifting exceptions (see chapter 10, *Renaissance Reprobates*; and chapter 32, *Fake Music*). Much more worrying currently are "fake news" and outright untruths in the political realm. The power of the "Big Lie" has forever been a malign influence, and our propensity to believe bizarre or unrealistic things we hear spoken as fact has always made human beings vulnerable to demagoguery. But in a world in which citizens increasingly receive their information from partisan sources while being told to distrust the more balanced mainstream media (see chapter 50, *Fake Journalism*), our society as a whole has become dangerously exposed to political misrepresentation and manipulation. Where the con's mark is the entire population, we all need to be especially on our guard.

So what can we conclude? As they have been since the beginning, people today are wildly variable in temperament. And while most of us instinctively shrink from major fraud—perhaps not least because the chances of getting away with it in the long run are pretty slender—some will continue to be naturally inclined toward it, especially when opportunity beckons. The bottom line is that as long as there is a market for anything, there will be a supply. And there will even be those prepared to fraudulently create a market. Fortunately, for the same reason that in nature predators are always much thinner on the landscape than their prey, it is reasonable to predict that in human society such reprehensible activities will remain the province of a relative few.

But, just as fraud, fakery, and fallacy all point toward a series of dichotomies in human experience—between the con and the mark, between the faker and the client, between the cynical and the credulous—the subjects of this book also evoke something that is universal in the human condition.

As far as we can tell, we human beings are alone in being able to conceive of things that lie well beyond our material grasp. We can imagine soaring like Superman, while risking life and limb every time we put on a wingsuit; we can imagine rising to the top, while being stifled by an unfeeling boss; we can dream of political utopias, while helplessly watching the world go to hell in a handbasket; we can imagine an all-powerful creator, while being unable to mitigate disaster.

That human powerlessness to accomplish everything we can imagine almost inevitably leads to a state of existential dissatisfaction. If we wish to achieve contentment we have only two choices: we can either accept our limitations and leave our unachievable aspirations safely stowed away (while acting on those we feel attainable), or we can use our powers of imagination to rely on snake oil, promised lands, fleeting fame, revolution, conspiracy theories, or lying politicians to provide temporary relief. The fraudsters will always have a niche, though let us hope it will never be more than that.

To end this book on what we hope will be a high note, we will repeat that not all fraud ultimately detracts from the general quality of life. Indeed, some has enhanced that quality, or at worst has contributed to general amusement. And it was in that spirit, as we announced in our preface, that we buried a tiny fraud of our own somewhere in the text of this book. We hope you'll have spotted it, but if by chance you didn't, check the Pepys quote on page 44. We made a tiny addition to Pepys's account of his activities on December 6, 1665. The Duke did not show him Michelangelo's much-lamented Cupid. As far as is known, it remained in Whitehall Palace until it was incinerated in the fire of 1698.

FURTHER READING

PREFACE

Bolt, Roelf, 2014. *The Encyclopaedia of Liars and Deceivers.* Translated by Andy Brown. London: Reaktion Books.

Gardner, Martin. 1957. *Fads and Fallacies in the Name of Science.* New York: Dover Publications.

MacDougall, Curtis D. 1958. *Hoaxes.* New York: Dover Publications.

MacKay, Charles. 1841. *Extraordinary Popular Delusions and the Madness of Crowds.* London: Richard Bentley.

I. OTHER ANIMALS:
EVOLUTION OF THE CON
<4 BILLION YEARS AGO

Byrne, Richard, and Andrew Whiten. 1992. "Cognitive Evolution in Primates: Evidence from Tactical Deception." *Man* New Series 27 (3): 609–27.

Carlson, Albert, and Jonathan Copeland. 1978. "Behavioral Plasticity in the Flash Communication Systems of Fireflies." *American Scientist* 66: 320–46.

Coyne, Michael J., Barbara Reinap, Martin M. Lee, and Laurie E. Comstock. 2005. "Human Symbionts Use a Host-Like Pathway for Surface Fucosylation." *Science* 307: 1778–81.

Hauber, Mark, and Rebecca Ilner. 2007. Coevolution, communication, and host chick mimicry in parasitic finches: Who mimics whom?. https://www.research gate.net/publication/225475541_Coevolution_ communication_and_host_chick_mimicry_in_ parasitic_finches_Who_mimics_whom.

Hoover, Jeffery P., and Scott. K. Robinson. 2007. "Retaliatory Mafia Behavior by a Parasitic Cowbird Favors Host Acceptance of Parasitic Eggs." *Proceedings of the National Academy of Sciences, USA* 104: 4478–83.

Knodler, Leigh A., Jean Celli, and B. Brett Finlay. 2001. "Pathogenic Trickery: Deception of Host Cell Processes." *Nature Reviews Molecular Cell Biology* 2: 578–88.

Searcy, William A., and Stephen Nowicki. 2005. *The Evolution of Animal Communication: Reliability and Deception in Signaling Systems.* Princeton, NJ: Princeton University Press.

2. APOCALYPTICISM:
THE END OF THE WORLD
AS WE KNOW IT 2800 BC

Camping, Harold. 2005. *Time Has an End: A Biblical History of the World 11,013 BC–2011 AD.* Great Barrington, VT: Vantage.

DiTommaso, Lorenzo. 2016. *The Architecture of Apocalypticism: From Antiquity to Armageddon. Vol 1.* New York: Oxford University Press.

Freeman, Charles. 2009. *A New History of Early Christianity.* New Haven, CT: Yale University Press.

Henry, Matthew, ed. 2014. *Book of Revelation.* Seattle, WA: CreateSpace Independent Publishing.

Iliffe, Rob, and Scott Mandelbrote. 2017. Catalogue of Newton's Alchemical Papers. The Newton Project. http://www.newtonproject.ox.ac.uk/texts/ newtons-works/alchemical

Miller, Robert J., ed. 1994. *The Complete Gospels.* San Francisco: HarperSanFrancisco.

Nelson, Chris. 2011. A Brief History of the Apocalypse. www.abhota.info.

Pappas, Stephanie. May 10, 2011. "The Draw of Doomsday: Why People Look Forward to the End." *Live Science.* www.livescience.com/14179-doomsday-psychology-21-judgment-day-apocalypse.html.

Weber, Eugen. 1999. *Apocalypses: Prophecies, Cults, and Millennial Beliefs through the Ages.* Cambridge, MA: Harvard University Press.

White, Michael. 1999. *Isaac Newton: The Last Sorcerer.* Boston: Da Capo.

3. PSEUDOARKEOLOGY:
THE ARK AT THE END OF THE RAINBOW 275 BC

Alter, Robert, ed. 1997. *Genesis: Translation and Commentary*. New York: W. W. Norton.

Carroll, Robert Todd. 2003. "Noah's Ark." In *The Skeptic's Dictionary*. Hoboken, NJ: Wiley.

Feder, Kenneth. 1998. *Frauds, Myths and Mysteries: Science and Pseudoscience in Archaeology*. Mountain View, CA: Mayfield.

Frazier, Kenneth. 1994. "The Sorry Saga of CBS and Ark Pseudoscience: Network Drops Two Sun Programs, Keeps One." *Skeptical Inquirer* 18 (2): 117–18.

Lippard, Jim. 1993. "Sun Goes Down in Flames: The Jammal Ark Hoax." *Skeptic* 2 (3): 22–33.

Mitchell, Stephen, trans. 2006. *Gilgamesh: A New English Version*. New York: Atria Books.

Parkinson, William. 2004. "Questioning 'Flood Geology': Decisive New Evidence to End an Old Debate." *National Center for Science Education Reports*, 24 (1): 24–27.

Ryan, William, et al. 1997. "An Abrupt Drowning of the Black Sea Shelf." *Marine Geology* 138: 119–26.

4. PREDETERMINED COMBAT:
GLADIATORS AND PRO WRESTLERS 260 BC

Christesen, Paul, and Donald Kyle. 2014. *A Companion to Sport and Spectacle in Greek and Roman Antiquity*. Hoboken, NJ: Wiley Blackwell.

Fagan, Garrett. 2011. *The Lure of the Arena: Social Psychology and the Crowd at the Roman Games*. Cambridge: Cambridge University Press.

Grabianowski, Ed. 2016. "How Pro Wrestling Works." *HowStuffWorks*. http://entertainment.howstuffworks.com/pro-wrestling.htm.

PWMania.com. February 24, 2016. "Roman Reigns Gets Blood Capsule Slipped to Him on WWE Raw." www.pwmania.com/roman-reigns-gets-blood-capsule-slipped-to-him-on-wwe-raw-video.

Young, Emma. January 19, 2005. "Gladiators Fought for Thrills, Not Kills." *New Scientist*. www.newscientist.com/article/mg18524834-400-gladiators-fought-for-thrills-not-kills.

5. SELLING EMPIRES:
THE JULIAN PURCHASE AD 193

Bingham, Sandra J. 2013. *The Praetorian Guard: A History of Rome's Elite Special Forces*. Waco, TX: Baylor University Press.

Birley, Anthony R. 1999. *Septimius Severus: The African Emperor*. New York: Routledge.

Echols, Edward C., trans. 1961. *Herodian of Antioch's History of the Roman Empire from the Death of Marcus Aurelius to the Accession of Gordian III*. Berkeley: University of California Press.

Gibbon, Edward. 2001. *The History of the Decline and Fall of the Roman Empire. Vol. 1*. New York: Penguin Classics.

Kelly, Christopher. 2007. *The Roman Empire: A Very Short Introduction*. New York: Oxford University Press.

6. CRYPTOZOOLOGY:
THE LOCH NESS MONSTER AD 563

Adomnàn of Iona. 1995. *Life of St. Columba*. Translated by Richard Sharpe. New York: Penguin Classics.

Campbell, Steuart. 1997. *The Loch Ness Monster: The Evidence*. Amherst, NY: Prometheus Books.

Dinsdale, Tim. 1976. *Loch Ness Monster*. London: Routledge & Kegan Paul.

Hall, Jamie. 2005. "Lake Monsters." The Cryptid Zoo. www.newanimal.org/lake-monsters.htm.

Scott, Peter, and Robert Rines. 1975. "Naming the Loch Ness Monster." *Nature* 258: 466–68.

Victor, Daniel. April 13, 2016. "Loch Ness Monster Is Found! (Kind of. Not really.)" *New York Times*.

Wilder, Billy, dir. 1970. *The Private Life of Sherlock Holmes*. United Artists.

7. SACRED RELICS:
THE PRECIOUS PREPUCE AD 800

de Voragine, Jacobus. 1993. *The Golden Legend: Readings on the Saints*. 2 vols. Translated by William Granger Ryan. Princeton, NJ: Princeton University Press.

Geary, Patrick J. 1991. *Furta Sacra: Thefts of Relics in the Central Middle Ages*. Princeton, NJ: Princeton University Press.

Holmes, William, ed. 1997. *The Lost Books of the Bible Being All the Gospels, Epistles, and Other Pieces Now Extant Attributed in the First Four Centuries to Jesus Christ, His Apostles and Their Companions*. New York: Bell.

Jacobs, Andrew. 2012. *Christ Circumcised: A Study in Early Christian History and Difference*. Philadelphia: University of Pennsylvania Press.

Palazzo, Robert. 2005. "The Veneration of the Sacred Foreskin(s) of Baby Jesus—A Documented Analysis." In *Multicultural Europe and Cultural Exchange in the Middle Ages and Renaissance*, edited by J. P. Helfers, 155–76. Turnhout, Belgium: Brepols.

Shell, Marc. 1997. "The Holy Foreskin; or, Money, Relics, and Judeo-Christianity." In *Jews and Other Differences: The New Jewish Cultural Studies*, edited by Jonathan Boyarin and Daniel Boyarin, 345–59. Minneapolis: University of Minnesota Press.

Thiede, Carsten Peter, and Matthew d'Ancona. 2003. *The Quest for the True Cross*. New York: Palgrave Macmillan.

8. GENDER BENDING:
POPE JOAN AD 855

Cooney, Kara. 2015. *The Woman Who Would Be King: Hatshepsut's Rise to Power in Ancient Egypt*. New York: Broadway Books.

Hildegard of Bingen. 2002. *Selected Writings*. Edited by Mark Atherton. New York: Penguin Classics.

New, Maria. 2011. "Ancient History of Congenital Adrenal Hyperplasia." In *Pediatric Adrenal Diseases*, edited by Lucia Ghizzoni et al., 202–11. Basel: Karger.

New, Maria, and Elizabeth Kitzinger. 1993. "Pope Joan: A Recognizable Syndrome." *Journal of Clinical Endocrinology and Metabolism* 76: 3–13.

Royidis, Emmanuel. 2003. *Pope Joan*. Translated by Lawrence Durrell. London: Peter Owen.

Stanford, Peter. 1999. *The Legend of Pope Joan: In Search of the Truth*. New York: Henry Holt.

9. SINDONOLOGY:
THE SHROUD OF TURIN AD 1390

Damon, Paul, et al. 1989. "Radiocarbon Dating of the Shroud of Turin." *Nature* 337: 611–15.

de Voragine, Jacobus. 1993. *The Golden Legend: Readings on the Saints*. 2 vols. Translated by William Granger Ryan. Princeton, NJ: Princeton University Press.

Haberman, Clyde. June 11, 1989. "Despite Tests, Turin Shroud Is Still Revered." *New York Times*.

Leclercq, Henri. 1907. "The Legend of Abgar." In *The Catholic Encyclopedia*. Vol. 1. New York: Robert Appleton Company.

Wilson, Ian. 1991. *Holy Faces, Secret Places*. Garden City, NY: Doubleday.

Wilson, Ian. 2011. *The Shroud: The 2000-Year-Old Mystery Solved*. New York: Bantam.

10. RENAISSANCE REPROBATES:
MICHELANGELO'S CUPID AD 1488

Conway, Roderick Morris. November 23, 2002. "A Gathering of Renaissance Masters." *New York Times*.

Norton, Paul F. 1957. "The Lost Sleeping Cupid of Michelangelo." *Art Bulletin* 39 (4): 251–57.

Pepys, Samuel. 1970–1983. *The Diary of Samuel Pepys: A New and Complete Transcription*. Vol. 6. Edited by Robert Latham and William Matthews. Berkeley: University of California Press.

Shattuck, Kathryn. April 18, 2005. "An Ancient Masterpiece or a Master's Forgery?" *New York Times*.

Vasari, Giorgio. 1988. *The Lives of the Artists*. Vol. 1. Translated by George Bull. London: Penguin Classics.

11. FRAUDULENT ETHNICITY:
PSALMANAZAR AD 1703

Collins, Paul. 2001. *Banvard's Folly*. New York: Picador.

Keevak, Michael. 2004. *The Pretended Asian: George Psalmanazar's Eighteenth-Century Formosan Hoax*. Detroit: Wayne State University Press.

Lynch, Jack. 2005. "Forgery as Performance Art: The Strange Case of George Psalmanazar, 1650–1850." In *Ideas, Aesthetics, and Inquiries in the Early Modern Era*, vol. 11, edited by Kevin L. Cope. New York: AMS Press.

Psalmanazar, George. 1704. *An Historical and Geographical Description of Formosa of himself from the reflections of a Jesuit...Illustrated with several cuts*. 2010 Reprint. Farmington Hills, MI: Gale Ecco.

12. ROMANTIC SUICIDE:
THOMAS CHATTERTON AD 1770

Ackroyd, Peter. 1996. *Chatterton*. New York: Grove Press.

Cook, Elizabeth, ed. *John Keats: The Major Works, Including Endymion, the Odes and Selected Letters*. New York: Oxford University Press.

Groom, Nick, ed. 1999. *Thomas Chatterton and Romantic Culture*. New York: Palgrave Macmillan.

Poetry Foundation. Accessed 2016. "*Thomas Chatterton*." www.poetryfoundation.org/poems-and-poets/poets/detail/thomas-chatterton.

Shelley, Percy Bysshe. 1887. *Adonais—An Elegy on the Death of John Keats*. www.poetryfoundation.org/poems-and-poets/poems/detail/45112.

Timmons, J. W. 1999. *A "Fatal Remedy": Melancholy and Self-Murder in Eighteenth-Century England*. Princeton, NJ: Princeton University Press.

13. COUNTERFEIT WINE:
THOMAS JEFFERSON'S LAFITE
AD 1784

Keefe, Patrick Radden. September 3, 2007.
"The Jefferson Bottles." *New Yorker,* 1–10.

Robinson, Jancis, ed. 2006. *The Oxford Companion to Wine.* 3rd ed. New York: Oxford University Press, 4, 26–27.

Steinberger, M. June 2010. "What's in the Bottle?" *Slate.* www.slate.com/articles/life/drink/2010/06/whats_in_the_bottle.html.

Tattersall, Ian, and Rob DeSalle. 2015. *A Natural History of Wine.* New Haven, CT: Yale University Press.

Wallace, Benjamin. 2008. *The Billionaire's Vinegar.* New York: Crown.

14. PSEUDOSHAKESPEARE:
THE BOY WHO WOULD BE BARD
AD 1795

Ireland, William Henry. 1794. "*Vortigern, an Historical Play.*" Reproduced by Vortigern Studies. Accessed 2017. www.vortigernstudies.org.uk/artlit/vortigern.htm.

Ireland, William Henry. 1796. *Miscellaneous Papers and Legal Instruments Under the Hand and Seal of William Shakespeare.* Beinecke Rare Book & Manuscript Library. Accessed 2017. http://brbl-dl.library.yale.edu/vufind/Record/3582266.

———. 1874. *Confessions of William-Henry Ireland: Containing the Particulars of His Fabrication of the Shakespeare Manuscripts.* Reproduced by Archive.org. Accessed 2017. https://archive.org/details/confessionsofwil01irel.

Shea, Christopher. October 24, 2016. "New Oxford Shakespeare Edition Credits Christopher Marlowe as a Co-Author." *New York Times.*

Stewart, Doug. 2010. *The Boy Who Would Be Shakespeare: A Tale of Forgery and Folly.* Boston: Da Capo.

15. CRYPTOANTHROPOLOGY:
THE SAGA OF BIGFOOT AD 1811

Bigfoot Field Research Organization. 2017. "Geographic Database of Bigfoot / Sasquatch Sightings & Reports." www.bfro.net/gdb.

Gisondi, Joe. 2016. *Monster Trek: The Obsessive Search for Bigfoot.* Lincoln: University of Nebraska Press.

Krantz, Grover S. 1999. *Bigfoot Sasquatch: Evidence.* Blaine, WA: Hancock House.

Redfern, Nick. 2015. *Bigfoot Book: The Encyclopedia of Sasquatch, Yeti and Cryptid Primates.* Detroit: Visible Ink.

Sykes, Bryan. 2016. *Bigfoot, Yeti, and the Last Neanderthal: A Geneticist's Search for Modern Apemen.* Newburyport, MA: Disinformation Books.

Than, Ker. August 20, 2008. "Bigfoot Hoax: 'Body' Is Rubber Suit." National Geographic News. http://news.nationalgeographic.com/news/2008/08/080820-bigfoot-body.html.

16. IMAGINARY LANDS:
POYAIS AD 1822

Daily Grifter. 2010. "Gregor MacGregor: The Prince of Poyais." http://thedailygrifter.blogspot.com/2010/06/gregor-macgregor-prince-of-poyais.html.

Economist. December 22, 2012. "The King of Con-Men."

Love, Dane. 2007. *The Man Who Sold Nelson's Column and Other Scottish Frauds and Hoaxes.* Edinburgh: Birlinn.

Moen, Jon. October 2001. "John Law and the Mississippi Bubble: 1718–1720." Mississippi History Now. www.mshistory.k12.ms.us/articles/70/john-law-and-the-mississippi-bubble-1718-1720.

Sinclair, David. 2004. *The Land That Never Was: Sir Gregor MacGregor and the Most Audacious Fraud in History.* Boston: Da Capo.

17. ALTERNATE REALITIES:
FAKED PHOTOGRAPHS AD 1840

Bronx Documentary Center. 2015. "Altered Images: 150 Years of Posed and Manipulated Documentary Photography." www.alteredimagesbdc.org.

Brugioni, Dino A. 1999. *Photo Fakery: The History and Techniques of Photographic Deception and Manipulation.* Dulles, VA: Brassey's.

Cooper, Joe. 1998. *The Case of the Cottingley Fairies.* Eureka, CA: New York: Pocket Books.

Doyle, Arthur Conan. 2006. *The Coming of the Fairies.* Lincoln: University of Nebraska Press.

Fourandsix Technologies. Accessed 2017. "Photo Tampering Throughout History." http://pth.izitru.com.

Gernsheim, Helmut, and Alison Gernsheim. 1956. *L.J.M. Daguerre (1787–1851), the World's First Photographer.* Wenatchee, WA: World Publishing.

Griffiths, Frances, and Christine Lynch. 2009. *Reflections on the Cottingley Fairies: Frances Griffiths—In Her Own Words.* Warsaw, ONT: JMJ Publications.

Kaplan, Louis. 2008. *The Strange Case of William Mumler, Spirit Photographer.* Minneapolis: University of Minnesota Press.

King, David. 1997. *The Commissar Vanishes: The Falsification of Photographs and Art in Stalin's Russia.* New York: Metropolitan Books.

Lemagny, Jean-Claude, and Andre Rouille. 1987. *A History of Photography*. New York: Cambridge University Press.

Natale, Simone. 2016. *Supernatural Entertainments: Victorian Spiritualism and the Rise of Modern Media Culture*. University Park: Pennsylvania State University Press.

18. AERIAL FEATS:
EDGAR ALLAN POE AND THE GREAT BALLOON HOAX AD 1844

Goodman, Matthew. 2008. *The Sun and the Moon: The Remarkable True Account of Hoaxers, Showmen, Dueling Journalists, and Lunar Man-Bats in Nineteenth-Century New York*. New York: Basic Books.

Poe, Edgar Allan. 1844. "The Balloon-Hoax." Reproduced by Poestories.com. Accessed 2017. http://poestories.com/read/balloonhoax.

———. 2012. *Complete Tales and Poems*. New York: Fall River Press.

———. 1850. "The Imp of the Perverse." Reproduced by Poestories.com. Accessed 2017. http://poestories.com/read/imp.

———. 1850. "The Unparalleled Adventure of One Hans Pfaall." Reproduced by The Edgar Allan Poe Society of Baltimore. Modified January 12, 2016. http://www.eapoe.org/works/tales/unphlle.htm.

Sassaman, Richard. 1993. "The Tell-Tale Hoax." *Air & Space* 8 (3): 80–83.

19. COMMUNING WITH THE DEPARTED:
SPIRITUALISM AND EVOLUTION AD 1848

Albanese, Catherine L. 2007. *A Republic of Mind and Spirit: A Cultural History of American Metaphysical Religion*. New Haven, CT: Yale University Press.

Bown, Nicola, Carolyn Burdett, and Pamela Thurschwell, eds. 2004. *The Victorian Supernatural*. Cambridge: Cambridge University Press.

Davenport, Reuben Briggs. 2014. *The Death-Blow to Spiritualism: Being the True Story of the Fox Sisters, as Revealed by Authority of Margaret Fox Kane and Catherine Fox Jencken*. Charleston, SC: Nabu Press.

Diniejko, Andrzej. 2013. "Sir Arthur Conan Doyle and Victorian Spiritualism." The Victorian Web. www.victorianweb.org/authors/doyle/spiritualism.html.

Doyle, Arthur Conan. 1926. *The History of Spiritualism*. 2 vols. New York: Doran.

Milner, Richard. October 1996. "Charles Darwin and Associates, Ghostbusters." *Scientific American*, 72–77.

———. 2015. "Wallace, Darwin, and the Spiritualism Scandal of 1876." *Skeptic* 20 (3): 29–35.

20. DIDDLING:
THE ORIGINAL CON MAN AD 1849

American Social History Productions. 2017. "'Arrest of the Confidence Man'—New York Herald, 1849." Reproduced by Lost Museum Archive. http://lostmuseum.cuny.edu/archive/arrest-of-the-confidence-man-newyork-herald.

Johnson, James F., and Floyd Miller. 1961. *The Man Who Sold the Eiffel Tower*. Garden City, NY: Doubleday.

Konnikova, Maria. 2016. *The Confidence Game: Why We Fall for It…Every Time*. New York: Viking.

Melville, Herman. 1991. *The Confidence-Man: His Masquerade*. New York: Penguin Classics.

Paulhus, Delroy L. 2014. "Toward a Taxonomy of Dark Personalities." *Current Directions in Psychological Science* 23 (6): 421–26.

Poe, Edgar Allan. 1843. "Raising the Wind; or, Diddling Considered as One of the Exact Sciences." *Philadelphia Saturday Courier* XIII (655). Reproduced by The Edgar Allan Poe Society of Baltimore. Modified August 17, 2015. www.eapoe.org/works/tales/diddlnga.htm.

Usher, Shaun. 2012. "10 Commandments for Con Men." Lists of Note. www.listsofnote.com/2012/02/10-commandments-for-con-men.html.

21. PSEUDOARCHAEOLOGY:
THE DAVENPORT TABLETS AD 1867

Adovasio, J. M., and Jake Page. 2003. *The First Americans: In Pursuit of Archaeology's Greatest Mystery*. New York: Modern Library.

Dillehay, Thomas D. 2000. *The Settlement of the Americas: A New Prehistory*. New York: Basic Books.

Feder, Kenneth L. 2005. *Frauds, Myths, and Mysteries: Science and Pseudoscience in Archaeology*. New York: McGraw-Hill.

Fell, Barry. 1976. *America B.C.: Ancient Settlers in the New World*. New York: Quadrangle/New York Times Books.

McKusick, Marshall Bassford. 1991. *The Davenport Conspiracy Revisited*. Ames: Iowa State University Press.

Priest, Josiah. 2005. *American Antiquities and Discoveries in the West*. Colfax, WI: Hayriver Press.

Silverberg, Robert. 1968. *Mound Builders of Ancient America: The Archaeology of a Myth*. Greenwich, CT: New York Graphic Society.

Squier, Ephraim G., and Edwin H. Davis. 1998. *Ancient Monuments of the Mississippi Valley*. Washington, DC: Smithsonian Books.

Stanford, Dennis, and Brian Bradley. 2002. "The Solutrean Solution." *Scientific American Discovering Archaeology* 2: 54–55.

Williams, Stephen. 1991. *Fantastic Archaeology*: *The Wild Side of North American Prehistory*. Philadelphia: University of Pennsylvania Press.

22. ULTIMATE DIETS:
BREATHARIANISM AD 1869

BBC News. September 21, 1999. "Woman 'Starved Herself to Death.'" http://news.bbc.co.uk/2/hi/uk_news/scotland/453661.stm.

Brumberg, Joan Jacobs. 2000. *Fasting Girls*: *The History of Anorexia Nervosa*. New York: Vintage Books.

Inedia Musings. 2015. *Complete Science of Breatharianism*. Richmond/Surrey, UK: The Book Shed.

Jasmuheen. 2011. *Ambassadors of Light*: *Living on Light*. Buderim, AUS: Self Empowerment Academy.

Jauregui, Andres. February 28, 2014. "'Breatharian' Barbie Valeria Lukyanova Says She Wants to Live Off Light and Air Alone." *Huffington Post*. www.huffingtonpost.com/2014/02/28/breatharian-barbie-valeria-lukyanova_n_4873706.html.

Yahoo News. October 25, 1999. "Fresh-Air Dietician Fails TV Show's Challenge." www.caic.org.au/miscult/breatharians/Fresh-air%20dietician%20fails%20TV%20show%27s%20challenge.htm.

23. DEATHBED CONVERSIONS:
THE LADY HOPE AD 1882

Clark, Ronald W. 1985. *The Survival of Charles Darwin*: *A Biography of a Man and an Idea*. London: Weidenfeld and Nicolson.

Darwin, Charles. 1958. *The Autobiography of Charles Darwin 1809–1882*. London: Collins.

———. 2003. *The Origin of Species*. 150th anniv. ed. New York: Signet Classic.

Malec, Grzegorz. 2015. "Charles Darwin and Lady Hope—The Legend Still Alive." *Hybris* 29: 126–48.

24. FORGED DOCUMENTS:
THE PRIORY OF SION AD 1886

Baigent, Michael, Richard Leigh, and Henry Lincoln. 1982. *The Holy Blood and the Holy Grail*: *The Secret History of Christ*, *The Shocking Legacy of the Grail*. London: Jonathan Cape.

Brown, Dan. 2003. *The Da Vinci Code*. New York: Doubleday.

Introvigne, Massimo. 2005. "Beyond *The Da Vinci Code*: History and Myth of the Priory of Sion." CESNUR International Conference. www.cesnur.org/2005/pa_introvigne.htm.

Polidoro, Massimo. 2004. "The Secrets of Rennes-le-Château." *Skeptical Inquirer* 28 (6). www.csicop.org/si/show/secrets_of_rennes_le_chacircteau.

Wilson, Ian. 1984. *Jesus: The Evidence*. New York: Harper and Row.

Wrixon, Fred B. 2005. *Codes, Ciphers, Secrets and Cryptic Communication*: *Making and Breaking Secret Messages from Hieroglyphs to the Internet*. New York: Black Dog & Leventhal.

25. PUBLIC CREDULITY:
POLITICAL LIES AD 1888

Foner, Philip S. 1972. *The Spanish-Cuban-American War and the Birth of American Imperialism 1895–1902*. 2 vols. New York/London: Monthly Review Press.

Moïse, Edwin E. 1996. *Tonkin Gulf and the Escalation of the Vietnam War*. Chapel Hill: University of North Carolina Press.

Nyhan, Brendan, and Jason Reifler. 2010. "When Corrections Fail: The Persistence of Political Misperceptions." *Political Behavior* 32 (2): 303–30.

On the Media. 2016. "A Recent History of Political Lies." Podcast and transcript online at www.wnyc.org/story/on-the-media-2016-07-08.

Tattersall, Ian. 2012. *Masters of the Planet: The Search for Our Human Origins*. New York: Palgrave Macmillan.

Wilson, Joseph. 2004. *The Politics of Truth*. New York: Carroll & Graf.

26. POLITICAL PERSECUTIONS:
THE DREYFUS AFFAIR AD 1894

Arendt, Hannah. 1951. *Antisemitism: Part One of the Origins of Totalitarianism*. New York: Harcourt Brace Jovanovich.

Begley, Louis. 2009. *Why the Dreyfus Affair Matters*. New Haven, CT: Yale University Press.

Burns, Michael. 1991. *Dreyfus: A Family Affair, 1789–1945*. New York: HarperCollins.

Whyte, George R. 2008. *The Dreyfus Affair: A Chronological History*. New York: Palgrave Macmillan.

27. FINANCIAL FRAUD:
THE SCAMMER SCAMMED AD 1899

Gribben, Mark. Accessed 2017. "The Franklin Syndicate." The Malefactor's Register. http://malefactorsregister.com/wp/the-franklin-syndicate.

Henriques, Diana B. 2012. *The Wizard of Lies: Bernie Madoff and the Death of Trust*. New York: St. Martin's Griffin.

Markopolos, Harry, and Frank Casey. 2010. *No One Would Listen: A True Financial Thriller*. New York: John Wiley & Sons.

Soltes, Eugene. 2016. *Why They Do It: Inside the Mind of the White-Collar Criminal*. New York: PublicAffairs.

Zuckoff, Mitchell. 2005. *Ponzi's Scheme: The True Story of a Financial Legend*. New York: Random House.

28. FAKE PALEOANTHROPOLOGY:
PILTDOWN AD 1908

De Groote, Isabelle, et al. 2016. "New Genetic and Morphological Evidence Suggests a Single Hoaxer Created 'Piltdown Man.'" *Royal Society Open Science* 3: 160328.

Spencer, Frank. 1990. *Piltdown: A Scientific Forgery*. Oxford: Oxford University Press.

Tattersall, Ian. 1995. *The Fossil Trail: How We Know What We Think We Know About Human Evolution*. New York: Oxford University Press.

Weiner, Joseph. S., and Chris B. Stringer. 2003. *The Piltdown Forgery*. 50th anniv. ed. Oxford: Oxford University Press.

29. ARCTIC EXPLORATION:
ROBERT PEARY AD 1909

Amundsen, Roald. 1912. *The South Pole: An Account of the Norwegian Expedition in the 'Fram,' 1910–12.* 2 vols. London: John Murray.

Bartlett, Robert A. 2006. *The Log of Bob Bartlett: The True Story of Forty Years of Seafaring and Exploration*. Paradise, Newfoundland: Flanker Press.

Bruni, Frank. April 30, 2016. "The Many Faces of Dennis Hastert." *New York Times*.

Bryce, Robert. 1997. *Cook and Peary: The Polar Controversy Resolved*. Mechanicsburg, PA: Stackpole Books.

Davies, Thomas D. 1990. "New Evidence Places Peary at the Pole." *National Geographic* 177 (1): 46–60.

Henson, Matthew. July 17, 1910. "Matt Henson Tells the Real Story of Peary's Trip to the Pole." *Boston American*.

Herbert, Wally. 1988. "Did Peary Reach the Pole?" *National Geographic* 174 (3): 387–413.

Huntford, Roland. 2001. *Nansen*. London: Abacus.

———. 1980. *Scott & Amundsen: The Race to the South Pole*. New York: G. P. Putnam's Sons.

National Geographic. Peary Arctic Expedition. www.nationalgeographic.com/photography/photos/north-pole-expeditions/.

Peary, Robert. 1910. *North Pole: Its Discovery in 1909 Under the Auspices of the Peary Arctic Club*. New York: Frederick A. Stokes.

Rawlins, Dennis. 1973. *Peary at the North Pole: Fact or Fiction?* Fairfield, CT: R. B. Luce.

Rensberger, Boyce. November 2, 1988. "Explorer Bolsters Case Against Peary." *Washington Post*.

Roberts, David. 2001. *Great Exploration Hoaxes*. New York: Modern Library.

Uusma, Bea. 2014. *The Expedition: The Forgotten Story of a Polar Tragedy*. London: Head of Zeus.

30. QUACK MEDICINE:
RADIONICS AD 1910

Abrams, Albert. 2010. *The Electronic Reactions of Abrams*. Whitefish, MT: Kessinger.

Hudgings, William. 1923. "Dr. Abrahms Electron Theory." Reproduced by Sympathetic Vibratory Physics. Accessed May 30, 2017. www.svpvril.com/Abrahm.html.

Lescarboura, Austin C. September 1924. "Our Abrams Verdict: The Electronic Reactions of Abrams and Electronic Medicine in General Found Utterly Worthless." *Scientific American*: 158–60.

Macklis, Roger M. 1993. "Magnetic Healing, Quackery, and the Debate About the Health Effects of Electromagnetic Fields." *Annals of Internal Medicine* 18: 376–83.

Sinclair, Upton. 2015. *The Book of Life*. www.gutenberg.org/ebooks/38117.

31. MYTHOGENESIS:
THE SIX MONA LISAS AD 1911

Decker, Karl. June 25, 1932. "Why and How the Mona Lisa Was Stolen." *Saturday Evening Post*.

Nilsson, Jeff. December 7, 2013. "100 Years Ago: The Mastermind Behind the Mona Lisa Heist." *Saturday Evening Post*.

Scotti, R. A. 2009. *Vanished Smile: The Mysterious Theft of Mona Lisa*. New York: Knopf.

32. FAKE MUSIC:
FRITZ KREISLER AD 1913

Biancolli, Amy. 1998. *Fritz Kreisler: Love's Sorrow, Love's Joy.* Portland, OR: Amadeus.

Burwick, Frederick, and Paul Douglass, eds. 1988. *A Selection of Hebrew Melodies, Ancient and Modern, by Isaac Nathan and Lord Byron.* Tuscaloosa: University of Alabama Press.

Campbell, Margaret. 1981. *The Great Violinists.* New York: Doubleday.

Guardian Music. May 1, 2015. "Milli Vanilli Man Attempts Comeback—with the Man Who Actually Sang the Songs." *Guardian.* www.theguardian.com/music/2015/may/01/milli-vanilli-fab-morvan-comeback-man-who-actually-sang.

Kreisler, Fritz. 1915. *Four Weeks in the Trenches: The War Story of a Violinist.* Boston and New York: Houghton Mifflin.

Riding, Alan. February 17, 2007. "A Pianist's Recordings Draw Praise, but Were They All Hers?" *New York Times.*

Schoenbaum, David. November 9, 2012. "Dietmar Machold, Dealer of Expensive Violins, Gets 6 Years in Prison in Austria." *Washington Post.*

33. PSEUDOPLANETOLOGY:
FLAT AND HOLLOW EARTHS AD 1914

Adams, Frank Dawson. 1954. *The Birth and Development of the Geological Sciences.* New York: Dover Publications.

Burroughs, Edgar Rice. 2006. *At the Earth's Core.* West Valley City, UT: Waking Lion Press.

Gardner, Martin. 1957. *Fads and Fallacies in the Name of Science.* 2nd ed., rev. New York: Dover Publications.

Garwood, Christine. 2008. *Flat Earth: The History of an Infamous Idea.* New York: Thomas Dunne Books.

Griffin, Duane. 2012. "What Curiosity in the Structure: The Hollow Earth in Science." In *Between Science and Fiction: The Hollow Earth as Concept and Conceit,* edited by Hanjo Berressem, Michael Bucher, and Uwe Schwagmeier, 3–34. Münster, Germany: Lit Verlag.

Halley, Edmond. 1692. "An Account of the Cause of the Change of the Variation of the Magnetick Needle, with an Hypothesis of the Structure of the Internal Parts of the Earth." *Philosophical Transactions of the Royal Society of London* 17 (195): 563–78.

Miller, Jay Earle. October 1931. "$5,000 for Proving the Earth a Globe." *Modern Mechanics and Inventions:* 70–74, 200–4.

Standish, David. 2006. *Hollow Earth: The Long and Curious History of Imagining Strange Lands, Fantastical Creatures, Advanced Civilizations, and Marvelous Machines Below the Earth's Surface.* Cambridge, MA: Da Capo.

Symmes, Americus. 1878. *The Symmes Theory of Concentric Spheres, Demonstrating that the Earth Is Hollow, Habitable Within, and Widely Open About the Poles.* 2nd ed. Louisville, KY: Bradley and Gilbert.

[Teed, Cyrus], and Ulysses Morrow. 1975. *The Cellular Cosmogony; or, The Earth a Concave Sphere.* Edited by Robert Fogarty. Philadelphia: Porcupine Press.

34. FAKE ART:
TRIBUTE OR EXPLOITATION?
AD 1936

Ewell, Bernard. 2014. *Artful Dodgers: Fraud and Foolishness in the Art Market.* Bloomington, IA: Abbott Press.

Hamlin, Jesse. July 29, 1999. "Painting Forger Elmyr de Hory's Copies Are Like the Real Thing." *San Francisco Chronicle.*

Irving, Clifford. 1969. *Fake! The Story of Elmyr de Hory, the Greatest Art Forger of Our Time.* New York: McGraw-Hill.

Lopez, Jonathan. 2009. *The Man Who Made Vermeers: Unvarnishing the Legend of Master Forger Han van Meegeren.* New York: Mariner Books.

35. DIALECTICAL BIOLOGY:
LYSENKOISM AND ITS CONSEQUENCES AD 1938

Carey, Nessa. 2013. *The Epigenetics Revolution: How Modern Biology Is Rewriting Our Understanding of Genetics, Disease and Inheritance.* New York: Columbia University Press.

Ings, Simon, 2016. *Stalin and the Scientists: A History of Triumph and Tragedy.* New York: Atlantic Monthly Press.

Kammerer, Paul. 1923. "Experiments on Clona and Alytes." *Nature,* 2823 (112): 826–27.

Koestler, Arthur. 1973. *The Case of the Midwife Toad.* New York: Vintage.

Koltzoff, Nikolai K. 1934. "The Structure of the Chromosomes in the Salivary Glands of Drosophila." *Science* 80 (2075): 312–13.

Lamarck, Jean Baptiste. 2015. *Zoological Philosophy: An Exposition with Regard to the Natural History of Animals.* London: Forgotten Books.

Lysenko, Trofim. 1948. *The Science of Biology Today.* New York: International Publishers.

Muller, Hermann J. 1948. "The Destruction of Science in the USSR." *Saturday Review of Literature* XXXI (49): 13–15, 63–65.

Noble, G. Kingsley. 1926. "Kammerer's Alytes." *Nature* 2962 (118): 209–11.

Soyfer, Valery N. 2001. "The Consequences of Political Dictatorship for Russian Science." *Nature Reviews Genetics* 2: 723–29.

Zirkle, Conway, ed. 1949. *Death of a Science in Russia: The Fate of Genetics as Described in* Pravda *and Elsewhere*. Philadelphia: University of Pennsylvania Press.

36. COUNTERFEIT CADAVERS:
"THE MAN WHO NEVER WAS"
AD 1943

Macintyre, Ben. 2011. *Operation Mincemeat: How a Dead Man and a Bizarre Plan Fooled the Nazis and Assured an Allied Victory*. New York: Harmony Books.

Montagu, Ewen. 1953. *The Man Who Never Was*. Philadelphia: J. B. Lippincott.

Smyth, Denis. 2010. *Deathly Deception: The Real Story of Operation Mincemeat*. New York: Oxford University Press.

37. INVENTED IDENTITIES:
KORLA PANDIT AD 1948

de Clue, David. 2006. "Korla Pandit (aka John Roland Redd, aka Juan Rolando)." Official Korla Pandit Website. www.korlapandit.com/historyparttwo.htm.

Smith, R. J. 2001. "The Many Faces of Korla Pandit." *Los Angeles* 46 (6): 72–77, 146–51.

Turner, John. May 31, 2016. "How a Black Man from Missouri Passed as an Indian Pop Star." *Atlas Obscura*. www.atlasobscura.com/articles/how-a-black-man-from-missouri-passed-as-an-indian-pop-star.

Zack, Jessica. August 15, 2015. "Exotic Korla Pandit Hid Race Under Swami Persona." *San Francisco Chronicle*.

38. MISGUIDED ARCHAEOLOGY:
A LION IN WINTER AD 1964

Adovasio, J. M., and David Pedler. 2016. *Strangers in a New Land: What Archaeology Reveals About the First Americans*. A Peter N. Névraumont Book. Richmond Hills, ONT: Firefly Books.

Haynes, Vance. 1973. "The Calico Site: Artifacts or Geofacts?" *Science* 181: 305–9.

Johanson, Donald, and Blake Edgar. *From Lucy to Language. Rev. ed*. A Peter N. Névraumont Book. New York: Simon & Schuster.

Leakey, Louis S. B., Ruth DeEtte Simpson, and Thomas Clements. 1968. "Archaeological Excavations in the Calico Mountains, California: Preliminary Report." *Science* 160: 1022–23.

Leakey, Louis S. B., Ruth DeEtte Simpson, Thomas Clements, Rainer Berger, and John Witthoft. 1972. *Pleistocene Man at Calico*. San Bernardino, CA: San Bernardino County Museum Association.

Leakey, Mary. 1984. *Disclosing the Past*. London: Weidenfeld and Nicolson.

Morell, Virginia. 1996. *Ancestral Passions: The Leakey Family and the Quest for Humankind's Beginnings*. New York: Simon & Schuster.

Simpson, Ruth DeEtte. 1980. *The Personal History of the Early Years of the Calico Mountains Archaeological Site*. http://calicoarchaeology.com/pdf/deesimpson.pdf.

39. CIRCUMNAVIGATIONS THAT WEREN'T:
THE SAD SAGA OF DONALD CROWHURST AD 1968

Finkel, Donald. 1987. *The Wake of the Electron: A Narrative Poem*. New York: Atheneum.

Harris, John. 1981. *Without Trace: The Last Voyages of Eight Ships*. London: Methuen.

McCrum, Robert. April 4, 2009. "Deep Water." *Guardian*.

Nichols, Peter. 2001. *A Voyage for Madmen*. New York: HarperCollins.

Stone, Robert. 1998. *Outerbridge Reach*. Boston: Houghton Mifflin.

Tomalin, Nicholas, and Ron Hall. 1970. *The Strange Last Voyage of Donald Crowhurst*. London: Hodder and Stoughton.

40. LUNACY:
CONSPIRACY THEORIES AD 1969

Fox, Josh. December 28, 2012. "10 Reasons the Moon Landings Could Be a Hoax." ListVerse. http://listverse.com/2012/12/28/10-reasons-the-moon-landings-could-be-a-hoax.

Interesting Things. 2013. "Skeleton on the Moon." http://interestingthings.info/mildly-interesting/skeleton-on-the-moon.html.

National Geographic Magazine. 2009. "Eight Moon-Landing Hoax Myths—Busted." http://news.nationalgeographic.com/news/2009/07/photogalleries/apollo-moon-landing-hoax-pictures/.

Nyhan, Brendan, and Jason Reifler. 2010. "When Corrections Fail: The Persistence of Political Misperceptions." *Political Behavior* 32 (2): 303–30.

Shermer, Michael. December 1, 2014. "Why Do People Believe in Conspiracy Theories?" *Scientific American*. www.scientificamerican.com/article/why-do-people-believe-in-conspiracy-theories/.

Uscinski, Joseph E., and Joseph M. Parent. 2014. *American Conspiracy Theories*. New York: Oxford University Press.

41. HUMAN VARIATION:
THE FALLACY OF RACE AD 1972

Cavalli-Sforza, Luigi Luca, and Francesco Cavalli-Sforza. 1995. *The Great Human Diasporas: The History of Diversity and Evolution*. Reading, MA: Addison-Wesley.

Cavalli-Sforza, Luigi Luca, Paolo Menozzi, and Alberto Piazza. 1995. *The History and Geography of Human Genes*. Princeton, NJ: Princeton University Press.

Haeckel, Ernst. 1884. *The History of Creation; or, the Development of the Earth and Its Inhabitants by the Action of Natural Causes*. Vols. 1 and 2. New York: Amazon Digital Services.

Jablonski, Nina. 2006. *Skin: A Natural History*. Berkeley: University of California Press.

Lewontin, Richard. 1972. "The Apportionment of Human Diversity." *Evolutionary Biology*, 6: 381–98.

Prado-Martinez, Javier, et al. 2013. "Great Ape GeneticDiversity and Population History." *Nature* 499: 471–75.

Sussman, Richard W. 2014. *The Myth of Race: The Troubling Persistence of an Unscientific Idea*. Cambridge, MA: Harvard University Press.

Tattersall, Ian, and Rob DeSalle. 2011. *Race?: Debunking a Scientific Myth*. College Station: Texas A&M University Press.

42. ETERNAL LIFE:
THE FROZEN SELF AD 1976

Altman, Lawrence K. July 26, 1988. "The Doctor's World; Ingenuity and a 'Miraculous' Revival." *New York Times*.

Cryogenic Society of America, Inc. 2017. www.cryogenicsociety.org.

Ettinger, Robert C. W. 1964. *The Prospect of Immortality*. New York: Doubleday.

Thomson, H. 2016. "The Big Freeze: Inside Timeship's Cryogenic Revolution." *New Scientist* 231 (3080): 26–31.

43. HOMEOPATHY:
THE MEMORY OF WATER AD 1988

BBC Horizon. 2002. "Homeopathy: The Test—Transcript." www.bbc.co.uk/science/horizon/2002/homeopathytrans.shtml (archived).

Davenas, Eau, et al. 1988. "Human Basophil Degranulation Triggered by Very Dilute Antiserum Against IgE." *Nature* 333: 816–18.

Ennis, Madeleine. 2010. "Basophil Models of Homeopathy: A Sceptical View." *Homeopathy* 99 (1): 51–56.

Maddox, John, James Randi, and Walter W. Stewart. 1988. "'High-Dilution' Experiments a Delusion." *Nature* 334: 287–90.

National Health and Medical Research Council. 2015. *Evidence on the Effectiveness of Homeopathy for Treating Health Conditions*. Canberra, AUS: National Health and Medical Research Council NHMRC Publication.

44. PSEUDOPALEONTOLOGY:
"ARCHAEORAPTOR" AD 1997

Dingus, Lowell, and Timothy Rowe. 1998. *The Mistaken Extinction: Dinosaur Evolution and the Origin of Birds*. New York: W. H. Freeman and Company.

Mayell, Hillary. November 20, 2002. "Dino Hoax Was Made of Ancient Bird, Study Shows." *National Geographic News*. http://news.nationalgeographic.com/news/2002/11/1120_021120_raptor.html.

Pickrell, John. November 15, 2014. "How Fake Fossils Pervert Paleontology." *Scientific American*. www.scientificamerican.com/article/how-fake-fossils-pervert-paleontology-excerpt/.

Rowe, Timothy, Richard A. Ketcham, Cambria Denison, Matthew Colbert, Xu Xing, and Philip J. Currie. 2001. "The *Archaeoraptor* Forgery." *Nature* 410: 539–40.

Simons, Lewis M. 2000. "*Archaeoraptor* Fossil Trail." *National Geographic* 197 (10): 128–32.

Sloan, Christopher P. 1999. "Feathers for *T. rex*? New Birdlike Fossils Are Missing Links in Dinosaur Evolution." *National Geographic* 196 (5): 98–107.

45. UNRELIABLE MEMORIES:
FAKE MEMOIRS AD 1997

Barthes, R. 1967. "The Death of the Author." *Aspen*. Reproduced by Literarism. December 30, 2011. http://literarism.blogspot.com/2011/12/roland-barthes-death-of-author.html.

Capote, Truman. 1965. *In Cold Blood*. New York: Random House.

Defonseca, Misha. 1997. *Misha: A Mémoire of the Holocaust Years.* Gloucester, MA: Mount Ivy.

Frey, James. 2003. *A Million Little Pieces.* New York: Doubleday Books.

Jack, Ian. June 17, 2011. "Albania's 'Second Greatest Living Writer' Was a Hoax, but Does It Really Matter?" *Guardian.*

Johnston, Ian. August 23, 2014. "Fake Memoirs: Academic Says We Should Not Disregard Books Because They Unexpectedly Change Genre." *Independent.*

Jones, Margaret B. [Margaret Seltzer]. 2008. *Love and Consequences: A Memoir of Hope and Survival.* New York: Riverhead Books.

Rosenblat, Herman. 2008 [withdrawn prior to publication]. *Angel at the Fence: The True Story of a Love That Survived.* New York: Berkley Books.

The Smoking Gun. January 4, 2006. "A Million Little Lies: Exposing James Frey's Fiction Addiction." www.thesmokinggun.com/documents/celebrity/million-little-lies?page=0,0.

46. IRRATIONAL HYSTERIA:
VACCINES AND AUTISM AD 1998

Deer, Brian. 2011. "How the Case Against the MMR Vaccine Was Fixed." *British Medical Journal* 342 (5347): 77–82. Online at www.bmj.com/bmj/section-pdf/186183?path=/bmj/342/7788/Feature.full.pdf.

———. January 11, 2011. "Timeline." *British Medical Journal.* Reproduced by Campbell M. Gold.com. Accessed May 30, 3017. www.campbellmgold.com/archive_blowing_in_the_wind/mmr_timeline_jan_2011.pdf.

DiResta, Renée, and Gilad Lotan. 2015. "Anti-vaxxers Are Using Twitter to Manipulate a Vaccine Bill." *Wired.* www.wired.com/2015/06/antivaxxers-influencing-legislation/.

Dominus, Susan. April 20, 2011. "The Crash and Burn of an Autism Guru." *New York Times Magazine.* www.nytimes.com/2011/04/24/magazine/mag-24Autism-t.html.

Godlee, Fiona, Jane Smith, and Harvey Marcovitch. 2011. "Wakefield's Article Linking MMR with Autism was Fraudulent." *British Medical Journal* 342: 64–66.

Sifferlin, Alexandra. March 17, 2014. "4 Diseases Making a Comeback Thanks to Anti-Vaxxers." *Time.* http://time.com/27308/4-diseases-making-a-comeback-thanks-to-anti-vaxxers.

Wakefield, Andrew J., et al. 1998. "Ileal-Lymphoid Nodular Hyperplasia, Non-specific Colitis, and Pervasive Developmental Disorder in Children." *Lancet* 351: 637–41 [retracted].

47. PEER REVIEW:
JAN HENDRIK SCHÖN AD 2000

Beasley, Malcolm R., Supriyo Datta, Herwig Kogelnik, Herbert Kroemer, and Don Monroe. 2002. "Report of the Investigation Committee on the Possibility of Scientific Misconduct in the Work of Hendrik Schön and Coauthors." Bell Labs. http://w.astro.berkeley.edu/~kalas/ethics/documents/schoen.pdf.

Chang, Kenneth. May 23, 2002. "Similar Graphs Raised Suspicions on Bell Labs Research." *New York Times.*

Murray, Cherry A., and Saswato R. Das. 2003. "The Price of Scientific Freedom." *Nature Materials* 2 (4): 204.

Reich, Eugenie Samuel. 2009. *Plastic Fantastic: How the Biggest Fraud in Physics Shook the Scientific World.* New York: Palgrave Macmillan.

Schön, Jan Hendrik, Christian Kloc, and Bertram Batlogg. 2000. "Fractional Quantum Hall Effect in Organic Molecular Semiconductors." *Science* 288 (5475): 2338–40. [Retracted]

Wade, Nicholas, and Choe Sang-Hun. January 10, 2006. "Researcher Faked Evidence of Human Cloning, Koreans Report." *New York Times.* www.nytimes.com/2006/01/10/science/10clone.html.

48. BOGUS SECURITY:
FAKE BOMB DETECTORS AD 2001

al-Salhy, Suadad. January 24, 2010. "Iraq Official Warned Against Anti-bomb Device Buy." uk.reuters.com/article/uk-iraq-britain-explosives-idUKTRE60N1MF20100124.

Higginbotham, Adam. July 11, 2013. "In Iraq, the Bomb-Detecting Device That Didn't Work, Except to Make Money." *BusinessWeek.*

Smith, Richard. March 21, 2013. "Jim McCormick: Con-Man Sold Golf Ball Finders as Bomb Detectors in 'Diabolical' £60m Scam Which Put Lives at Risk." *Daily Mirror.*

49. FAKED DEATHS:
PSEUDOCIDE AD 2002

Applebaum, Anne. December 10, 2007. "Getting Away from It All: Why Do So Many of Us Want to Disappear and Start Over?" *Slate.* www.slate.com/articles/news_and_politics/foreigners/2007/12/getting_away_from_it_all.html?y=1.

Askwith, Richard. October 10, 1999. "The Vanishing Season." *Independent on Sunday.*

Bhattarai, Abha, and Nelson D. Schwartz. July 3, 2008. "Fund Manager Who Faked His Suicide Surrenders." *New York Times.*

Forsyth, Frederick. 1972. *The Day of the Jackal*. New York: Viking Press.

Greenwood, Elizabeth. 2016. *Playing Dead*: *A Journey Through the World of Death Fraud*. New York: Simon & Schuster.

Knapp, Samuel L. 1858. *The Life of Lord Timothy Dexter, with Sketches of the Eccentric Characters That Composed the Associates, Including His Own Writings*. Boston: J. E. Tilton.

Pierce, Emmet. 2011. "Faking Death to Collect Life Insurance Money: A Life on the Run." Insure.com. www.insure.com/life-insurance/faking-death-for-life-insurance-money.html.

White, James. December 9, 2011. "'Faking your own death is easy…but coming back is hard!' Canoe Man John Darwin Boasts of How He Walked Around Home Town Disguised as an Old Man." *Daily Mail*. www.dailymail.co.uk/news/article-2072033/Canoe-man-John-Darwin-describes-easy-fake-death-life-insurance-payout.html.

50. FAKE JOURNALISM:
STEPHEN GLASS, JAYSON BLAIR, AND THEIR LEGACY AD 2003

Barry, Dan, David Barstow, Jonathan D. Glater, Adam Liptak, and Jacques Steinberg. May 11, 2003. "Correcting the Record; *Times* Reporter Who Resigned Leaves Long Trail of Deception." *New York Times*.

Blair, Jayson. 2004. *Burning Down My Masters' House*: *My Life at the* New York Times. London: New Millennium.

Connolly, Kate, et al. December 12, 2016. "Fake News: An Insidious Trend That's Fast Becoming a Global Problem." *Guardian*.

Fisher, Marc, John Woodrow Cox, and Peter Hermann. December 6, 2016. "Pizzagate: From Rumor, to Hashtag, to Gunfire in D.C." *Washington Post*.

Glass, Stephen. 2003. *The Fabulist*. New York: Simon & Schuster.

Mnookin, Seth. 2004. *Hard News*: *The Scandals at* The New York Times *and Their Meaning for American Media*. New York: Random House.

Morrison, Blake. March 19, 2004. "Ex-USA TODAY Reporter Faked Major Stories." *USA Today*.

EPILOGUE

Kaiser, David. 2009. "Physics and Pixie Dust." *American Scientist* November–December, 496–98.

Knowles, Eric S., and Jay A. Lin. 2004. "Approach-Avoidance Model of Persuasion: Alpha and Omega Strategies for Change." In *Resistance and Persuasion*, edited by Eric S. Knowles and Jay A. Linn. Mahwah, NJ: Lawrence Erlbaum Associates, pp. 117–48.

Konnikova, Maria. 2016. *The Confidence Game: Why We Fall For It…Every Time*. New York: Viking.

ACKNOWLEDGMENTS

For crucial assistance in obtaining illustrations, and for kindly providing valuable background information, the authors warmly thank: Dave Bergman; Sarah J. Biggs at the British Library; Albert D. Carlson at Stony Brook University; Albert D. Carlson III; D. Chris Cottrill at the National Air and Space Museum; Christina M. Deane at the University of Virginia Library; Simon Flavin at Mirrorpix; Mark Forgy, author of *The Forger's Apprentice*; Brad Goldstein at Resilience Communications, LLC; Michael Jones McKean at Virginia Commonwealth University; Bryan Kasik at the University of Virginia; Bill Koch; Eric Loss at Pangaea Exploration; Melissa Merson Ellison; Richard Milner/Milner Archive; Martin Mulholland of the U.S. Secret Service; Jamie Nathan at the National Library of Israel; David R. Nevraumont; Guy Newman at Alamy Stock Photo; Robert Newman at Biblical Theological Seminary; Pamela Patton at Princeton University; Timothy Rowe of the High-Resolution X-ray Computed Tomography Facility at the University of Texas at Austin; Mike Sampson of the U.S. Secret Service; Julie Stoner at the Library of Congress; Chris Stringer and the Natural History Museum, London; John Turner; and Michelle Wright at the Library of Congress.

We are deeply indebted to Dinah Dunn of Black Dog and Leventhal, not only for her support and enthusiasm for the book, but most especially for her expert editing instincts. Also at Black Dog and Leventhal, we are grateful to production editor Melanie Gold and copyeditor Laura Cherkas for their thoughtful notes and at Red Herring to Carol Bobolts for the book's stylish design.

Our gratitude is also due to Jane Dystel and Miriam Goderich, agents extraordinaire. We lucked out.

And finally, we thank Jeanne Kelly for her many excellent suggestions, and Ann Dana Carlson for listening patiently to endless tales of human folly, illusion, and deception.

INDEX

Illustrations are indicated in **bold**

PHOTO CREDITS